Reclaiming Your Dream

...AWAKEN HOPE AND REALIZE YOUR DESTINY

by Ann Platz

Harrison House
Tulsa, Oklahoma

07 06 05 04   10 9 8 7 6 5 4 3 2 1

Reclaiming Your Dream—
Awaken Hope and Realize Your Destiny
ISBN 1-57794-480-1
Copyright © 2004 by Ann Platz
1266 West Paces Ferry Road, #521
Atlanta, Georgia 30327-2306

Published by Harrison House, Inc.
P. O. Box 35035
Tulsa, Oklahoma 74153

Dedication

Reclaiming Your Dream is lovingly dedicated to a woman I love and greatly admire—Anne Severance—my friend, trusted advisor, editor extraordinaire, prayer partner, sister in Christ, and co-laborer in kingdom work.

Contents

Acknowledgments

With a grateful heart I want to acknowledge the people who have provided so much assistance in making this book a reality.

I am eternally grateful for the trust and blessing that the Lord has given me with the opportunity to tell my story and the stories of others who have reclaimed their dream.

I am so grateful to you, Bill Fowler, for seeing the heart and need for a book on reclaiming one's dream. I thank you and your incredible team at Harrison House for giving me the opportunity to partner with you in extending the kingdom of God through the printed word. To each of you, I thank you!

To my husband, John Platz, *I thank you* is not enough word power for who you are and the servant heart you have for kingdom work. *I love you* does not cover my feelings for you either. You are the best husband a woman could dream of! Thank you from the bottom of my heart!

To my daughters, Margo McDonald and Courtney Jones, I impart the blessing of a mother to each of you. I am so proud of your boldness to tell your stories in this book. May you always be "overcomers" and women of great faith and abundant love. My hope is for you to be giant oaks for the Lord and kingdom women who make a difference in the lives of others.

To my son-in-law, Nelson McDonald, I love you and thank God for you. You are an answer to my prayers and a huge part of the reclaiming of Margo's dream. Thank you!

Thank you to each woman who has so graciously contributed to this book of hope. I love and admire each of you and value you as a friend and co-laborer in kingdom work. I pray that God will expand your ministries and spheres of influence and that this book will be a catalyst that greatly blesses you in your spiritual journey.

To the women who mentor me and encourage me, I thank you for your support and love. To my family and friends, especially my seven grandchildren, thank you for sharing me! To my office staff, many, many thanks!

To my audience—friends I have not yet met in person, but who kindly communicate that my books have made a difference in their lives—this one is for you! Thank you!

Introduction

"Ann!" she exclaimed as she spotted me in a parking lot in downtown Atlanta. "I can't believe I ran in to you today. I've been meaning to write to thank you for changing my life!"

I had recognized the attractive brunette as a woman who had attended a seminar I had conducted several weeks earlier. But her startling remark caught me off guard.

"And just how did I manage to do *that?*" I asked, chuckling.

"Well, after experiencing your 'Reclaiming Your Dream' Retreat, I went right home and started a landscape and garden business, a goal I never expected to achieve. You encouraged me to dust off my dreams and try!"

This is only one of many such comments I have received over the past few months. One woman rekindled her childhood dream and opened a boutique. Another discovered that she was a gifted writer and began her first book. Another was so encouraged by the seminar that she decided to pursue a college degree at the age of sixty-two!

For as long as I can remember, I have been an encourager, looking for hidden gifts in others and helping to bring them forth. These recent fruits of my labor have fueled my desire to extend my audience to include both men and women of all walks of life. From that desire, this book was born.

Dreams are much more than wishing on a star, reaching for the moon, setting earthly goals, or striving to accomplish selfish ambitions. Dreams are seeds of destiny planted in the soil of the spirit by God Himself.

In my more than twenty-five years of interior design work—from the most palatial mansions to corporate board rooms to one-room apartments—I have enjoyed the process of helping to make dreams come true. In more recent years, I have moved into a new phase of ministry—communicating the transforming love of God through speaking, writing, and mentoring. Each client I contact, each seminar attendee I meet, is a dreamer in search of a dream. What a joy it is when the Lord allows me to "interpret" the dream, sharing with others the truth that it is not creature comforts—accessories, fine furnishings, lovely fabrics—that bring us the most joy, but discovering God's design for our lives.

Somewhere along the way, however, many of us either lose the original vision or fall victim to the doomsayers whose negativism destroys our dreams. This book is an attempt to point the way back to recovering all that you were destined to be.

In Part I, "Dream-Maker," you will discover that the dream for your life began in the heart of God. You are here on purpose. You were no accident of birth. As believers, we are all His chosen children, co-heirs with Jesus, God's only begotten Son.

Though you have come into this world by divine design, you must be on the alert for the Dream-Stealers, those who, either inadvertently or purposely, set out to sabotage God's sublime plan. Part II, "The Dream-Stealers," addresses these agents of deception and suggests what we can do to resist their schemes or to launch spiritual damage control if they get away with their thievery.

In Part III, "Recovering the Dream," you will move from forgiving the past to future fulfillment. It is only then that you may become thoroughly equipped to help others reclaim their dreams or to move in the "Joseph anointing" that will literally touch the nations.

Throughout this book are testimonies of transformation and renewal. You may find your own story—or a similar one—on many of its pages and thrill to the discovery that what God has done for them, He can do for you. The prayers at the end of each chapter are directly from my heart to the heart of the Father, prayed with all the hope and joy, the desperation or expectation I was discerning at the time. I was carrying you to Him in intercession as I entered into His Presence. But you can use your own words and insert your specific need. Just pray, knowing that the Author of your dream also has all the answers to enable you to reclaim it.

But no book on reclaiming one's dream would be complete without the Bible story of that most renowned of all dreamers—Joseph. From his boyhood days as the favored son of his father to the infamous pit where he was abandoned to die by his brothers to the palace of the Egyptian pharaoh, we track his rise from near death to deliverance. In many aspects of Joseph's life, we find ourselves—and take courage.

Whatever your talent or calling, you must follow your unique path, march to the beat of your own drum, and never fear failure. Expand your knowledge of God and of who you are in Him. Explore your gifts and talents, acknowledge that His dreams for your life are far greater and grander than your own, learn to identify and forgive the dream-stealers, and ultimately you will be able to reclaim your lost and stolen dreams.

—Ann Platz

PART I

Dream-Maker

God may speak in one way, or in another,

yet man does not perceive it.

In a dream, in a vision of the night,

When deep sleep falls upon men…

Then He opens the ears….

JOB 33:14-16

So God created man in His own image;

in the image of God He created him;

male and female He created them.

Then God blessed them and said to them,

"Be fruitful and multiply;

fill the earth and subdue it...."

GENESIS 1:27,28

CHAPTER 1

Designer Original

I will praise You, for I am fearfully and wonderfully made....
My frame was not hidden from You, when I
was made in secret, and skillfully wrought....
Your eyes saw my substance, being yet unformed.
And in Your book they all were written, the days
fashioned for me, when as yet there were none of them.

PSALM 139:14-16

I still vividly remember those wonderful patchwork quilts Clara used to make. She would take a seat in a rocker next to her "old fashioned" black potbellied stove and sew on the patches when the chores were done. "Crazy quilts," she called them. And crazy they were! Reds, blues, browns, yellows, and oranges, all tumbled together with no rhyme or reason. A kaleidoscope of color, every texture imaginable—from taffeta and lace to muslin, side by side—stitched altogether by hand. Patterns galore! Nothing matched, yet amazingly everything matched.

I can see her nimble brown fingers now, tearing scraps of cloth, fitting the pieces in place like a giant puzzle, and adding her own unmistakable flavor and style in the way she finished off with wide, colorful, irregular stitches. I remember marveling at the material Clara chose: threadbare remnants of her worn-out garments, some things my mother had given her—including some old curtains—plus bits and pieces of my discarded party dresses and Sunday school outfits. Chuckling that trademark chuckle of hers, she would say, "You didn't know where those dresses had gone, now did you?"

I was born in the Low Country of South Carolina and blessed with the rich heritage of plantation farm life. As a child I often had nothing better to do on long, lazy summer evenings than to sit at the feet of my beloved nurse and companion, Clara Evins, and watch as she pieced together a tapestry of life. Quilts tell a story of life's journey—the irregular pathways, the inconsistencies, the flaws. And they were all there in Clara's quilts—the lights and the darks, the rips and tears, the proud and painful passage of time. None of her quilts was like any other, just as Clara herself was unlike anyone I have ever known. Each was unique, a one-of-a-kind, never-to-be-duplicated work of art, significant in this world of sameness.

You, too, are a Designer original, with a unique DNA and a built-in destiny. There has never been, nor will there ever be, another person exactly like you. You carry in your being the image of the divine, and somewhere deep within is the dream God planted in you.

Seize His Dream

I am convinced that most people spend their entire lives trying to answer two questions: 1) *How can I be happy?* and 2) *Why am I here in the first place?* If you are one of these, you are wasting precious time either floating aimlessly in a foggy limbo or rushing about, grabbing moments of pleasure to anesthetize your pain. God is just waiting for you to wake up and seize *His* dream. Since He is the only One who knows the end from the beginning,[1] He is the Source of the authentic dream for your life.

When God created the world, He already knew your name.[2] He knew how tall you would be, the color of your eyes, how many times you would stumble, and what it would take to shape you into a vessel ready to receive His love and His purpose. He knew the depth of your sin, the stubbornness of your will, the hardness of your heart…and He loved you anyway. He knew the times you would be wounded by others, the afflictions you would suffer, the injustices you would bear…and He provided a way out. He knew that on your way to realizing your dream, you would be waylaid by the dream-stealers…and He put in place a plan to reclaim it.

You are not alone. God has promised never to leave you nor forsake you.[3] Not only that, but you have the fellowship of others who have proven Him and found Him true. And that is the purpose of this book—to steer you back to the original dream and the Dreamer.

Beautiful Dreamer

We limit ourselves when we do not allow God to do the dreaming. His dreams are so much bigger and better than ours. He is the Maker of Dreams and the Keeper of Dreams, and He will hold them in reserve until the time is right to fulfill them. In fact, any dream for your life that does not line up with God's idea is doomed to failure, or at the very least, will not bring the abundant blessing He is so ready to give.

You may just think you know what is good for you. But hold on a minute. Consider His words to Job, a man in the Old Testament whom He described as "blameless and upright."[4]

"Where were you when I laid the foundations of the earth?…

Do you know how its dimensions were determined, and who did the surveying?

What supports its foundations, and who laid its cornerstone as the morning stars sang together and all the angels shouted for joy?

"Who decreed the boundaries of the seas when they gushed from the depths? Who clothed them with clouds and thick darkness

and barred them by limiting their shores…?

"Have you ever once commanded the morning to appear and caused the dawn to rise in the east?…

Have you ever told the daylight to spread to the ends of the earth, to end the night's wickedness?

"Have you visited the treasuries of the snow, or seen where hail is made and stored?…

Where is the path to the distribution point of light? Where is the home of the east wind?

Who gives intuition and instinct?

Who provides for the ravens when their young cry out to God…?

"Do you still want to argue with the Almighty? Or will you yield?... "
Job 38:4-10,12,13,22-24,36,41; 40:2 TLB

Just about the time I begin to think I'm running the show, I recall these poetic, yet powerful words from the book of Job and remember that I am incapable of dreaming this big. Since only the all-wise God knows all things, including how everything will turn out, I would be utterly foolish to substitute my dream for His.

When God dreamed...He spoke the world into being by the majesty of His breath!

When God dreamed...He established plant life and the animal kingdom!

When God dreamed...He set up whole civilizations!

When God dreamed...He had you and me in mind for all eternity!

One man who recognized the superiority of God's dream was George Müller, a nineteenth-century layman known for his incredible faith and his passion for the orphans of England. The dream God planted in Müller's heart was to establish an orphanage that would be operated entirely on faith. In his journals, before his death, he had recorded over 50,000 answers to prayer!

When asked how one determines the will of God (His dream), Müller listed the following:

- "Seek to have no will [dream] of your own, in order to ascertain the mind of God regarding any steps you propose to take....

- "Seek His help, and seek it earnestly, perseveringly, patiently, believingly, and expectingly, and you will surely, in His own time and way, obtain it....

- "Use scriptural means. Prayer, the Word of God, and His Spirit should be united together. We should go to the Lord repeatedly in prayer, and ask Him to teach us by His Spirit through His Word.... If we should think that His Spirit led us to do so and so, because certain facts are so and so, and yet His Word is opposed to the step we are going to take, we would be deceiving ourselves....

- "Quietly wait His time; for when it comes, God will help....

- "No situation, no business [no dream] will be given to me by God, in which I do not have time enough to care about my soul."[5]

Relinquishment, prayer, bathing oneself in the Word of God, a clear conscience, faith—George Müller discovered these secrets to success, abandoning his own dream and lining himself up with God's greater and grander one. Later in this book we will be taking a deeper look at each of these elements.

But what if this man had decided that he didn't need God's help in achieving his goals? What if he had figured that he could handle everything on his own? Or what if he had never consulted God at all? What if he had settled for the world's ideas of what would bring happiness and satisfaction? Two thousand children might have remained homeless. And fifty thousand prayers might never have been prayed. In addition, George himself would have missed the blessing of knowing that he was God's chosen vessel for a history-making endeavor that would fire the faith of Christians around the world.

When the Dream Is Delayed

In at least one phase of my life, I missed God's best for me. It all began with a college romance that ended in marriage. Starry-eyed and naive, I thought I had it all—handsome husband, dream cottage, and before long, two adorable daughters. But I had failed to factor in God's ideas about my life, His dream for my future.

I knew the biblical promise: "'For I know the plans I have for you,' says the Lord. 'They are plans for good and not for evil, to give you a future and a hope…when you pray, I will listen. You will find me when you seek me, if you look for me in earnest'" (Jer. 29:11-13 TLB). At least, I had read the words in some Sunday school lesson in the past. But I didn't realize that they applied to me.

So caught up was I in living the life of a young suburban housewife and mother, restoring and furnishing our home, whirling in all the right social circles, that prayer and looking for God "in earnest" were far from established disciplines, much less abandoning my own ideas about what would make me happy, as George Müller had recommended.

In fact, it was much worse than that. I wanted to do what *I* wanted to do—and I expected God to go along with my agenda. I wasn't willing to wait on Him. I *was* willing to disrupt my own destiny for "the pleasures of sin for a season.'"[6] Therefore, I married the wrong man for all the wrong reasons. I was willful and disobedient. I was outright rebellious!

When the winds blew, my house came tumbling down. After the marriage failed and my husband deserted me and our two babies, I was so devastated, so wounded, that I wasn't even aware that God's original dream was still intact, just waiting to be rediscovered.

For a while I wandered in the wilderness, much like the early children of Israel,[7] grumbling and complaining about this miserable state of affairs and feeling utterly rejected and humiliated. All of which led to more poor choices—horrible choices—that led me farther and farther down the path, away from God and hope.

During this time, however, I learned one lesson well: God still loved me even when I turned away. He knew that this would be a fallen world and that His children would taste of forbidden fruit. So He provided a Redeemer, His only Son. If you truly belong to Jesus, if you have ever accepted Him as your Savior, He will permit you to exercise your free will and continue in "sin for a season," if that is what you desire. But when you reach the end of yourself, when your heart is broken and repentant and your dreams are in splinters, if you will begin to look for Him in earnest, He will be there to help you pick up the pieces.

The dream does not end when you blow it; it is only delayed.

Joseph's Patchwork Coat

Every dream is an original, conceived in the heart of God for each of His children. Although my dream was delayed through circumstances of my own choosing and others were stolen by the thief of our souls, Satan, I can now see more clearly the original dream for my life and when it began to take shape in my heart.

At five, I was already fascinated by color and texture. I spent long hours playing house, designing my own rooms, and furnishing them with old bricks "upholstered" in cast-off remnants of fabric from Mother's past treasures and Clara's quilt scraps. So on the day we studied the life of Joseph in Sunday school, I was intrigued when our teacher passed out coloring book pictures of this biblical character and asked us to fill in his "coat of many colors" as the story was told.

Some of the children began applying the color in vertical stripes. Others chose to draw in horizontal stripes. Probably inspired by Clara's crazy quilts, I proceeded to design a patchwork coat, filling in the colors in paisleys and plaids and solids, connecting them with big, fat "stitches" of yellow and red as I had seen her do so many times before.

Fingers busy, we listened to the teacher who spoke of a little boy who lived in a very large family—ten older brothers and one younger—and of a father who loved him best. The father favored Joseph so much, in fact, that he made him a little coat the boy wore proudly. It did not help his brothers' feelings toward him when Joseph told them about a dream he had dreamed— that they would bow down to him someday.[8]

When the jealous older brothers heard this, they plotted to kill him. I was horrified, and shuddered a little, relieved that my own two brothers would never think of doing such a dreadful thing!

We continued to work on our pictures as the teacher told of the evil scheme. When Joseph went to see about his brothers, who were grazing the flocks in a far field, his colorful coat gave him away while he was still a good distance from them. "Let's kill him and tell Father a wild animal has devoured him," said one brother. "Then we'll see what will become of his dreams!"

"Oh, no," said another. "Let's just toss him into that empty well; that way he'll die without our touching him." As it turned out, that is exactly what the brothers did—although Joseph didn't stay long in the well. They sold him instead to a passing caravan of traders on the way to Egypt.[9]

I couldn't believe it! How must Joseph have felt when his wicked brothers threw him into that dark, damp place? How he must have pleaded with them to save him—not to leave him there to starve to death and break his poor father's heart—only to be sold to strangers and taken far from home!

The next part of the story was not much more hopeful. It tells how Joseph became a slave in a foreign country, was falsely accused of a terrible crime by his owner, and thrown into prison, where he remained for several years.[10] What had happened to Joseph's wonderful dream? I colored furiously, indignant over the injustice committed against a young boy who had done nothing wrong that I could tell.

But that was not the end. As I finished drawing in the stitching on Joseph's coat, I learned how much he loved God and listened to Him—even in the cold, damp prison. I learned that Joseph was given the ability to interpret dreams, helped some of his cellmates, and eventually even told Pharaoh the answer to a strange and troubling vision. I looked up when I heard my teacher say that afterward, Joseph was promoted to second in command under Pharaoh himself![11] Joseph then followed God's instructions to store up grain before a famine and was able to save his own family, including all the evil brothers, from starvation. By this time my mouth was as wide as my eyes! *So the dream came true, after all,* I thought in wonder.

Yes, the dream will "come true" when we are willing to give up our own selfish desires, when we listen to God and accept His ideas rather than our own, and when we trust Him to reveal the giftings that will be used to fulfill all that He has for us.

Back to the Beginning

In reclaiming God's perfect plan for your life, you frequently have to go back to the beginning. There simply are no shortcuts in life, only longer and more time-consuming routes. In fact, shortcuts are usually the longest possible way to get anywhere!

At one of my seminars that has been highly successful in helping people recover their dreams, I ask the participants to place themselves at the age of five. If there are those who have suffered a traumatic childhood, I suggest that they picture themselves in a safe place. "What do you look like? Describe the outfit you are wearing," I begin, instructing them to write down the description. "How are you entertaining yourself? Who are you pretending to be? What world are you creating around you? What do you want to be when you grow up?"

As the participants sit and contemplate, a strange phenomenon takes place. The revelation comes that they are not much different—both spiritually and in the natural world—from that child of long ago. Gifts and talents, desires of the heart, a hunger for God—all these are either in fruition or on their way to becoming reality. I have been amazed to hear from teachers who were "teaching" their dolls at the age of five and doctors who were putting splints on teddy bear paws. As for me, I was making a home comfortable and beautiful for all who were under my care.

In that age of innocence, you *were* what you would *become.* Now some twenty, thirty, forty, even fifty years later, you may be surprised to discover that the dream that was in seed has now blossomed to reveal the original dream in your young heart.

There are, however, exceptions.

As a conference speaker, I absolutely love the view from the podium. Looking out over a sea of faces—like so many flowers in a bouquet—I spot the drooping ones, the ones whose petals are still tightly closed, the blooms that have lost their luster. So nothing pleases me more than to see the transformation when the light finally penetrates and the seed finds fertile soil. In that moment of revelation, heads are lifted, frowns turn to bright beams, and dreams are reborn. This encourages me to believe that my message has connected.

After one particularly stirring session, when the anointing of the Holy Spirit had been particularly powerful, we took a short break before resuming the afternoon activities. As I stepped off the platform, a beautiful young woman (whom I knew from a local church) made a beeline for me and grabbed both my hands in hers. Fully expecting her to share some wonderful truth the Lord had just revealed to her, I was shocked to hear her blurt out, "I cannot tell you how deeply jealous I am of your childhood! It was all I could do to sit there and not run out of the room while you were speaking. Out of respect for you, I stayed."

Aghast, I could only listen as she continued, "You see, when I was five years old, my father sexually molested me, and I had to hide in a closet to escape from him. I have been struggling to recover ever since."

For once, I was speechless. My heart was pounding. I hadn't a clue what to say next! But I knew the One who could fill my mouth with just the right words for this precious soul. *Please, God, 911!* I prayed in desperation.

"Do you realize that the dream was not really stolen from you?" I found myself asking.

She wasn't about to settle for that. "Are you kidding? I didn't have time for daydreams. I was too busy hiding from my father and trying to protect my little sisters."

"But that was the enemy's strategy to destroy God's dream," I insisted. "Just look at your life now—you have a creative, dynamic husband who adores you, great friendships, and security and worth beyond this world's riches!"

This time she listened, then gave a little gasp. "You know...I think you're right."

I *knew* I was right because that message was straight from the throne room, in answer to my desperate cry. I breathed a prayer of thanksgiving and relief. It wasn't over. There was much more work to be done, but this dear one was on the way to rediscovering all that God had dreamed for her from the beginning. My eyes filled with tears as she turned and walked away. I was so glad that the Holy Spirit had brought her to this meeting.

Still, the image of that little girl hiding in a closet—like Joseph in the pit—haunted me...the fear, the rejection, the horror of that demonic plot! How could a father take advantage of his own child, or brother sin against brother? How could they attempt to rob a younger, weaker one of innocence, of life itself? Yet I was aware that some version of this story is all too often true. For far too many, the only dream they know is a nightmare! A new sense of compassion began to swell in my heart for those who have been so bruised, and it was then that I resolved to help them reclaim their dreams.

If you are one who has suffered at the hands of someone you trusted—if you have lost your vision or never discovered the dream the Father planned for you before He created the foundations of the world—then take a moment to catch your breath and pray this prayer with me:

Father God, I present myself to You as I quietly wait before You. Please take me back to a time and place of innocence and purity. Let me remember and relive the essence of who I was then and the dream You planted in my spirit, then show me where the dream is today. Allow me to feel safe with my memories and to recapture the small details—the thread, the color, the fabrics—and please, Father, most of all may I see Your fingers fashioning my life. In the powerful name of Jesus, I pray, amen.

Israel loved Joseph more than all his children,

because he was the son of his old age.

Also he made him a tunic of many colors.

But when his brothers saw that their father

loved him more...they hated him.

GENESIS 37:3,4

CHAPTER 2

The Search Begins

There are diversities of gifts, but the same Spirit.
There are differences of ministries, but the same Lord.
And there are diversities of activities…
But one and the same Spirit works all these things,
distributing to each one individually as He wills.

1 CORINTHIANS 12:4-6,11

How incredible you are! I may not have met you in person, but I already know a lot about you. Just think: God created you to be a distinct individual, yet positioned you in a certain family—with your own unique blend of parents, grandparents, and other forebears—to live in a particular geographical location in the world. If you are married, you have joined your lineage with that of your husband and together you have started another family tree. Even if you have a twin, there are no other fingerprints just like yours anywhere on the planet. Those distinctive fingerprints document, undeniably, who you are. And even if you happen to have the color of your mother's eyes and the shape of your father's, no two eyes are exactly alike. You were "…fearfully and wonderfully made…skillfully wrought…" (Ps. 139:14,15).

I wonder why God went to all that trouble to custom-design us when He could have used a simple pattern and just duplicated it over and over. I suppose He was too creative to settle for that. I believe, too, that He wanted to make an important statement: Each human being is precious to Him and eternally significant. In addition, since we are created in the image of the Triune God—Father, Son, and Holy Spirit, who continually interact with One Another[1]—I believe He wants us to relate to others and celebrate all the differences in our personalities and roles. Each one of us is a patch in His glorious quilt!

The search for self—who you are and where you fit into the grand design—is a lifelong pursuit. You may catch early glimpses of a pattern or a piece as you are growing up. But the truth is, God's dream for you is a part of your spiritual DNA. If it is not fully discovered or is lost somewhere along the way, you will never feel totally fulfilled until it is reclaimed.

Talent Scout

God's original dream for you—including your gifts and talents—cannot remain hidden. When you begin to seek who you are in the Lord, you will find out what you want to know. He promised, "Ask, and it will be given to you; seek, and you will find; knock, and it will be opened to you. For everyone who asks receives, and he who seeks finds, and to him who knocks it will be opened. If a son asks for bread from any father among you, will he give him a stone? Or if he asks for a fish, will he give him a serpent instead of a fish? Or if he asks for an egg, will he offer him a scorpion? If you then, being evil, know how to give good gifts to your children, how much more will your heavenly Father give the Holy Spirit to those who ask Him!" (Luke 11:9-13).

Did you notice something interesting about that last verse? Take another look. What kind of "good gifts" does it say that earthly fathers know how to give? "Bread...fish...egg"—good things, nourishing and pleasing food, especially when beautifully prepared and served. Now, what does the heavenly Father give those who ask Him? Not always exactly what we think we are looking for perhaps, but infinitely more satisfying. When you ask, you will not necessarily find a *thing,* but you will most certainly find a *Person*— One who has been called the Comforter, the Counselor, the Helper, the One who guides us into all truth.[2] When you are seriously searching for your spiritual identity (in the Lord), you will find the Holy Spirit!

He will help you ask yourself the right questions: *What is there about me that is unique? What sets me apart from everyone else? What can I do that will make a difference in the world?*

He will also guide you in interpreting the suggestions that come from others. Listen to what people say about you. For example, someone may remark, "I couldn't help overhearing you sing during the worship service this morning. You have a beautiful voice. You really ought to be a worship leader." Rather than passing the comment off as a casual compliment, think about it. It may be a directive from the Lord.

On the other hand, you may hear from "Joseph's brothers." (You'll hear about them later in this book.) Some people will be so resentful and envious of your gifting that they will not be able to acknowledge it. In that case, go back to the Source—the divine "Talent Scout"—and disregard the lies of the enemy.

Talent or Gift?

Suppose you like to cook. You have not bought into our fast-food culture, with its drive-through dining, but truly enjoy combining unusual ingredients to produce some exotic recipe and serving it with style. "Scratch" cooking, it's called; the no-packaged-mix, all-natural, time-consuming, old-fashioned technique of preparing good food. Your family is delighted, and you're everyone's pick for the church potluck dinners. Our family cook, Clara, had this kind of ability to whip up the most delectable delicacies ever to grace a table. Someone with an interest in the culinary arts may take French cooking classes and go right by the book but never achieve the same flair as Clara.

Is this a talent or a gift?

In the English language, we often use the words *talent* and *gift* interchangeably. Perhaps it would help if we paused long enough to distinguish between the two. Webster's dictionary sheds a great deal of light here. Under the word *gift,* these synonyms are listed: "...faculty, aptitude, bent, talent, genius, knack...," meaning "...a special ability for doing something...."[3] The distinction is that *talent* is "a marked natural ability that needs to be developed,"[4] while *gift* "...often implies special favor by God...."[5]

Clara, with no special lessons or instruction, was a gifted cook. I, on the other hand, don't cook much, but I can decorate food with the best of them! I have concentrated my time and energy in the area where God has gifted *me*. When someone sees a home I have designed and decorated for a client and exclaims, "What an interesting mix of color and fabric! How did you do that?" I can reply with absolute certainty, "It comes naturally. It is a gift from God."

Following the apostle Paul's admonition to his good friend Timothy, I did not "neglect the gift" (1 Tim. 4:14) but stirred it up[6] by studying art and design at the Atlanta Design Institute. I meditated on these things, giving myself entirely to them, that my "progress may be evident to all" (1 Tim. 4:15). Still, I'm very much aware that it was the Master Designer who gave me an eye for beauty and order in the first place.

A friend's son-in-law, Michael W. Smith, is a gifted pianist. This young man doesn't read music and he plays entirely by ear, but when he sits down to the piano or keyboard, magnificent, original melodies flow from his fingers. He lasted through one semester of college music theory, then quit to follow his dream with his God-given gift intact. In his case, had he *studied* music, he might have been conformed to the mold and lost the unique anointing that has set him apart from other talented musicians. He may not have pursued academic training in music, but he continues to "stir up" his gift by using his natural ability under the inspiration of the Holy Spirit. When asked about his amazing talent, he is the first to give the glory to his heavenly Father.

No doubt Paul was speaking of spiritual things when he cautioned Timothy in two different letters (1 and 2 Timothy) to keep growing and developing; however, the exhortation is applicable to the natural world as well. For example, although I had not the remotest idea that God would use my secular career in interior design as a platform to launch a ministry of spiritual transformation, that is exactly what happened. He gave me the gift, allowed me to further refine it, and took it to the next level, both spiritually and in the natural.

What about temperament? Aren't some people just "naturally" creative or practical, outgoing or contemplative, organized or casual, leaders or followers? And what does one's temperament have to do with gifts and talents and reclaiming your dream?

Profile of a Successful Dreamer

Several years ago the Lord led me to a book that changed my whole perspective on dreams and what drives us to fulfill them—*Spirit-Controlled Temperament* by Dr. Tim LaHaye.[7] I devoured that book, reading it straight through in a single sitting as the light bulbs came on one by one!

Dr. LaHaye, in his brilliant yet warmly compassionate style, taught me why people are so different. He quoted Hippocrates, the ancient Greek physician who proposed that there are four temperament types—choleric, sanguine, melancholy, and phlegmatic—based on certain body fluids, with many variations and blends of each type. This concept has since been disproved by the medical world, but the strange-sounding names have stuck.

In a nutshell, the *Choleric* is one who dreams big, sees the whole picture, and catches the vision. The *Sanguine* is more of a people person, flamboyant and outgoing, who wants to help others achieve their dreams. The *Melancholy* may have lost their dream, but they are busy analyzing and dissecting, and are conscientiously working toward recovery. The *Phlegmatic* is calm, easy-going, and can laugh in the face of the dream-stealers. The tricky part is that we are never just one of these types, but a blend of at least two, with one of them being predominant.

Dr. LaHaye goes on to say that, like the words *gift* and *talent,* there are three other terms we need to define clearly in order to be accurate in our search for wholeness—*temperament, personality,* and *character.*

- *Temperament* is a combination of inherited traits—your genetic predisposition. You can't do a thing about it!

- *Personality* is who you appear to be. You can manipulate your outward appearance by "putting on" a mask to make yourself more attractive or acceptable to others.

- *Character* is who you are when no one else is looking—the real you. Character is influenced by temperament and personality, but can only be truly changed by the power of the Holy Spirit.

Through this teaching, I have been able to analyze my temperament, my personality, and my character and, quite frankly, now better understand the intricate workings of who I am and where I fit into my family and the world. Rather than becoming impatient or judgmental of others' differences, I have gained a greater compassion for them. I have even found freedom to forgive when necessary. Can you grasp how huge that idea is and how it can literally change your life? It did mine.

I am writing these words through my tears as I consider the implications for you, the reader. What it took me 45 years to discover, I want to "download" in a few simple words. Along with your natural talents—known and unknown—God has strategically gifted you with all the resources necessary to realize or reclaim His original dream for your life. Your temperament—your inborn traits—and your personality, under the control of the Holy Spirit, can produce godly character, which will accelerate the process.

"You've Got What It Takes"

Sanguines and Cholerics are kissing cousins—the "green-light girls." Both are spontaneous and exuberant, true extroverts, while Melancholies and Phelgmatics proceed with caution, taking time to ponder and reflect. Most people, of course, are a composite of the four temperament types, which makes analysis a little more difficult.

Pause a moment to find yourself on the chart reprinted here by permission of the publisher.[8] First, identify your strengths to determine your own unique style. There are no right and wrong answers. Actually, this chart is a kind of camera for taking your personality picture and giving you a realistic view of yourself as others see you—and as God has created you.

Score Your Strengths and Weaknesses

STRENGTHS

SANGUINE	CHOLERIC	MELANCHOLY	PHLEGMATIC
Outgoing	Strong leader	Gifted	Calm and quiet
Responsive	Independent	Analytical	Easy-going
Warm, friendly	Visionary	Aesthetic	Dependable
Talkative	Practical	Self-sacrificing	Objective

| Enthusiastic | Productive | Industrious | Diplomatic |
| Compassionate | Decisive | Self-disciplined | Efficient |

WEAKNESSES

Undisciplined	Cold, unemotional	Moody	Unmotivated
Emotionally unstable	Self-sufficient	Self-centered	Procrastinator
Unproductive	Impetuous	Martyr complex	Selfish
Egocentric	Domineering	Unsociable	Indecisive
Exaggerates	Unforgiving	Critical	Fearful

Have you noticed that the list of "weaknesses" is actually a description of the unredeemed sin nature? If left unchecked and unchanged, we would act out of our sin more often than our strengths and never find or recover God's original dream for our lives. But "if we confess our sins, He is faithful and just to forgive us our sins and to cleanse us from all unrighteousness" (1 John 1:9). Take time right now to find yourself on this chart and ask God to forgive all your unrighteousness. This is the first step toward dream recovery.

So here is the big picture as the Creator sees it. Together, the variety of individuals He has created—in strong, bold strokes and muted, soft shades—make up a beautiful tapestry of temperaments.

The Sassy Sanguine—Woman of Passion and Life

The Sanguine stands out in a crowd. She's the life of the party, wearing the most brilliant colors—reds and purples and passionate pinks—and the heaviest scents. She is always onstage, the consummate entertainer, and loves nothing more than to charm her friends with a fascinating story or a song. She wants everyone around her to feel comfortable and special. Therefore, she goes out of her way to nurture and provide everything needed. She is Superwoman, living on the go and on the edge.

The Sanguine is free-spirited and sometimes has a childlike innocence that is irresistible, unless she is having one of her difficult days. Then she could be perceived as being a show-off, too talkative, unpredictable, or undisciplined. It must have been on a day like this that Mary of Magdala first met Jesus and was delivered of seven demons, after which she followed Him and willingly provided for Him out of her substance for the rest of His life.

(Luke 8:2,3.) It was she whose temperament was so transformed that after witnessing Jesus' mock trial and public humiliation, she stood by courageously at the foot of the cross to hear His last words and to weep with the other women. Then, with her spontaneity restored and channeled into useful service, Mary Magdalene, formerly possessed by demons, became possessed by the power of Resurrection morning and ran to tell the other disciples that their Master had risen from the dead! (John 20:11-18.)

When Jesus died, Mary Magdalene lost her Dream, but she didn't waste time whining about it. She prepared His body for burial, waited as long as possible at the tomb, hurried back on Easter morning, and was rewarded when her Dream was restored in three days! Her passion for Him matched His for her. One of the most moving passages in all the Bible is the story of Mary's encounter with Jesus at the garden tomb. She recognized Him only when He called her by name, "Mary!" (John 20:16.)

He calls your name, too. When a Sanguine loses her dream, she is like a forgotten starlet—remembering the days of old, but refusing to live in the present. Her dream slowly fades until it dims and is finally extinguished.

The Confident Choleric—
Woman of Courage and Strength

This is a true visionary, a woman with the inborn trait of leadership. She is decisive and practical, and doesn't cave in to the opinions of others. She loves a good challenge and rises to meet it with courage and strength.

The biblical model for this temperament type is Deborah, "a mother in Israel" (Judg. 5:7). In an era of Israel's history when national honor was at its lowest ebb and "the children of Israel did evil in the sight of the Lord" (Judg. 3:7), this courageous woman rose up as a prophet and judge, commanding great respect for her common-sense approach to solving problems. Even more astonishing was the fact that she rallied the small army of Israel and trained their general, Barak, who later defeated a greater enemy army of 900 iron chariots![9]

Deborah obviously had many natural gifts and talents. Among them, the Scriptures mention her musical ability. On the day of their great victory, she and General Barak wrote and performed a song. Although we don't know the melody, the powerful lyric was recorded in God's Word and will forever remain as a testimony to one whom some have called the first woman military commander and the first female Supreme Court Justice.

> "Awake, awake, Deborah! Awake, awake, sing a song…!
> "Thus let all your enemies perish, O Lord! But let those who love Him be like the sun when it comes out in full strength…."
>
> Judges 5:12,31

Under Deborah's anointed leadership, the "land had rest for forty years" (v. 31).

The downside to this temperament is that if the Holy Spirit has not been allowed to do His refining work, the very fire that drives the Choleric to succeed in life can flame up and erupt in anger. Even more dangerous than a hot temper and impetuous nature is the tendency to be self-sufficient—to be so cocky about attaining the dream that there is no need to seek the counsel of others or even to wait on God's timing. Although the Bible is silent about Deborah's weaknesses, she was human and no doubt had her share.

Apparently, though, she had learned that it was "'Not by might nor by power, but by My Spirit,' says the Lord of hosts" (Zech. 4:6). She recognized her need to wait until the Lord gave her specific wisdom before she offered advice or led her fellow Israelites into battle. I could learn a few things from Deborah.

As I read Dr. LaHaye's book, I saw the pattern pieces of my own life shift and join right before my eyes. I related to every trait of the Choleric he had described on those pages. I saw the profile of myself—the good, the bad, and the ugly! For the first time, I realized that my words could hurt others if they were not softened and chosen carefully with love as the covering, that my tendency to be stubborn and resistant could be harmful, so I should exercise caution in this area. Accepting this list of undesirable traits as true to my temperament style, I vowed to overcome them. This exercise has been greatly used as a corrective in my life.

I frequently take my "temperament temperature" and remember that God "made me this way" to accomplish the dreams He planted in my heart. I am no mistake. I am purposed, with a destiny as unique as I am. The same holds true for you, my friend. You are a woman of purpose and destiny, and you, too, can reclaim your dream.

The Mellow Melancholy— Woman of Spirit and Substance

Rather than seeking the limelight, Ms. Melancholy prefers to paint the scenery or edit the script for the school play. She sets a high standard for herself and is not content with mediocrity. She is more apt to be a thinker than a doer, but if she does something, she gives it 150 percent and insists on performing it perfectly and preferably ahead of schedule. Spiritual discipline comes a little more easily for her since she tends to live in the abstract. It should come as no surprise, then, that many missionaries and humanitarians are melancholy by nature, along with artists and musicians.

On the flip side, however, the Melancholy seldom knows how to protect herself. With no boundaries, she sometimes falls victim to burnout and stress-related diseases. She gives and gives until there is nothing left to give. Consequently, the enemy (Satan) has a field day and often succeeds in sidelining her on the eve of some important mission.

The Passive Phlegmatic—Woman of Peace and Grace

If there were a perfect temperament type, it would appear to be the Phlegmatic. She is sitting in the front row when the Sanguine needs an audience. She is tolerant and pleasant when the Choleric leads or loses her temper. She balances the Melancholy's moodiness with peace and contentment. She is the calm in the midst of the storm, always thinking and pondering, rather than shouting her opinions from the rooftops. But when she speaks, the world listens. Reflective and serene, this woman waits on the Lord for her orders and obeys them quickly.

The truth is that, in the natural, one can be too laid back, too submissive, allowing the enemy to run roughshod over her gentle spirit. Some people perceive the Phlegmatic as indifferent or uncaring, fearful or unenthusiastic, slow and sluggish. This is far from true when she is operating in her positive side. Her problem is that though she will never burn out, she may rust out!

Ignited by the fire of the Holy Spirit, however, this temperament type is like Mary, the mother of Jesus. Mary's womb was the chosen cradle for the Son of God. No woman could dream of a higher calling. Even her cousin Elizabeth recognized the mother of her Messiah when she exclaimed prophetically, "Blessed are you among women, and blessed is the fruit of your womb! But why is this granted to me, that the mother of my Lord should come to me? For indeed, as soon as the voice of your greeting sounded in my ears, the babe leaped in my womb for joy. Blessed is she who believed, for there will be a fulfillment of those things which were told her from the Lord" (Luke 1:42-45).

Mary's "dream," conceived by the Holy Spirit, was to give birth to the Savior of the world. Later Mary had other children, but it was Jesus who honored her most when, from the cross, He committed His mother into John's loving care.[10]

Dream Team—Co-Partnering With God

God, the Dream-Maker, is also the Keeper of your dreams. He has all the answers. He drew the blueprint for your life. With Him, there is everything you need; you lack "no good thing."[11] He meant for it to be that way. He created it that way. You don't accidentally bump into God. He is always there—in your past, present, and future. He has forgiven the past. He gives you the present, and He guards the gates to your future.

Joseph, the Old Testament dreamer, knew the Dream-maker well. He never took the low road—not even when faced with earthly temptation and premature death. He held on to the dream, believing that the One who had promised was faithful. In both the pit and the prison, Joseph trusted God. (Gen. 37,39-41.)

Joseph could easily have given up long before he saw his dream come true. Talk about dysfunctional families. Joseph's boyhood home was a powder keg just waiting for a match. And Joseph himself provided more than enough ammunition to touch off a family feud. Of course, it wasn't his fault that he was his father's favorite—the eleventh son, born in Jacob's old age to Rachel, his beloved wife. But perhaps young Joseph did not help matters any

when he paraded around in that colorful tunic his father had gᵢ
his brothers were tending the sheep out in the pasture.

And what of Joseph's brothers? Can you imagine having those ᵢ ᵢ
siblings in your family? One is bad enough, but ten! Here is a complete kaleidoscope of temperament types in all their weaknesses—from deception and
conniving to attempted murder and incest.

We are to see how partnering with God is the only way out of family
dysfunction. As His child, you have the Father's heart, the Father's eyes, and
the Father's hand to guide you out of the pit, through the wilderness, and into
the eternal home He has planned for you. But get ready for adventure ahead!
It's only beginning.

*Prayer for a Beautiful Beginning: Gracious Father, we bless You this day and
stand in awe of the magnificence of Your creativity. We thank You for making
us one-of-a-kind, special-order, not-to-be-duplicated vessels for Your glory.
We thank You that Your plan for each life includes pits and valleys, ups and
downs, and the long way around that eventually leads us back to You. Thank
You for Your timeless love, for Your unmerited favor, and for partnering with
us as we pursue the dream. Thank You for enough strengths to give us an
understanding of who You are and enough weaknesses to keep us constantly
aware that we need You. In the name of Jesus, amen.*

Now Joseph had a dream, and he told it to
his brothers; and they hated him even more.
And Pharaoh said to Joseph, "I have had a dream,
and there is no one who can interpret it.
But I have heard it said of you that you
can understand a dream, to interpret it."

GENESIS 37:5; 41:15

CHAPTER 3

Interpreting the Dream

"For I know the plans I have for you...plans to
give you a hope and a future."

JEREMIAH 29:11 NIV

The sky is the limit! Hitch your wagon to a star! Climb the ladder of success!
These tired clichés and many more represent the world's sales pitch to
the dreamer in you. You can write your own ticket to happiness, they say.
Create your own destiny. Make all your dreams come true, if you will only
believe in yourself, work hard enough, and take charge of your life. Sounds
good, doesn't it? Some of it even sounds true. Plays right into our twenty-
first century work ethic and the "me-first" mindset.

On the other hand, the world's view always falls short of the genius of
God. It is He, the original Dreamer, who created us in His image, deposited
His dream in our hearts, and sent the Holy Spirit to guide us to fulfillment.
His vision spans time and space, a vision so vast that it cannot be measured
by any instrument man can contrive.

Our problem is that we try to interpret the infinite with a finite mind. A
further complication is the difference between flesh and spirit. There is something profoundly different about how God thinks, reasons, operates,
sequences things, evaluates. Unfortunately, our perspective is hugely influenced by the wisdom of man and all that we have learned from our experience in a fallen world. So instead of seeing and interpreting from God's

perspective, "we see in a mirror, dimly" and we know only "in part" (1 Cor. 13:12). Because we live in a physical world and our senses are trained to discern the physical, we have become nearly blind to the spiritual realm, and our dreams can die a slow death as we settle for less than His glorious best.

The Impossible Dream

Dreams are more than myths and musings and the product of an active imagination. A dream is also more than a strongly desired purpose or goal, as worthy as that goal may be. The dream in God's heart—His vision for you— is the only one that really matters. By the world's system of values, it is an "impossible" dream. Check out Psalm 139 again for proof that He has a purpose for your life:

> "You made all the delicate, inner parts of my body and knit me together in my mother's womb.
>
> Thank you for making me so wonderfully complex! Your workmanship is marvelous—and how well I know it.
>
> You watched me as I was being formed in utter seclusion, as I was woven together in the dark of the womb.
>
> You saw me before I was born. Every day of my life was recorded in your book. Every moment was laid out before a single day had passed."
>
> Psalm 139:13-16 NLT

God knew you before you were born. He catalogued the number of your days before you had taken your first breath. He knows where you are going before you get there.

Ephesians 2:10 is similar: "For [you] are His workmanship, created in Christ Jesus for good works, which God prepared beforehand that [you] should walk in them." According to this verse, you were created for "good works"—a plan that God Himself designed for you "beforehand" or in advance! Do you realize that your unique life dream was in blueprint stage in God's mind long before you became aware of it? And if He conceived the plan, He can also interpret it for you.

Recently I read something by author Jim Monsor that explains this so well: "A spiritual illustration God taught me through my career relates to Design Specifications. Design specs are what an engineer develops at the start of a project. What is this machine or piece of equipment supposed to do when I am through designing and building it? How is it supposed to function? Is it supposed to process data? If so, how and in what manner? Where does the information come from and where does it go after I am done with it? God wrote design specs for each life before there was yet one day of it! He had a dream for your life. When He was busy forming the earth and the universe, He was also dreaming of you and planning what He wanted you to become, what role He wanted you to play. Over the past few years, one of my consistent prayers has been: 'God, when You dreamed of me, when You were writing the design specs for me, what did You envision? What did You have in mind when You laid the plans for my life? Lead me to fulfill Your dream for me.'"[1]

This is the key, the dream you should pursue, the one with eternity written into the "design specs," not the manmade, self-seeking, false security based on job performance, fear, youth and beauty, power and greed. If you will learn how to identify and interpret the real dream, it will take you places you have never been and accomplish the fantastic purpose for which you were created.

$\mathcal{J}oseph's$ $\mathcal{B}oyhood$ $\mathcal{D}ream$

Who would have thought that a shepherd boy from a nomadic tribe in the Middle East would rise to become second in command to the Pharaoh of Egypt! Joseph, the Old Testament dreamer, not only dreamed his own dreams but also helped others define their dreams on his way from the pit to the palace.

It all started on the hillsides of Canaan. God's dream for Joseph was already in place when he was out tending his father's flocks. Even then he was a leader. Latent within him were the temperament, the personality, and the character traits, ignited by the fire of a Holy Spirit anointing that would give him authority to command people instead of sheep. All he lacked at the moment was position.

I have already given you a glimpse of Joseph's home life. With that elaborate coat he wore as a constant reminder of his favored status in the family, it's no wonder his brothers could barely speak a civil word to him. And then there were those dreams of his.[2]

Twice he dreamed and quickly told his family all about his dreams. How his brothers' wheat sheaves bowed to his in the field, how even the sun, moon, and eleven stars bowed before him. Delusions of grandeur? Hardly. What the brothers interpreted as arrogance and pride was God's dream of greatness for Joseph and subsequently salvation for the entire family! But the prophetic dreams had not yet come to pass. It often takes time—sometimes months or even years—and all they knew was that this confident kid brother of theirs was getting on their nerves, and they'd had about all they could take of his bragging.

I wonder what Joseph must have been thinking when disaster so swiftly followed his dreams. Did he become discouraged or fearful when his older brothers, consumed by jealousy, actually plotted to kill him? As it was, they didn't get away with murder but threw him in a pit, a dry well used as a holding tank. They did soon succeed in getting him out of their hair permanently (or so they thought)—by selling him to a passing caravan of traders headed for Egypt.

Now, by biblical standards, Egypt has always symbolized the opposite direction of the believer's destiny. While on the outside everything looks seductively peaceful—music and laughter, beauty and bright lights, a land of plenty—the truth is that spiritual Egypt represents a dark place, filled with sin and evil, death and destruction. And that's where Joseph was bound. How could God's dream for him possibly come to pass in this godforsaken land?

How would you feel if, after discovering your dream, the rug is suddenly yanked out from under you—perhaps by financial setback, divorce, abuse, abandonment, or the death of a child—and you are in some far country, far from fulfilling your heart's desire? What would you do? Where would you turn?

You think you have problems? Consider Joseph's plight. He was despised, cast out of the family, sold to foreigners, sent to a strange land, and through an incident not of his own choosing, landed in jail. It appeared that he had lost everything—but he never lost the dream.

The Bible doesn't fill in all the blanks, but there are enough clues that we can piece together, like one of Clara's quilts, the story of Joseph's recovery in those "lost" years. In this book, we are going to learn that:

- *He was faithful to the vision and never gave up.* "…it was not you who sent me here, but God," he later told his brothers. "He has made me a father to Pharaoh, and lord of all his house, and a ruler throughout all the land of Egypt" (Gen. 45:8). The vision that had been so strong in his youth carried him through to its fulfillment, yet it took thirteen long years!

- *He trusted in God and obeyed His commands.* Whatever task was assigned him throughout his life—at home in Canaan, in Potiphar's house, in prison, in the palace—Joseph was diligent and conscientious to do it well. But his diligence went far beyond a natural desire to do a good job or become a man-pleaser. His primary motivation was pleasing God and following His instructions. This Joseph did despite all the negative circumstances of his life. He kept looking up!

- *He used his circumstances to bless others.* "…the Lord was with him [Joseph]; and whatever he did, the Lord made it prosper" (Gen. 39:23). If the Lord had not been with Joseph, he could never have endured prison life, yet he found ways to help others who were in the same condition.

We will find that during those prison years, Joseph used his gifts and talents for the benefit of his fellow prisoners. Unselfishly, he placed their welfare above his own.

Joseph was always a man of integrity, but that integrity was born of his belief that God had some great purpose for his life. Even when everything seemed hopeless, he managed to keep the vision—the dream—alive!

$\mathcal{D}$oes $\mathcal{G}$od $\mathcal{S}$till $\mathcal{S}$peak in $\mathcal{D}$reams and $\mathcal{V}$isions?

No book based on the life of Joseph, the dreamer, would be complete without taking a look at the controversial concept of dreams and visions. Are these manifestations simply the aftereffects of something you ate before going to bed or the result of having seen too many movies? Or does God still use the nighttime hours to communicate His thoughts to His children?

I am personally a believer in dreams and visions. I believe that God speaks through them today just as He did centuries ago. It seems the kind of thing God would do—to come to us at a time when there are fewer distractions, and we are at our most vulnerable. (Of course, the enemy knows this, too, and may take advantage of our vulnerability to torment us with disturbing dreams and nightmares.) But many Christians have reported that they hear from the Lord best while they are sleeping.

The most helpful book I have ever found on this subject is a little volume by James Ryle entitled *A Dream Come True: A Biblical Look at How God Speaks Through Dreams and Visions*.[3] If you have any interest at all in exploring this topic, I highly recommend getting your hands on a copy of this book! I would not give you two cents for anything that is not documented in Scripture, but James Ryle has made a thorough and careful study of this much-disputed topic and fully backs all comments and suppositions with the Word of God.

On the front cover of this book, Bill McCartney, founder of Promise Keepers, a Christian organization for men, writes that "James Ryle takes his unique, God-given ability for explaining truth and applies it to the mysterious and often misunderstood subject of dreams and visions. The results are inspiring!"[4] I agree. If I had not already experienced God's "voice in the night," I would have been convinced by the end of Chapter 1!

I can recall a vivid dream I had some years ago soon after God called me to a deeper walk with Him. In the dream I was seated in front of a typewriter, and as I sat there, staring at a blank piece of paper, the typewriter began typing out a message. I watched, mesmerized, as these words appeared, letter by letter: *You are going to be tested!*

It was one of those dreams that jars you awake, pulse racing, every sense on alert. I knew that I had heard from God, and it wasn't long afterward that all the forces of hell came against me. I was tested in every area of my life except my marriage, where John and I had a rock-solid relationship, built on our mutual faith in God. But other friends deserted me. Business colleagues caused problems. People spoke untruths about me. In retrospect, I know that the dream was sent as a prelude to those difficult times. God was actually letting me know how much He loved me by warning me in advance, helping me see what I was made of (He already knew), and reminding me that testing times have a beginning and an end. This one lasted two years, just in time to prepare me for the greatest test of all—my sister's death.

The confirmation that this was truly a prophetic dream from the Lord came one night at a church meeting in Atlanta, when a visiting apostle called me out of the audience, never having seen me before in his life, and declared, "The Lord says you passed the test!"

In his book, Ryle describes this kind of thing happening, referring to a passage in Job that I had somehow overlooked in my multiple readings of the Bible: "...God is greater than man....For God may speak in one way, or in another. Yet man does not perceive it. In a dream, in a vision of the night, when deep sleep falls upon men, while slumbering on their beds, then He opens the ears of men, and seals their instruction. In order to turn man from his deed, and conceal pride from man, He keeps back his soul from the Pit, and his life from perishing by the sword" (Job 33:12,14-18).

From this passage, Ryle states seven blessings that may result from dreams and visions. I will mention only three, in addition to the divine intervention that dreams can provide.

1. *Dreams can offer God's answers to our questions.*[5] We can wrestle with some issue—spiritual or natural—for days, then God may deliver the answer in a dream. This happened to me once when I landed a large design commission, one of the greatest joys of my design career. For this impressive residence, I was able to design thirty-nine rugs, including one for the Grande Salon. The dimensions were far too vast to call this a mere living room. The rug itself, a French Savonerrie, was to measure 32 by 28 feet. Even though I had had years of experience in rug design, I labored over this one, knowing the scale was so huge that any error would appear as if under a magnifying glass. Beyond the design I was expected to create, the colors had to be just right—the layering of creams and pinks and garnets achieved skillfully and exactly. I went to sleep at night, praying about this rug.

Then, one night in a dream, I saw it! God gave me the entire intricate design. It was beyond description, completely out of my range of ability. The color, the pattern, the completed rug was spread out before me, and the next morning I flew to get paper and a pen to record the vision while it was still fresh in my mind. When the sketch was presented to my clients, they declared it to be one of the most magnificent rugs they had ever seen. And during its manufacture at Lacey-Champion Carpets, Inc. in Fairmount, Georgia, even the mill workers crowded around to see "the rug God designed."

2. *Dreams can give us instruction in the things of God.*[6] My wonderful office assistant, Patricia, is a brilliant and talented coworker with children of her own. She tells of a dream she had recently in which she saw herself standing in her kitchen, designed as a solarium. The light was growing brighter and brighter, and she felt herself being drawn upward. In the dream she sensed that she was dying and panicked. "But, Lord, I haven't told my children all they need to know about You!"

Upon waking, Patricia realized that this dream had brought to her consciousness the desire of her heart, her deepest longings—that her children come to know the Lord as she knows Him. Stirred by this reminder of her mortality, she asked for more time to model the Christlike life for her children, to point them to the true Source of all their need, and as the Lord instructed Habakkuk, to "write the vision and make it plain" (Hab. 2:2).

Patricia is also a gifted Bible teacher and has taught from a Bible in which she has made many marginal notes. One of her dreams is to write a book based upon an idea that the Lord has revealed to her from her Bible teaching. Through God's divine appointment and in fulfillment of both dreams, she will be spending ten weeks during the summer with a learning disabled daughter at her new college, helping her with her academic courses and teaching her more about God from the margins of her Bible. There will also be time for writing!

3. *Dreams can preserve our soul from the pit.*[7] One of my dearest friends is Charlotte Hale, a writer for many prominent Christian leaders. We met when her career was at an all-time high, but her personal life was in shambles. Her dream of a lifelong marriage to a godly man was dissolving. It was obvious that *this* husband, who wanted out, would not be the one. And right now, she could not think beyond the moment, could not even recall the dream, although not a literal one.

I sailed over to her new apartment, where she stood, helpless and in the pit of despair, amid the packed boxes of odds and ends she had brought over from her former home. This was a considerable downsize from the lovely mansion she had shared with her ex-husband before their divorce. Now she was making do with half of their material possessions, trying to arrange them in some semblance of order.

As a writer who worked out of her home, she *needed* a home. She needed peace and order and serenity. At the moment she had none of the above, and she was in no condition to create order out of all that confusion. I gathered myself up and looked her right in the eye. "I am here on assignment," I told her. "I have a message for you. God is going to redeem the years the locusts have eaten. You will have that godly husband and houses—plural! So let's get organized." By the end of the day, we had fluffed and polished and brought about a small miracle, surrounding Charlotte with some of her dear and familiar things, and a rebirth of hope.

Charlotte needed someone that day—someone who not only could decorate her home, but someone who could remind her of her dream. Seventeen years later I can look back and see where God has redeemed every single area the enemy stole from her—the husband, the multiple homes (three!), the fulfilling career. And the bonus for me is that as her prayer partner and close friend, I feel as if all these wonderful blessings have come to me as well!

Do you understand, dear one, that while we may be talking about interpreting dreams experienced during sleep, the same principles apply to the interpretation of a life dream, as with Charlotte's? Only God Himself, the Dream-Maker, can interpret your dream. Interpreting dreams is His business. Only He is discerning and wise enough. In the process, He may send prophets and princesses to help, but ultimately He alone knows the end from the beginning. It is all part of the Dream-Maker's intricate design.

Hearing the Voice of the Interpreter

As you stay focused on God, become deeply rooted in His Word, and listen for His still, small voice (in your heart), He will give you the interpretation of your own dream.

A lovely spiritual daughter of mine, Victoria, a former prostitute and strip dancer, has established a ministry, Victoria's Friends, to bring other young women out of that lifestyle. One of them is Chandra, a stripper in a downtown club. With a lot of quick money and the security that bought for herself and her three young children, Chandra thought she was living her dream. When she discovered Jesus through Victoria's ministry, she left the old lifestyle behind, at least until she encountered a bump in the road. She was moving toward healing when she got her feelings hurt by a Christian couple with whom she was living.

About this time Victoria brought Chandra to a "Beauty for Ashes" conference where I was the speaker. During a time of ministry, Chandra approached me in the line for prayer for her broken heart and wounded emotions. I knew that the Lord was dealing with her, yet I could read the total despair and confusion in her demeanor. She was a step away from plunging into the pit.

When Victoria later told me that Chandra was tempted to go back to the only life she knew, I swung into action and arranged a conference call. "Chandra," I began, "what is this I hear? Just what are you thinking?"

With tears, she confessed, "This isn't worth it. I'm going back to dancing."

What she meant was that she was tossing aside her new birth experience and going back to Egypt! I knew that if she did that, she would be choosing death, not life. She needed an interpreter to translate the dream. What did it all mean? How would she make it?

"Chandra," I said, speaking with the bold authority the Lord gave me at that moment just for her, "there is no way you're going back. I will stand in the gap for you and walk you through this. We'll put a net around you and draw you close. Victoria and I will be God's hand extended."

By now she was sobbing. In the background I could hear the voices of her children, needing her attention. God's dream for this girl was in jeopardy, and He had tapped Victoria and me to interpret. We stormed heaven in Chandra's behalf, then arranged a meeting for Sunday. After another prayer for serenity and peace, we said good night and promised to stay in close touch.

The next day Chandra e-mailed Victoria: "Is this a dream? I'm calm! I can't believe I'm so calm!"

Yes, Chandra, it is a dream, God's dream for you. You're moving—out of your dark pit and the prison of rejection and heartache—from Egypt to the Promised Land.

Prayer for Interpretation of the Dream: **Father God, we thank You that You are** the Interpreter of our dreams. No one else knows the end from the beginning. No one else cares so intimately about all the details of our lives and knows so well the powerful potential within us. Thank You for speaking to us in the dark of night, while we are slumbering, and in the daytime vision. Thank You for warning us, for directing us, for protecting us, for instructing us, and for helping us avoid the pits and pitfalls of life. Help us to hold Your dream close to our hearts and bring Your anointed ones to lead us out, to set us free, to heal us, and to bring us into that place with You where we become whole. We thank You that, in the darkest hour, You allow the song to break forth, the dance to begin, and the dream to be resurrected. In Jesus' name, amen.

Then Jacob tore his clothes, put sackcloth on

his waist, and mourned for his son many days.

And all his sons and daughters arose to comfort him;

but he refused to be comforted, and he said,

"For I shall go down into the grave to my son

in mourning." Thus his father wept for him.

GENESIS 37:34,35

CHAPTER 4

Relinquishing the Dream

*"I have been crucified with Christ; it is no longer
I who live, but Christ lives in me; and the life which
I now live in the flesh I live by faith in the Son of God,
who loved me and gave Himself for me."*

GALATIANS 2:20

Her demeanor was downcast. Her eyes, deep pools of murky, muddy brown. Her posture spoke of both defeat and defiance. But there was more to Chandra's story, and we were willing to wage warfare to ensure a happy ending.

Victoria, my faithful spiritual daughter, had dutifully issued an invitation to the girl to attend the Sunday worship service at our church. After lunch, we reconvened for prayer at my house. For three hours, we prayed and wept, engaging the enemy in fierce spiritual "hand-to-hand" combat[1] for Chandra's very soul. There was no doubt that if she left that day without Jesus, she would return to a lifestyle of the living dead.

Finally, she broke, renouncing her sinful past and accepting Jesus Christ as her Savior, her Rescuer, her Knight in shining armor. It was as if He galloped into my living room on a white horse and scooped her up into His arms. In the face of such true and unconditional love, she melted. Before the afternoon was over, she had also received the baptism of the Holy Spirit to empower her to live this new life and was delivered of three demonic strongholds that had set themselves up in her life at her invitation—perversion and lust, witchcraft, and a rebellious spirit. The unexpected bonus was that her little eight-year-old son, who had been back in my bedroom with his four-year-old sister and my husband, was also saved! What victory! What celebration! You could have heard the shouts all the way to the new Jerusalem[2] as we rejoiced with the angels in heaven!

The transformation in Chandra was instantaneous. Her eyes lost their jaded dullness. Even the color changed. With the new life that now pulsated throughout her being, they sparkled like green diamonds. If I hadn't seen it for myself, I would have been skeptical that such change could be possible so quickly.

What happened? What miracle was accomplished on that Sunday afternoon, and how did it all come about?

I Die to Myself

The key to Chandra's breakthrough came when she was willing to relinquish her own dream of security, wealth, and power and exchange it for God's dream for her life. That kind of relinquishment involves dying to self, letting go of your own agenda, surrendering the sins and claims of the past in order to embrace the glorious dream God has envisioned for your future. Chandra is going to find that the life of the believer brings more excitement and drama than anything she has left behind. But she will also find a few surprises.

As we have already learned, in almost every case, the world's view is the exact opposite of God's view. Jesus said, "'...My strength is made perfect in weakness,'" to which Paul quickly replied, "Therefore most gladly I will rather boast in my infirmities, that the power of Christ may rest upon me. Therefore I take pleasure in infirmities, in reproaches, in needs, in persecutions, in distresses, for Christ's sake. For when I am weak, then I am strong" (2 Cor. 12:9,10).

Jesus also said, "...I did not come to bring peace but a sword" (Matt. 10:34), and "He who finds his life will lose it, and he who loses his life for My sake will find it" (v. 39). Riddles? Puzzles? No, simply the mysteries of God, hidden from those who do not have spiritual eyes to see or ears to hear.

Solving these mysteries, as the Holy Spirit leads u
the Dream, the Great Adventure God has planned fo

Self will always be your greatest enemy—*your*
your plans, *your* selfish ambition. All that is to be drop
coat on a spring day. Paradoxically, you will only b   *your*
maximum potential when you confess your weakness a_   _.c willing to die
to any dream but God's. The process might be painful as you surrender pet
habits and hopes, but it will free you to view life from His perspective.

One of the most powerful aids in overcoming strongholds, such as the
ones that imprisoned Chandra, is praying the Word of God back to Him. Beth
Moore, a gifted writer and Bible teacher, offers a treasure trove of practical
prayers in her best-selling book, *Praying God's Word.* An example is this
prayer based on Romans 6:11-14.

Christ Jesus, I count myself dead to sin but alive to God in You.
Therefore I will not let sin reign in my mortal body so that I obey its evil
desires. I choose not to offer the parts of my body to sin, as instruments of
wickedness, but rather I offer myself to God, as one who has been brought
from death to life I offer the parts of my body to You as instruments of right-
eousness. Sin shall not be my master, because I am not under the law but
under grace. Amen.[3]

Joseph's prison years were brought about by the false accusation of a
woman who tried to seduce him. He chose not to offer the parts of his body
to sin, as instruments of wickedness,[4] but was faithful to honor God in every
circumstance—even the most difficult tests. Just as the enemy sets us up for
disaster when we sin, so God uses every good decision we make to advance
His dream. Strange as it may seem, Joseph's wise choice propelled him into
prison, but God used him mightily there. From the time he had his two
dreams until the time of their fulfillment was thirteen years. But those dreams
came to pass because Joseph chose to believe and surrender all to God.

9 Surrender

Another way of expressing what happened to Chandra—and Joseph—is
surrender. The word *surrender* implies that there has been some kind of
struggle before the decision was made to give in to a greater authority. Before

ing her will to that of Jesus Christ, Chandra had to weigh her losses. e felt that as a stripper, the pay was good and the hours were short. Although it wasn't exactly a dream job, she could support her children, with time and money left over to dress well and enjoy life. As long as she could maintain her youth and beauty, it seemed to her that she would "have it made." If she quit her job, she would have to find other work—soon! Nor was she prepared for the current slow market. It wouldn't be easy, but she made the right decision to follow Jesus and submit to His dream for her life.

Our modern-day picture of surrender may stem from film footage of wars fought in faraway places or movies and television depicting cops and robbers. Men armed with guns, the "bad guys" with hands in the air, a visual statement that says, "You win. I give up. Your strength and power are greater than mine. I will no longer fight back."

In the spiritual realm, the message goes much deeper. When the battle is over, when you stop fighting with God, He opens the door to kingdom treasures that cannot be seen with the natural eye. As you give Him permission to be the Lord of all of your life, you will find that surrender is victory! In fact, without it, you cannot proceed to the next level of God's dream for you.

I recall another scenario of surrender. This battlefield was not the mountains or fields of Korea or Afghanistan or the desert lands of Iraq, but the posh living room of an elegant grande dame, the mother of a friend of mine. Still strikingly beautiful, this woman had been a New York model at one time but was now battling terminal cancer. Her daughter had invited John and me over on a Saturday afternoon in the hope of winning her mother to the Lord.

Having lost all of her hair during chemotherapy, this charming woman looked chic and stylish in a lovely robe and matching turban. Ever the gracious hostess, she insisted on serving tea and engaging in conversation. My husband, however, was on a mission and didn't want to miss this opportunity to minister. In spite of the fact that I was picking up all kinds of signals that she wasn't interested in "spiritual talk," John persisted. Finally, clearly uncomfortable, she excused herself to "rest awhile" and withdrew from the room, leaving her daughter to entertain us.

When we began to laugh hysterically over some hilarious incident that had happened recently, suddenly without warning the mother returned, taking a seat as far from John as she could get. "I haven't heard laughter in so long. Just what were you girls talking about anyway?" she asked.

Before we could reply, John pulled from his pocket a copy of the Sinner's Prayer that he always carries with him. "I want to read you something," he told her, and before she could object, he proceeded to do just that.

She was spellbound. "That is the most beautiful prayer I've ever heard," she admitted. My heartbeat quickened! I knew that I was about to witness a miracle!

John pinned her with his gaze. "God wants to heal you," he said. "He heals emotionally, spiritually, and physically. But before you can receive all that He has for you, you have to pray this prayer and let Him into your heart."

To my amazement, she agreed. Of course, it was the physical healing she was after, but when she came to the phrase "I surrender," she began to weep. This charming hostess, who knew just what to say in any social setting, had no words—until now—to express that she was at the end of herself, with no hope. Over the next four months her life radically changed. She began listening to praise music, soaking in the healing Word of God, and fellowshipping with the Lord.

It is always God's desire that we are healthy and whole in our spirit, soul, and body: "Beloved, I wish above all things that thou mayest prosper and be in health..." (3 John 2 KJV). He also tells us in Ecclesiastes 3:2 that there's "a time to be born, and a time to die..." meaning that death is a season of life. And so it was for my friend's mother. At the end of those four months, she went home to be with the Lord.

At her death, God opened the gates of heaven and welcomed this unlikely angel—His child—home. It's just sad that it had taken the pit of cancer, a terrible condition that can make one feel as if they are in a prison of hopelessness, to bring her to His dream of salvation and right relationship with Him.

In retrospect, I see a poignant touch from the Lord in this story. Another sign of surrender is "waving the white flag." I can just see this lovely woman lifting a white hanky from among her exquisite collection to signal the end of her struggle. Her daughter gave me one of those handkerchiefs, lavished with Belgian lace, as a token of her victory that memorable day!

I Yield

We are so conscious of time. How quickly it flies! How little there seems to be of it. How we would love to freeze some precious moments for savoring. Then there are those minutes and hours that crawl by, times when we are waiting for a doctor's diagnosis, when a loved one's life hangs in the balance, when the answer to a prayer has not yet come. To yield has several meanings. One is "...to surrender or submit (oneself) to another...."[5] It can also be to take a little time—as in braking your car at a caution light—to pause, to slow down.

With this in mind, another term for yielding might be "time lapse." A time lapse is a necessary part of spiritual growth. It allows God an opportunity to work in your behalf, to do the refining and pruning necessary to shape you for your destiny. You might be spending time in a place of confinement, as Joseph did. If so, it is your choice to moan and complain or to grow and become great. Joseph chose to grow, to allow God time to mature him, to yield himself to the process of becoming. I'm sure that as a boy with big dreams, he really had no clue that someday he would be second only to Pharaoh, that he would be one of the two most powerful men in the land of Egypt. He just took each day as it came, accepting each challenge with integrity, being molded into a vessel fit for God's use.

You are great in God's eyes when you answer His call. You need not be the president of a company or a member of the country club or the woman of the year. You need not measure up to some well-known, admired personality who is in the public eye. Your job is to be the best *you* that you can be—to bloom where you are planted, to be faithful in the little things, to yield to the Master's voice and to His touch.

These time lapses, these refreshing pauses—even if you are spending them in bed during an illness or in limbo because you have been laid off at work—will test your character, to see how far you've come in the Lord and how far you have yet to go. These are times of increased heat and pressure, times of questioning yourself and others, times of exploration and discovery. It is in these times that you will develop your greatest spiritual muscle. Being unable to withstand God's (seeming) silence, we can prevail in prayer, beating our fists on the gates of heaven until we hear from Him.

This is preparation time, time to yield. Like Queen Esther, who spent a full year in the extensive beauty regimen required of a young woman in competition for the affections of the king,[6] you are being groomed to win the crown.[7] And you never know when the time is up, when your name will be called.

One "time lapse" for me lasted seven years. After being abandoned by my first husband and left penniless with our two small daughters, I prayed for God to send someone into my life to love us. This prayer was not uttered immediately, of course, but long after I had begun to pick up the pieces of my shattered life.

Soon after my first husband left for good, I drove the 45 miles home to "Willbrook," our family farm about an hour from Charleston, South Carolina, to see my mother and father and to receive some measure of comfort from them. But it was a month before my younger sister's wedding, and Mother had just returned from a trip to Europe to find that much had fallen through the cracks while she was gone.

"Darling, half of the invitations were lost in the mail, and the cleaners have lost the guest room curtains!" she explained. Presents were piled high, and thank-you notes had to be written.

"Mary Ashley and I simply have so much to do. I hope you understand…this is just not a good time for a visit."

Poor Mother. I should have sympathized with her plight. Not so very long ago, she was orchestrating the details for my wedding. But all I could think of was my own crisis. All I could hear were her last words: "Not a good time." My heart was breaking, but this was not a good time. Neither of us had any idea that day just how prophetic her statement would be.

How interesting that it was Mother who was with me seven years later when my eyes fell on John Platz in the VIP room at JFK Airport in New York as we were preparing to make a trip to Israel. John—the fulfillment of my prayer and dream for a life mate, the person with whom I would co-partner in ministry. I soon learned that he had been widowed a year and a half earlier.

"I knew almost immediately when I heard him say that his wife died the year before that you would marry," Mother told me later.

Mother and I don't often travel together, and it was unusual that she was with me at this particular time. But that, too, was part of God's design. God placed her there to behold my destiny and to propel me into it.

Eliza, a precious mentor of mine, had handed me the brochure, describing this trip to the Holy Land. I knew to pay attention. Eliza always offered advice with wisdom and forethought. And Mother encouraged me to go— even offered to accompany me. Mother is a very savvy, seasoned traveler. She has been to many of the most exotic places in the world, traveling to Russia, to just about all the countries on the continent of Europe, and on extended visits to Japan and France. Even when she came out of open-heart surgery, her first words were, "Does this mean I'm not going to China this year?" But Israel had escaped her notice until the prime moment in time— God's time and His timing. "For some reason," she told me, she had a tremendous desire to go to Israel, and so we went!

I recalled the story of Ruth and Naomi. How, after the death of her husband, Ruth had traveled with her mother-in-law back to Bethlehem, Naomi's hometown. You probably remember those famous lines of Ruth from Scripture: "Entreat me not to leave you, or to turn back from following after you; for wherever you go, I will go; and wherever you lodge, I will lodge; your people shall be my people, and your God, my God" (Ruth 1:16). Now here we were—my mother and I—on another historic journey. Yet this time God was leading me away from my mother's house and into a deeper relationship with Him. I had the feeling that neither of us—Mother nor I— would ever be the same.

Is it not stunning how God redeems everything and everyone? Just look at the picture of who is there with you witnessing the moment. Watch how God *includes*, never *excludes*. My mother had spoken some words earlier in my life about time: "This is just not a good time...." That was *not* the time— the world's answer to crisis. *This was* the divinely appointed time—God's answer. His answer is always restoration and healing, and He says, "Come home to Me!" Mother was in this picture on purpose. God wanted her to witness His providential hand in my life. She saw the moment of connection between John and me, even prophesied our union. She knew that it was a divine appointment and that my life was redeemed from the pit! Praise God!

We'll watch that picture unfold again when Joseph is reunited with his brothers. They will see God's redemption in his life and bear witness to the awesome power of the Almighty in that yielded vessel. Only He can perform such miracles so that in the end, everyone wins!

I Submit

If there is anything on earth that some women refuse to do, it's to submit! The very word itself conjures up images of dictatorial employers or spouses, lording it over someone weaker—and in their eyes, at least—inferior. I'm no militant feminist, but that thought even makes *my* blood boil!

But I have good news for you. I saved this word for last because the whole process of relinquishing your dream for God's dream, as you know, is a series of steps—dying to self, surrender, yielding—and finally, perhaps the most difficult and dramatic of all: submission. But I believe that once you are able to see the true spiritual significance of this act, you will never again have a problem with it.

You see, God's perspective on submission is giving way before a force that one can no longer resist. His love expressed in His Son, Jesus Christ, is absolutely irresistible! The opposite of submitting is holding out, refusing to let go, insisting on your own way. Yet, why would anyone choose their own way when God's way is so infinitely more fulfilling and rewarding?

Recently, during an afternoon visit at my house, I was counseling a spiritual daughter who had strayed from her Christian roots and was dabbling in the New Age philosophy. Thirty-something, she is bright and beautiful, but a little on the stubborn side.

"The reason I'm here," she began, "is because I know you have the answer. I can look at your life—you're so…together—and I see that you have it."

Without hesitation, I replied, "Yes, I do have the answer, and I'll tell you what it is. You must submit—that means recklessly abandon yourself—to Jesus Christ. If you don't, you'll never get back on track."

She paused in thought, tapping one polished nail on the table. "But there are some things about the New Age movement that are very positive and very good."

Again the words flew out of my mouth, and I knew it was a steady stream of divine revelation for this precious one. "I'm sure you're right." I picked up the glass of water before me, noting its clarity. "What you're experimenting with is like this glass—except that a certain percentage of it is liquid, pure and clear, and the rest is poison. That's what the New Age movement is."

I waited for this to sink in before continuing. "We are at the point where we don't need to move forward until you are ready to relinquish everything to Jesus Christ. He's your Advocate with the Father, to bring you back to Him. You want to know why I am 'successful'? It's because of Jesus, and He's the only Way *you're* going to get there. By the way," I added, "you just *thought* it was your idea to come here today. I have news for you." I smiled at her reaction of surprise. "It was the Holy Spirit who prompted you. You can't know Jesus without having interacted with Him."

Before she left that day, she had prayed the Sinner's Prayer, asked me for a copy to take to the gentleman she was dating, and promised to stay in touch. I told her that I would be praying that she would hunger and thirst for the Word of God and that she would stay immersed in the Word until she learned all that God had for her. A week later I received a note, telling me that she was "hungering and thirsting for more of Him and couldn't get enough!"

Relinquishment brings us into a new relationship with the Lord and with others, gives us new eyes to see, and a desire to invest in the eternal. Until you know the love of God, you don't know anything about love at all. Before that, everything is self-love, self-absorption, self-help.

By the time I was thirty, I was ready to relinquish my selfish self. I was tired of struggling to have my own way, tired of trying to manage my own life, tired of focusing inward. I was especially weary of trying to patch up my broken dreams. I was ready to step into the dream God had for me.

Elisabeth Elliot, lecturer, teacher, and one of the most popular Christian writers of our time, speaks of this final step of faith in her book *Discipline: The Glad Surrender,* "Why then, instead of taking Christ at His word, do we prefer to argue ('it's too hard, too restrictive, it isn't my thing'), to claim our 'rights,' to muddle through on our own? In this way paradise was lost. It is the same enemy who comes to us today with the same lie ('you shall not die, but live'). Yet still faithfully Jesus calls to life and to utter bliss those who will follow His way. Granted, it is the way of the cross, but only that way leads to the resurrection."[8]

Prayer of Relinquishment: Gracious Father, I come to You today as a wounded warrior, a veteran of many wars, a soldier who has fought a long battle. I come with flag in hand and heart. I relinquish the war that was never meant to be won, the burden that is too heavy to carry and too expensive to keep. I gladly surrender the chambers of my heart, my wounded past, my fractured memories...all to You! With Your help, I am willing to die to my selfish dreams. I surrender. I yield. I submit to Your greater vision. I abandon myself to You for my safety and Your glory. Give me the humility of heart that only You can give, the restoration needed for my life, and the pathway You have chosen for my footsteps. From this day forward, I choose to follow Your dream. In Jesus' name, amen.

PART II

The Dream-Stealers

"Here comes that master-dreamer…let's kill
him and toss him into a well and tell
Father that a wild animal has eaten him.
Then we'll see what will become of all his dreams!"

GENESIS 37:19 TLB

"Now Joseph had a dream, and he told it to his brothers; and they hated him even more. And his brothers said to him, 'Shall you indeed reign over us? Or shall you indeed have dominion over us?' So they hated him even more for his dreams and for his words."

GENESIS 37:5,8

CHAPTER 5

Unmasking the Dream-Stealers, Part 9: In the Most Unexpected Places

"The thief does not come except to steal, and to kill, and to destroy. I have come that [you] may have life, and that [you] may have it more abundantly."

JOHN 10:10

In identifying the dream-stealers, you need to remember that your life dream—that utilizes all the talents and abilities God has given you to bless others and bring glory to Himself—is targeted for extinction by the enemy of your soul. So don't be surprised when someone or something comes along to pluck it right out of your heart.

Some dream-stealers are obvious:

- the jealous friend
- the unfaithful spouse
- the financial reversal
- the serious illness
- a teacher who tells you that you are not qualified to reach your goal

Others are subtler:

- a passing remark
- betrayal of a sibling
- a perceived criticism
- an inferior grade in school

As a younger woman, I never considered myself to be a writer. Actually, no teacher had to call this to my attention. It was there in black and white on my report card! Spelling was my nemesis. Nor was I in the accelerated English class, as some of my friends were. It was a subtle statement. It was certainly easy for me to assume that I should never aspire to write for publication. I had no doubt that the right-brain creativity was present, but I was lacking in technical skills. Not until a mentor recognized this part of the vision for my life and challenged me to dream big did I allow myself to ponder the possibility.

Now, with eleven books in print, I have to laugh at my earlier reservation. In retrospect, I can now see the potential. The five-year-old with paintbrush in hand, dabbing bold splashes of color on paper, would one day wield a pen with the same flair and flamboyance. As for spelling, that's why writers have editors and spell check!

What about unrealistic expectations? Did you think your high school sweetheart was dream husband material because he was the quarterback for the football team or the best dancer at the prom—only to discover after marrying him that your dream was, in reality, a nightmare? Or maybe you didn't make it into a certain college. Did that brand you as "not smart enough," or "not good enough"? These thoughts, at a subliminal level, can shape your opinion of yourself and sabotage your dream.

A dream must be nurtured and kept alive. What happens to us in early childhood is so important. Therefore, some of us may have to look no farther than our own doorstep to find a dream-stealer. As we explore these very personal areas, ask the Lord to heal that very spot. Listen to His words (in your heart) as He speaks to your wounded place, and allow Him to help you reclaim your dream.

Problems at Home

He was a small-town boy, one of many who played with his brothers and sisters in the dusty streets and helped with the chores. His father ran a business out of the home, so the children learned early the value of a strong work ethic and honest dealings. Still, a cloud hovered over the little family. Rumor had it that his mother was a "loose woman," that he had even been conceived out of wedlock. The stigma of that shame followed him, compounded by the fact that his siblings regarded him as a dreamer, too idealistic for any practical purpose.[1]

Yet the dream burned in his heart, not to be extinguished by any rumor or family squabble. And he went on to fulfill his destiny so that you and I might fulfill ours. Who was He? By now you have probably guessed. It was Jesus, the Son of the living God.

As one of the great theologians of the twentieth century, Oswald Chambers, put it, "For thirty years Jesus lived at home with brothers and sisters who did not believe in Him, and when He began His ministry they said He was mad…. We say, 'When I was born again I thought it would be a time of great illumination and service, and instead of that I have had to stay at home with people who have criticized me on the right hand and on the left; I have been misunderstood and misrepresented.' Do we think our lot ought to be better than Jesus Christ's?"[2]

Dear one, you're not the only one with problems at home. Jesus had some, too!

Why is it that those who are supposed to know us best and love us most are among the ones the enemy often uses to delay or destroy the dream? Remember that little snake in the first garden? Well, that serpent was the master deceiver, Satan in disguise, the one who caused the first couple to have their first fight. The woman listened to his lie—if she ate the fruit of a certain tree in the garden, she would be as wise as God—and believed it. Like many women, she couldn't keep the news to herself, so since there was only one other person on earth to tell, she told her husband. He fell for it, too. This created a separation from God, who had created all things for their good and His glory, and thus began all the troubles in the world. (Gen. 3.) Of course, this is a very simplified version of sin.

God had told Adam and Eve, "...Be fruitful and multiply..." (Gen. 1:28), but even that command was corrupted. When they were evicted from their "garden apartment" and started a family, their firstborn son proceeded to murder his younger brother out of jealousy and spite. Is it any wonder, then, that we have gone on to multiplied sorrows (Gen. 3:16)?

A quick scan of the Bible, the story of God's loving plan to redeem fallen man, will reveal that one family after another started out with all good intentions to honor His original dream—His covenant made with Abraham—only to succumb to their own fleshly nature or to stumble into one of Satan's pits. Take Joseph's ancestors, for example.

His great-grandfather Abraham lied about his relationship to his wife to save his own skin.[3] Years later, Grandfather Isaac did the same thing with his wife Rebekah.[4] And his father, Jacob? Well, therein lies a story in itself.

Bad Dad?

God did not choose Jacob because of what he already was but because of what he was capable of becoming. Jacob, like all the rest of us, was not perfect. Far from it.

On the LaHaye Temperament Scale that we discussed earlier, Jacob would probably be a Choleric-Melancholy—a rare combination of leadership qualities and sensitive introspection. He could be described as fire and flame. It was Jacob who was so anxious to be born that he grabbed his twin brother Esau's heel, as if he were trying to thrust himself into the world first and reverse the birth order.[5] Jacob's action was an early sign of his future character as an artful, selfish, crafty man.[6]

He was his mother's (Rebekah's) favorite, and she was so determined that Jacob should have his father's blessing that she connived to get it. Jacob was deceptive and manipulative, yet later when the tables were turned—when he himself was duped by his Uncle Laban to marry the older daughter, Leah, instead of her younger sister, Rachel—Jacob was patient enough to work another seven long years to marry his true love.[7]

I suppose, when you think about it, Jacob was set up to be a deceiver. Not only did he "inherit" his basic sin nature from the evil one, but both parents also engaged in deceitful practices. Deception ran in the family! In

Numbers 14:18 the Bible refers to generational traits like this that are passed down in families: "The Lord is longsuffering and abundant in mercy, forgiving iniquity and transgression; but He by no means clears the guilty, visiting the iniquity of the fathers on the children to the third and fourth generation."

Jacob's one redeeming feature, however, was his consuming passion to encounter God. Jacob set out for the land of his fathers not only to flee from Esau's threats to kill him for tricking their father into giving him Esau's blessing,[8] but also he was not satisfied with a secondhand faith. Soon he stopped for the night to rest and dreamed of a stairway to the stars. Angels were ascending and descending a ladder that stretched to heaven's gate, where God was standing. Jacob heard God declare to him, "...I am the Lord God of Abraham your father and the God of Isaac; the land on which you lie I will give to you and your descendants. Also your descendants shall be as the dust of the earth...and in you and your seed all the families of the earth shall be blessed" (Gen. 28:13,14).

With the Abrahamic covenant confirmed, Jacob named the place "Bethel," meaning "house of God."[9] "...Surely the Lord is in this place, and I did not know it...How awesome is this place! This is none other than the house of God, and this is the gate of heaven!" (Gen. 28:16,17). In this moment of revelation, we see the sensitive nature of this man who was searching for his spiritual roots—actually, searching for his life dream, which he found literally "written in the sky" by the Lord Himself at Bethel.

Despite this supernatural experience and one other—when he wrestled with God and was left with a limp for a while and a name change to Israel[10]—we will see that Jacob was not a particularly strong role model for his twelve sons. In our fatherless culture, where many men have completely abdicated their responsibility or have failed to acknowledge their own children, Jacob doesn't seem so unusual. In fact, from the overall picture of his destiny as a "father of the faith," it appears that he must have been better than most. At least, he surpassed one father I heard about.

A precious friend of mine knows all about dads who are "dream busters." Carol Johnson dreamed of offering healthful, homemade bread to people in the marketplace because she realized that in America we have relinquished our responsibility for baking "daily" bread to commercial food processors that strip away vital nutrients in order to achieve longer shelf life.

By offering her nutritious bread and the Bread of Life, Jesus Christ,[11] simultaneously, she saw an opportunity for providing both physical and spiritual nourishment, reaching those who might otherwise never enter a church.

But before her venture was off the ground, a dream-stealer was busily at work—her dad. Her father cautioned her about leaving a "sure thing"—a fabulous job in medical sales at a six-figure income—and told her she was crazy to pursue this idea. What she needed desperately was to hear, "Go for it! You can do it! I'm so proud of you!" But there was never an encouraging word, and she was forced to drop the subject around him altogether.

In the meantime, Carol separated herself from her father for a time, buried herself in the Word, and attended church faithfully. Through it all, the Lord kept confirming to her to "press on." Literally, she had to choose between her earthly father and her heavenly Father. The choice is now obvious, although a few months before he died, Carol's dad spoke the long-overdue words she was hungry to hear.

The greatest lesson that came from the long waiting season before her ministry was launched, she testifies, is that preparation is necessary to the dream. God was preparing the moment for her and her for the moment. During this time the enemy was relentless in his attempt to kill her dream and shipwreck her faith. She had to repeatedly remind the devil that he could not steal her purpose, her destiny.

Recently Carol told me, "I had no idea three years ago, when I followed the call of God on my life, that we would be on The 700 Club, that Pat Robertson[12] would mention my ministry in his new book, that we would be shipping this bread nationally, or that so many people would want to franchise. God, in His infinite wisdom and creativity, can bring things to pass that we could never dream or imagine!"

If you have unresolved problems with your father, let the heavenly Father speak encouragement to your heart right now: *"My child. My little one. My under-shepherd. My dear friend: You are many things to Me, just as I am many things to you. My love for you is deep and tender.… How can I tell you that though I desire holiness, and while I desire fruit in your life, still My love for you is not contingent upon anything you attain?… I love you because you are My child. I love you because I am your Father. I love you with Calvary love. At a great price I redeemed you—because I have always loved you."[13]*

$\mathcal{M}essy$ $\mathcal{M}othering$

Fathers are not the only ones who can sin against their families by robbing their children of a dream. Unfortunately, mothers, too, can be the perpetrators of this kind of emotional domestic "violence." Some moms can be indifferent to their children's deepest needs, preoccupied with work or other activities, selfishly introverted, or physically absent during many of the childhood years.

My daughter Margo and I recently ran into a friend of ours at a conference. This friend's mother, by the world's standards, had it all—glamour, accomplishment, material possessions, position in the community, long-term marriage, and grown children. But upon closer inspection, the picture was fragmented and not at all what it appeared to be. This woman was masking much of who she was, a woman truly unable to love. She had a narcissistic personality disorder, which caused her to try to fill her life with material things and relationships to feed this empty desire to be loved and adored.

Her neediness had led her to a life of self-centeredness, secret alcoholism, and adultery. Her inability to mother her children caused an unnatural distancing from them in the early stages of their lives, thereby causing the children to connect emotionally with the father and bond with others who were there to nurture and care for them. This mother could justify all of her sins and neglect as someone else's fault, never hers.

As her children grew, she chose favorites and caused rivalry to spring up among them. To complicate the family dynamics, she fed and fueled the fire even more by changing her will several times. This mother was physically absent for long periods of time, claiming sickness and stress or a desire to travel and see the world—this is truly the epitome of messy mothering!

As my friend began to tell her story, I reminded her that God chooses our parents, a fact over which we have no control. God purposes who our mothers will be and why, although it may take a lifetime to connect all the links. For example, while Joseph certainly would have chosen nicer brothers, God used these sibling relationships to refine and position him for kingdom purposes.

I encouraged my friend to pray for her mother and to look to God to supply what her mother had failed to provide. One day she would be able to understand the mystery of her family of origin. Until then, she should press on toward the high calling of Jesus Christ and obey His command: "Do good to those who hate you, bless those who curse you, and pray for those who spitefully use you…and your reward will be great" (Luke 6:27,28,35).

There can be victory in our relationships if we understand the enemy's setup to take our dreams. This evil plan often works through those we love or who are positioned to love us.

I recently met another woman who, as a girl, had dreamed of becoming a dancer. In punishment for coming home late from school one day, her mother had stopped her dance lessons. Now, forty years later, this woman was still devastated, her dream crushed.

Tears spilled down her cheeks as I looked her directly in the eye and said, "God is bringing back your dream. Reclaim it!"

She began to weep as she envisioned the return of a lifelong passion. For her, dance was not appearing at Carnegie Hall, but self-expression, breaking free of a restriction imposed by her mother. If that mother could only have known what she was doing that long-ago day. She had shut her daughter down, had captured and contained that free spirit, and locked it away for a generation.

On this day, I hoped to break through to the young dreamer. "Dance, darling!"

I'm a mother, too. To my daughters, Margo and Courtney, whose creativity is alive and freely expressed through many outlets, I say, "I'm so proud of you! I knew you could do it! Dance!" To my spiritual daughters, many of whom are victims of childhood abuse or neglect, I say, "I love you! I believe in you! Dance!" To you who have lost the creative drive or purpose God planted in your heart years ago, I say, "Dance! Don't let your dream die or be stolen by an authority figure or financial circumstances. Dance! Gather a group of little girls and start your own dance team. Organize one at the church and worship God with all of your being. Dance!" Reclaim your dream!

Be encouraged by God's mothering message to you: *When you cast yourself upon Me as a baby upon a mother's breast, then shall you know surely that I have been constantly at your very side; that I have never deserted you. My love for you is of such nature and intensity that it would be impossible for you to ever escape My thoughts, or My longing for you to ever waver. My arms are already outstretched to receive you. Only believe. My arms shall gather you, and I shall never let you go.*[14]

"O Brother, Where Art Thou?"

As you already know, Joseph was born into a "dysfunctional family" long before the term was popular. He lost his mother when his younger brother, Benjamin, was born. His father was devastated by her death and took consolation in his first wife, Leah, and some concubines. With Jacob's large brood of boys and a daughter named Dinah, combined with managing the herds and farmhands, one wonders if there was much time for proper parenting. Jacob was a God-fearing man, which weighs heavily in his favor. But it was no secret that Joseph was his favorite son, and this didn't help Joseph's standing with his ten older brothers. In fact, it was a point of contention among them that led to much bickering and ill will, particularly when he gave Joseph, then a teenager, the infamous multi-colored coat.

A rundown of the family roster with some commentary on his big brothers' misdeeds will show you just what Joseph was up against:[15]

- Reuben—*Notice* (The meaning of his name tells a sad story of unrequited love: The Lord has noticed my trouble, and now my husband will love me [Gen. 29:32, author paraphrase]); eldest son of Jacob and Leah, "the unloved wife"; committed a form of incest with one of his father's concubines; guilty of aiding in the conspiracy to kill Joseph, lying, hatred, and theft.

- Simeon—*Jehovah Heard* (Because the Lord has heard that I am unloved, He has given me another son [Gen. 29:33, author paraphrase]); second son of Jacob and Leah; avenged his sister Dinah's rape by killing all the males in the city; guilty of conspiracy to kill Joseph, lying, hatred, theft, and violence.

- Levi—*Attachment* (Surely now my husband will feel affection for me, since I have given him three sons! [Gen. 29:34, author paraphrase]); third son of Jacob and Leah; avenged his sister's rape by killing all the males in the city; guilty of conspiracy to kill Joseph, lying, theft, hatred, and violence.

- Judah—*Praise* ("...Now I will praise the Lord..." [Gen. 29:35]); fourth son of Jacob and Leah; guilty of conspiracy to kill Joseph, lying, hatred, theft, and violence.

- Issachar—*Wages* (God has repaid me for giving my maid to my husband [Gen. 30:18, author paraphrase]); fifth son of Jacob and Leah; guilty of conspiracy to kill Joseph, lying, hatred, theft, and violence.

- Zebulun—*Gifts* (God has given me good gifts for my husband; now he will honor me for giving him six sons [Gen. 30:20, author paraphrase]); sixth son of Jacob and Leah; guilty of conspiracy to kill Joseph, lying, hatred, theft, and violence.

- Dan—*Justice* (God has given me justice and given me a son [Gen. 30:6, author paraphrase]); son of Jacob and Rachel, by Bilhah; guilty of conspiracy to kill Joseph, lying, hatred, theft, and violence.

- Naphtali—*Wrestling* ("...I am in a fierce contest with my sister and I am winning!" [Gen. 30:8 TLB]); son of Jacob and Rachel, by Bilhah; guilty of conspiracy to kill Joseph, lying, hatred, theft, and violence.

- Gad—*Lucky* ("...'My luck has turned!'" [Gen. 30:11 TLB]); son of Jacob and Leah, by Zilpah; guilty of conspiracy to kill Joseph, lying, hatred, theft, and violence.

- Asher—*Happy* ("What joy is mine! The other women will think me blessed indeed!" [Gen. 30:13 TLB]); son of Jacob and Leah, by Zilpah; guilty of conspiracy to kill Joseph, lying, hatred, theft, and violence.

- Benjamin—"...(*'Son of my sorrow'*)..."; Joseph's little brother was born on the way to Bethlehem, but his mother died in childbirth, and his father named the newborn, "...('Son of my right hand')" (Gen. 35:18 TLB).

From these descriptions it seems as if Joseph's older brothers were a savage, bloodthirsty lot with little to commend them. The meaning of their names, in italics, gives interesting insight, showing yet another dimension to Joseph's hectic home life. His mother and her sister, Leah, were in competition for his father's attentions by seeing who could produce the most heirs! In the seasons when they were barren, they simply loaned him their servant girls. With all that rivalry and jealousy in the tent, it must have been difficult for the boys to learn everything they should about godly living from their parents. So it is no small wonder that Joseph, at seventeen, could hear the voice of God in a dream and surrender to the call, or that the dream was immediately attacked by the dream-stealers—Satan and a band of ten rogue brothers!

In all fairness, I should remind you that Reuben was smitten with remorse after plotting to kill young Joseph and persuaded the others to throw their brother into a deep pit instead; secretly he planned to return later and release him. Later, in Egypt, it was Reuben who was the most concerned for their father back home and offered to remain as a hostage while the caravan returned to Canaan to fetch him.

This and a few other noteworthy acts of kindness on the part of some of the brothers is all we have to indicate that God had any decent material at all with which to work in forming the nation that would be called Israel, after Jacob's new name. What an unlikely patriarch! And what improbable candidates for leadership. Who would have voted them into office? Yet these very men, and two others who would come later—Joseph's sons, Ephraim and Manasseh—would be the forerunners of the twelve tribes of Israel! God truly is in the transformation business!

If you have ever felt unworthy, unloved, or unappreciated, you will surely find yourself somewhere in this cast of characters. Take a moment to catalog your own sins. Can you identify with Levi or Leah, Reuben or Rachel? Right now, ask God to search your heart and expose any dark corner. Then repent, and listen as He responds to your heart's cry:

"If you confess your sins, I am faithful and just to forgive you your sins and to cleanse you from all unrighteousness…. O My child, obey My words. Do not wander in unbelief and darkness, but let the Scripture shine as a light upon your path. My Word shall be life to you, for My commandments are given for your health and preservation. I have challenged you to pray, so that I may respond and help you…. I have asked you to forgive, in order to make your heart fit to receive my forgiveness."[16]

A Child's Prayer: Gracious, loving Abba Father, thank You for being our total provision for life…our "All We Need!" We come to You this moment as children in need of a Protector and Keeper of Our Dreams. Thank You for being the stable Father and consistent Parent to us as the dream-stealers march through our lives, intent on trampling down our homes and hearts...stealing and plundering our precious possessions and dreams. You were there standing guard over us when we did not even know who You really were. We felt Your Presence but did not know You! Help us see beyond the devastation and destruction the dream-stealers cause, and take us to the place where only You can lead...the higher place of grace and mercy where truth and peace reign over the enemy of our souls and where we can sing and dance before You forever and ever. In the name of Jesus, Your dear Son, I pray, amen.

And Reuben said to them, "Shed no blood,

but cast him into this pit which is in the wilderness,

and do not lay a hand on him...."

Then they took him and cast him into a pit....

GENESIS 37:22,24

CHAPTER 6

Unmasking the Dream-Stealers, Part II: In the Wilderness

"Fear not...I will help you," says the Lord
and your Redeemer, the Holy One of Israel.
"I will open rivers in desolate heights, and fountains
in the midst of the valleys; I will make the wilderness
a pool of water, and the dry land springs of water."

ISAIAH 41:14,18

At "Willbrook" where I grew up, the landscape beyond the cultivated lawn, beyond the hundred-year-old camellia bushes and the boxwoods around the "big house," was all open fields, bordered by thick, dark woods. When my sister and brothers and I would play in the tangled underbrush in that forest of tall pines, it was easy to lose our way, to become disoriented. What a relief when we would finally break through to a familiar path that led home!

A wilderness may be thickly wooded, like the one at "Willbrook," or it may be as in biblical times, a vast, empty expanse of sand. In the desert there is no provision. The merciless sun at noon brings stifling heat, and the night-time, bitter cold. Sandstorms and windstorms send swirling sand to obscure the horizon and give the wandering nomad no sure landmark.

It was in a desert scenario that Joseph found himself in a deep pit. Once this pit had held water to slake the thirst of traveling shepherds or tradesmen. Now it was his makeshift tomb. Joseph had been overcome, stripped of the wonderful coat his father had given him, and cast there by his strong brothers with the intent to kill him. There was no way out. He could see nothing around him. He could only look…up. What divine provision!

I love uncovering the schemes of the enemy of our souls, discovering pearls in unexpected places and dropping them in your path, standing by as you "get it" and rise above your circumstance to grasp the hand of God and move on toward fulfilling your dream. Some wonderful mentors have done that for me through the years, and now I find it incredibly satisfying to walk alongside you—to point out the pathway…and the pits.

In the last chapter, we took a look at some people—often those closest to us—who can betray our trust. What is so surprising is that these are the very people we expect to love us, support us, champion our cause, and cheer us on when all else fails. Sadly, we have learned that is not always the case.

In addition to people, there are well-conceived plots designed by the enemy to trip us up along the way. These dream-stealers are hiding in the circumstances of life. They are wrong choices, life events, interruptions, and trouble of all kinds that rob us of purpose and hold our dreams hostage. They are life's pits, and they are often found in the wilderness. But as you are about to see, God can lift us up out of even the deepest, darkest pit!

The Pit of Poverty

You can have no money and be rich; you can lack for nothing this world has to offer and be impoverished. The real test lies in who you are within. Jan Tennyson has always been rich—in abundant talents and gifts, in great kindness and love, and in the grace of God.

God's hand has been on her since the beginning. His hand was on her when she was placed in a New York Foundling Home as an infant after her mother suffered a nervous breakdown and had to be institutionalized. His hand was on her when she was moved to a low-income foster home, where she was criticized and seldom encouraged. His hand was on her when she was considered a misfit in society, when everyone knew that she really didn't "belong." Rather than complain about her lot, however, Jan consistently found the good in every situation, took advantage of the music lessons offered her, and focused on finding others' gifts and talents.

While she was only a child herself, she gathered the other neighborhood children on the front "stoop" of her Brooklyn row house and asked, pointing to one after another, "What are you best at? What would you like to do?" Even then, she was scouting out possibilities. A talent show was planned once, at which the local parish priest said, "This event happened all because of one little girl who whispered an idea in my ear." God was whispering in Jan's ear, planting the dream of orchestrating great things for Him.

At that early age, she couldn't know that, in the United States alone, 27 million children—38 percent—would be living in poverty when she was old enough to do something about it, that the child poverty rate would be highest for African-American and Latino children, or that "with the recent economic downturn, there is a risk the United States will abandon the policies that have helped families create better lives for themselves!"[1] She was too busy making plans and dreaming dreams to wallow in self-pity. God was preparing her for the day when she would step into her destiny.

When her birth mother died, Jan went to the hospital and asked to see her records. "I had to know why she had decided to put me in the Foundling Home. I had to know who I was. I spoke with the Catholic sisters, who graciously opened their files. Inside a little box, on four index cards, was the sum total of my life. I learned that my father and siblings—two brothers and a sister—had lived at Mt. Loretto on Staten Island. This New York City sanctuary for the children of families who were very poor and could not provide for them was founded by a Catholic father who rescued the children selling papers on the street corners.

"When I made a trip by ferry to the island, I took a bus to the orphanage. All the way I imagined what I might find when I got there. At the end of the island was a hillside. I left the bus and proceeded to climb the hill. There I was met by a nun who offered to show me the chapel where my father worshiped as a boy.

"'And upstairs,' she told me, 'we have a little museum with artifacts and pictures of what it looked like when he lived here—before we lost part of the orphanage in a fire.' In that room my life changed." Choked up, Jan could hardly go on.

I understood why when she explained, "On the walls were pictures of little boys sleeping in the stairwells of New York. Their expressions were haunted, their eyes wide with hopelessness. The caption over these pictures read: 'Children Without Dreams.'"

It should not be surprising that Jan has founded an organization called "Dare to Dream," a nonprofit foundation designed to help young people living in shelters, foster homes, and orphanages to know they can strive for and achieve a brighter future. Through this faith-based ministry, Jan uses her gifts as an inspirational speaker, pianist, choreographer, seminar leader, and writer to offer a message of faith and hope, challenging her audiences to discover their plan and purpose. Jan has performed in Carnegie Hall, in the jungles of Costa Rica, and in the schools of Mexico. She has visited the streets of Paris and the palaces of Russia. She has ministered in the orphanages and hospitals of Romania, the earthquake zones in Turkey, and is coordinating relief efforts to children in Africa. Who would ever have suspected that God would use a little girl from Brooklyn to impact the world for generations to come!

Although she did not have a good example of a Christian home growing up, Jan is sure that "someone in the world must have been praying for me. I have always wanted to do something exciting and challenging, to go for the outrageous!" God orchestrated the "outrageous" when He tapped Jan Tennyson to reach for the stars. She does not look for a game plan or approval from people, only from the One who created and commissioned her. He tells her what to do "one day at a time," then equips her to do it.

"The Lord has taught me to love those who don't deserve it. People need an intercessor, not a judge," says this woman, who once received an incredible amount of verbal abuse and rejection. She understands pain. While ministering one day to an unbeliever who was living a gay lifestyle, Jan says that she felt the favor of God resting upon her and an inaudible Voice saying, *Thank you, Jan, for loving them for Me.*

What a testimony—from an orphanage to international ministry! Out of the pit and into the palace.

The Pit of Divorce and Separation

For some of us, all our girlhood dreams of knights in shining armor and happily-ever-afters grudgingly give way to the grim reality of failure and unfaithfulness. The "I dos" become "I don'ts"—"I don't love you anymore. I don't want to be married. I don't need you. I don't even like you!" But on your wedding day, with the stars in your eyes and lulled by the strains of Mendelssohn, those are the last words you would ever expect to hear.

On that day you willingly yoke your dream to that of another person. You become one—legally, in the eyes of the state; physically, as in "one flesh" when the marriage is consummated; and spiritually, in the eyes of God when the marriage vows are spoken. It is how God feels about divorce that should concern us the most. Jesus Himself said, "…'a man shall leave his father and mother and be joined to his wife, and the two shall become one flesh'? So then, they are no longer two but one flesh. Therefore what God has joined together, let not man separate" (Matt. 19:5,6).

I wonder how many couples actually consider the meaning of those words and the One who spoke them before they take their vows. I know I didn't. On the day of my wedding to my first husband, I was too excited about the festivities of the day and about not having to say good night at the end of the evening! I wasn't pondering the significance of the "blood covenant" I was making with this man.

But that is exactly why separation and divorce are so horrific. The tearing apart of the marital covenant is much like the ripping of flesh. Divorce is as painful as surgery without anesthesia! And don't let anyone fool you with that ridiculous statement, "Oh, ours was an amicable divorce." There is rarely the divorce that qualifies as amicable! Divorce can cause more devastation and more long-term trauma than death. It is from the pit, and it is a pit into which as many Christians stumble and fall as worldly people. Lord, forgive us for not believing You meant it when You warned us not to allow man (or woman) to "separate" us from one another! Tragic as it is, divorce has become too comfortable a part of our culture. Even the Word, however, makes allowances for some divorce, but it is the exception rather than the rule.

In my collection of friends (and I do "collect" friends; they are my most prized treasures!), Kati is one rare woman of grace and courage. She grew up dreaming of finding the "perfect" husband, having "perfect" children, and taking care of a "perfect playhouse" for as long as they both should live. She married her high school sweetheart, and they settled into their first home to start a family. Kati bustled about—June Cleaver apron, pearls, and all—to fulfill her dream, fully expecting the accolades for her "perfect" performance to follow. But, much to her surprise, the script changed right before her eyes.

When I asked her when the dream had begun to fade, she said, "Last year, after thirty years of marriage, when I learned that my husband was having an affair."

I was saddened to hear of her pain and wanted to know how she had managed. "Who was with you? Who were your encouragers?"

"My two sons and my family, especially my sister; some incredibly faithful and loving friends who encouraged me not to give up; some prayer warriors who did not even know me personally but prayed anyway; and my best Friend, Jesus, who held my hand and never let it go."

She went on to tell me of her initial denial, the anger, the disgust, and all the other emotions that accompany the shock of betrayal. Eventually she was able to ask God to reveal His perfect will, His best for this mess. She didn't have to wait long for His answer: *Rebuild,* He said in that still, small voice in her heart. It seemed impossible, but she had vowed to love her husband "for better or worse," and she wasn't about to let Satan steal what God had given her.

"It was extremely difficult and very frustrating," Kati admitted. "After all, I considered myself a good wife and mother. I had tried so hard, expecting that all the pieces of our life would just fall into place if I played my part well. But I didn't figure on my husband having an affair. Still, I knew that I could either use this for my good or let it destroy my faith.

"So, after the first shock of my husband's betrayal, *I* began by asking God to show me where I needed to change. My flesh wanted revenge, but with God's help, I began to forgive my husband, vowed to love him uncon- ditionally and stand by him, and prayed for him in a way I never had before—that God would break him to the core of his being so he could be renewed and refilled. I had to be willing to lay down my life and my dream for someone who had broken my heart. Oddly enough, his restoration suddenly became more important to me than my own self-protection.

She continued, "The Scripture the Lord kept bringing to me was: '...Don't be afraid. Just stand where you are and watch, and you will see the wonderful way the Lord will rescue you today...The Lord will fight for you, and you won't need to lift a finger!'" (Ex. 14:13,14, TLB). I realized that my dream—the "perfect" marriage—was an idol, and I needed to repent, take my position in prayer, and trust God for the rest. It isn't easy, but I am learning that *He* is really all I have and all I will ever need."

Kati's husband has come back home, and they both have some forgiving to do in a valiant effort to heal their marriage. It seems they are headed in that direction. There is now hope for a "happy ending" after all. Only God could have given my friend this kind of determination and faith and helped her walk it through. Before the day was over, though, I would hear another story in which the wife, raw and bleeding from a bitter betrayal, is still wrestling with a decision after thirty-plus years of marriage.

"Sheila"[2] had just discovered that her husband is spending time with another woman while she is away on mission trips or, more recently, caring for her dying parents. Sheila has always been faithful to the call on her own life, which was confirmed by her minister grandfather when she was very young. She learned to love the Word of God at his knee and always preferred Bible stories over children's stories such as "Snow White." Although Sheila could not preach—since in those days it was generally not considered "proper" for young women to pursue that calling—she decided that the next best thing would be to *marry* a preacher.

Two years after her marriage, her husband was stricken with a serious heart condition, and Sheila nursed him back to health. For a while after his recovery, they traveled together all over the country, conducting a healing ministry. Then, suddenly and without explanation, he began pulling away.

The mystery has been solved, as week after week, new indiscretions have begun to surface. While Sheila has not spied on him, the Lord has constantly brought to her attention her husband's moral lapses—a phone bill listing numerous calls made to "the other woman," a hotel confirmation for two, a bag of pornographic videos from an adult bookstore. If anyone ever had biblical grounds for divorce, Sheila does!

But the Lord had other ideas. God ordered my steps[3] to intersect Sheila's path during a divine appointment.

"When I met Ann Platz at a woman's conference," Sheila writes, "heaven collided with earth! I was standing in line waiting for an autographed copy of her book *The Best Is Yet To Come,* missing the point and plotting how I could drive my car off the bridge near my house when I got home. I asked Ann if she would pray with me when she finished signing the books. Ann took one look at my face and said, 'Yes. Just wait over there.'

"Ann didn't know me, had never met me, but when she prayed, she called out the spirit of suicide and death, and went to work cleaning me up! By the time she'd finished praying for me, my legs were too weak to stand. She prayed for me like I had never been prayed for before. She called forth my gifts and talents, and I heard her say something about my anointed ministry to women. I was sent home refreshed, renewed, and re-fired to do kingdom work.

"God could have 'upside-downed' me many times in my marriage, but He sent His 'handmaiden of mercy' to do it. Ann picked the weeds out of my life—told me to read the book of Isaiah, told me to listen to praise music, to pray for my husband, *then leave him in God's hands!* When I berated myself for not being strong enough or good enough, she told me to stop arguing with God—that He had great things for me! She has kept in touch almost every day for two years. The things I knew as a little child are being rebirthed in me. I'm still in pain and my circumstances haven't changed...*but I have!*"

As if this were not fantastic news enough, I was to hear more from this amazing woman:

"You wouldn't know me today, Mama Ann. I'm not the same Sheila. I'm belly down, face on the floor. God is going to meet me at my need! Today I have an appointment with my husband's mistress. She called me to counsel her about her thirteen-year-old son. Oh, her son is not her problem. I know what this is about. But the Lord said to me, 'As a pastor, as a pastor's wife, you separate her from the enemy she is to your marriage. So I'll do it, Mama Ann, no matter how hard it is. The devil won't take another thing from me!"

There it is, dear one—how to avoid the pit of divorce. You avoid it by taking your husband off that pedestal. You love him and pray for him and forgive him, if you need to, but don't you idolize him! And don't leave as long as there is hope! You watch how the Lord brings His chosen people into your life to sharpen you and hone you for Himself. Ultimately, *He* is your Husband,[4] and everything in your marriage is to reflect *that* relationship. When God releases you from a marriage, you will know it, and He will give you the grace and the mercy to live again.

Not all women are called to stay in an adulterous marriage with an unrepentant husband who is refusing to follow God's commandments. But Sheila has been commissioned to stay and stand. She is glowing and growing in spite of the circumstances in her marriage. Her life and Christian witness are a blessing and testimony to the faithfulness of God. She has chosen to walk out of the wilderness into the light!

I love these words written by well-known author Frances Roberts but coming to you from the heart of your Bridegroom: *"O my beloved, abide under the shelter of the lattice, for I have betrothed you to Myself, and though you are sometimes indifferent toward Me, My love for you is at all times a flame of fire. My ardor never cools. My longing for your love and affection is deep and constant. I love you, and if you can always feel My heartbeat, you will receive insight that will give you sustaining strength.... I am your Husband; I will protect you, care for you, and make full provision for you.... Set your heart to be at peace and to sit at My feet. Come away, My beloved."*[5]

The Pit of Illness

If the enemy can't sideline you one way, he will try another. Judging from the shortage of medical personnel and the waiting rooms overflowing with sick people, physical illness is a common method of stealing your dream and neutralizing your effectiveness.

There are dozens of good books on the subject of health and nutrition, but recently I discovered a title by a medical doctor that piqued my curiosity. *What the Bible Says About Healthy Living*[6] was written by Dr. Rex Russell, a board-certified radiologist who completed his residency at Mayo Clinic. Driven by his own health problems—diabetes, abscesses, arthritis, deterioration of eyesight, arteries, kidneys—to find answers not available from the medical community, this young man began exploring the Word of God. And he came up with some unexpected treasures, but not before an angry outburst or two. While reading Psalm 139, he came across verse 14, where David the psalmist is praising God because he is "fearfully and wonderfully made." Dr. Russell looked up in disbelief and addressed the Almighty: "If we are so wonderfully made, why am I so sick? God, why didn't You give us a way to be healthy?"

He explained, "My heavenly answer came in the form of a quiet question in my mind. *Rex, the Questioner said, have you really read My Instruction Book?*

"Of course, I held a Bible on my lap, but I was skeptical that what I might find inside its pages would help. How could a book written between 2,000 and 6,000 years ago possibly have any relevant health information?... I was also a little afraid. Even if the Bible were to point me to some answers, would they be taken as ridiculous by other physicians?"[7]

Yet, during a period of four years, Dr. Russell decided to read God's Word to see what it had to say about his condition. Because he had not been helped by human ideas about health, he prayed for wisdom from God. "Gradually I came to understand that God gave His laws to protect people," Dr. Russell writes, "and that astounding measures of health are available to those who obey these laws, whether they are believers or not."[8] Now following his decision to adopt the Bible's teaching on diet and healthy living, his diabetes is under control and all other related ailments are gone!

While unhealthy diet and lifestyle cause some illnesses, others are rooted in conflict. And when all three play a part, the result can be fatal—or nearly fatal!

Not long ago, after I had spoken at a woman's seminar in Texas, I saw a slim, attractive woman approaching with a big smile on her face. She seemed vaguely familiar, but I couldn't place her until she came up for prayer.

"You don't recognize me, do you? I'm Ann Reynolds—a hundred pounds less of me than when we last met!"

I was astounded! This woman didn't look as if she'd had a sick day in her life, yet I remembered her story well. Ann was only 42 when she had a massive coronary that robbed her of 70 percent of her heart function. She was told she probably wouldn't make it, and if she did, she would definitely not be able to work again. Ha! Those doctors didn't know Ann Reynolds—or the power of her God!

A quick analysis of her lifestyle should explain the reason for her first heart attack: a high-stress job as supervisor of a medical lab, where she worked seven days a week; a five-pack-a-day cigarette habit since the age of sixteen; a rocky marriage (her husband visited her only twice in the eight weeks she was hospitalized—and one of those times was to announce that he was taking the boys fishing!); and the weight problem. That was 1987.

In 1990, over a six-week period, Ann lost her job of 25 years; on the same night that her mother passed away in a nursing home, her husband announced that he was leaving her for the love of his life; her eldest son and his wife moved to Houston, the middle son drove off to college, and the youngest started seventh grade. When Ann stopped by to ask her therapist if she could possibly be losing her mind, the answer was, "No, but you've sure broken the record for the most life stresses in the shortest time span!"

Ann was not hospitalized at this point, but she was in the deepest pit of her life. Like Joseph, she looked up and found the Source of her strength. Along with her faith, she was, and is, surrounded by a host of praying friends.

Later on, Ann was diagnosed with congestive heart failure and was slated for a heart transplant. Advised to lose weight in preparation for the surgery, she tackled that assignment with all the gusto she brings to any new endeavor. She did so well that her health improved, and she was removed from the list as a candidate for the transplant!

Ann's dream was initially stolen by her dad's illness. That emotional and financial devastation hindered her plans for college, but not for long. Driven to shoot for the stars, she proceeded to go to school anyway, found a job with the Dean of Women, and went on to graduate. With the support of such "earth angels" sent from God, Ann has built one business after another, partnering with many of the very doctors—the brightest and best in their fields—who are helping her recover her health.

Now she is realizing that God's original dream for her is still intact. Through her illness, she has developed compassion for other hurting people and is using her gift of intercession to lift them in prayer. Not only that, but her sense of humor helps to keep things in perspective.

"Oh, I suppose I have a few limitations," says this charming woman with a twinkle in her eye and a characteristic chuckle. "I can't square dance because it makes me breathless. And I can't sing in the church choir, but I never could sing anyway. I'm practicing my breathing, though, because praise is a big part of my life. I can always find something to thank God for. He didn't make me sick, but He's showing me how to stay active and alive in spite of it!"

Ann is one of the most "alive" persons I know. I am so proud of her! She squeezes the essence from every moment of life because she has come so close to death. Like Ann, we can practice good dietary habits, stop smoking, take up jogging or some other form of exercise, follow the biblical rules for healthy living, and otherwise cooperate with God in maintaining our mortal body. But only He has the answer to total healing. As someone once said, "For those who believe in Him, God always heals. The healing will come either as a miracle on earth or in eternity with Him in heaven."

The Pit of Depression

Heart trouble, cancer, and arthritis are not the only ailments many people face in a lifetime. There are also varying degrees of mental illness that often defy diagnosis and make life maddening for both patient and caretaker.

My own precious daughter Courtney suffered the symptoms of a particularly mystifying brain disease from the time she was in her teens. I simply didn't know what to do with her when she stayed out by the pool until two in the morning or, at the opposite end of the spectrum, lay in bed lifeless for hours. I was at my wit's end. Here was this exquisitely beautiful young woman with an IQ at genius level who seemed determined to destroy her life! It's one thing to be physically ill. I could have understood that. But it's another to be mentally ill. I didn't have enough life experiences to diagnose or understand what was wrong. I felt unqualified to be her mother. I felt helpless and afraid of what would happen to her if we did not get help. Talk about a guilt trip!

In the process of trying to help her, we both did a lot of research. We sought medical and spiritual counsel. Courtney was 28 years old when the diagnosis came. It was somewhat reassuring to learn that "depression is not a sign of weakness or a lack of character or courage."[9]

So many people suffer with similar disorders, and they go undiagnosed most of their lives. Abraham Lincoln and Winston Churchill are two men of great stature who are known to have suffered from serious depression. And what about Jeremiah, David, and Paul—three Bible personalities whose temperaments seemed prone to depression at times. Jeremiah was known as the "weeping prophet." David cried out, "Why be downcast? Why then be discouraged and sad?... Yet I am standing here depressed and gloomy..." (Ps. 42:5,6 TLB). And who could ever forget Paul's inner turmoil when he groaned, "O wretched man that I am! Who will deliver me from this body of death?" (Rom. 7:24).

Let's dispel some other myths, while we're at it. "Depression is *not* abnormal. If you feel depressed, you're in the company of over six million other Americans. Depressed people are *not* crazy. And, best of all, depression is *not* hopeless!"[10]

Depression is also not easy to define. You might say, "I'm a failure" or "I feel lonely" or "I'm just no good" or "It's all my fault" or "I'd be better off dead," and any one of these statements, taken by itself, is no cause for alarm. But if you experience all of these feelings—or several of them—on any consistent basis, you may be a candidate for treatment. Everything from staying busy to reading self-help books to talking things through with a counselor are recommended therapies for depression. But the best therapy is seldom mentioned by secular counselors. Prayer, reading God's Word, seeking help from other believers who have had this experience—these hold the real key to a lasting solution.

On the other hand, my daughter did not respond to anything we found in our early research. I already knew that her behavior was not simply rebellion, although it sure looked like it at times. And her mood swings became more and more erratic, something we learned to call "rapid cycling."[11] In fact, there was a name for her problem: bipolar disorder, a more severe mental illness than depression. Bipolar involves both depression and mania—the frantic activity that results in such outbursts as Courtney flinging herself into the swimming pool at unearthly hours or storming out of the house in tears! We also learned that there is treatment. On the human level, it involves careful monitoring of medications, along with psychotherapy. On the spiritual level, I was called upon to surrender my daughter to the Lord.

I'll never forget the day I finally made that difficult decision. I called Courtney and we chatted awhile, then I casually dropped a bomb. "You'll never guess what I did today! I totally gave you over to the Lord." This was not an overnight decision. After years of watching her fight for peace and normalcy to no avail, I knew I had to trust God with the most difficult thing in my life to surrender—my daughter's emotional stability. I handed her over to Him. I delivered her from my hands to His. I was not withdrawing my love, but instead, joining forces with the Giver of love.

"What do you mean?" Courtney was dumbfounded. "That's the worst thing I ever heard! Are you not even going to pray for me anymore?" She told me later that this was the scariest moment of her life. She felt completely unprotected and vulnerable.

"It simply means, darling, that I've given you to Him for safekeeping. He can take better care of you than I."

Quite frankly, I was completely exhausted trying to keep up with her roller-coaster emotions. I didn't have anything else to give, and I knew her heavenly Father had all the answers. Now, in obedience, I was simply standing and waiting to see the redemption of the Lord.[12] That's when He began to move so powerfully on her behalf.

I have asked Courtney to tell her story, as much in depth as she chooses, so you will have the benefit of becoming educated as to the truth about Bipolar disease. Too many people tend to blame the patient when what they need is unconditional love. I hope that you will understand and be blessed by her transparency.

Courtney's Story

"I knew something wasn't quite right for a long time. I didn't think I had normal depression because it wouldn't go away. There would be periods of time when I would seem to be fine, but always my body and brain would crave some kind of stimulant. Mine was alcohol and drugs. I discovered later through counseling that the first drink or drug a bipolar person takes is the first time they feel normal or at peace. This is why we are so easily addicted.

"With bipolar disease, it's the best of times and the worst of times. You swing between extreme emotional highs and extreme lows. For every high—just like the law of gravity—you'll have a low just as low. You could be on top of the world one minute and flat in bed the next. The manic stage is a thrill. You feel great and have all this energy. And then there are the down times.

"For the first two or three years, before we had a diagnosis, I struggled with telling anybody what I was going through. I would get so mad at Mom. She'd say, 'I want you to get your pretty little self out of that bed and do something!' What she didn't know was that I couldn't move at those times. I felt paralyzed.

"It helped when I was taught that this disease is not curable, but you can learn to live with it—and live well.[13] It's like having a leg amputated and having to adjust to using crutches, or modifying your lifestyle after a heart attack. Mental illness, though, has such a stigma, and if people only knew the truth, they could be more helpful. I'm aware that this disease is really stressful on all those who love me. But what I need to hear is not, 'I'll love you if you don't embarrass me or if you'll measure up to my expectations.' What I need is love with no strings attached.

"When someone asked me to describe my lowest low, I suppose it would have to be a day when I was on my way to buy drugs. The neighborhood looked like a hurricane had just blown through. People with blank stares were wandering up and down the street, and I remember wondering, briefly, if these were the people who sleep under bridges. I walked into an old tenant house—tin roof, no windows, no electricity. I wasn't thinking about where my children were or whether I'd run into someone in the car on the way home. The only thing on my mind was getting something to make the pain go away. Many years later I am now on prescription medication and not 'hooked' on anything. I have fought my way back to recovery one day at a time.[14]

"As for my faith? I'll have to admit that I really wasn't mad at my family, even though I learned that bipolar disease can be genetic. I was mad at God! I was raised in a Christian family, so I couldn't understand why He had let this happen to me. *This is a loving God?* I thought. *Um-hum. Then why am I being punished?*

"But I see now that everything in my life has happened for a reason. Even the poor choices I made when I was at the worst stage of my illness.

There is not a doubt in my mind—I would not be the person I am today without having gone through that pain! I can also appreciate my spiritual heritage and realize that my parents gave me the courage to resist the temptation to take my own life. Even though the suicide rate is high for bipolar patients, I would never think of it! It would be such a selfish thing to do and horrible in God's eyes. Funny, even when I was mad at Him, I would never have considered displeasing Him that way.[15]

"I don't believe in luck. I know I'm blessed to be alive! I believe that God is with me, no matter what. Whether I'm up or whether I'm in the pit, He's there.

"Mom gave me a beautiful quotation that I had framed so I can see it all through the day. It really touches me:

> This is my life—one day at a time. This is enough.
>
> Don't look back and grieve over the past, for it is gone.
>
> And do not be troubled about the future, for it has not yet come. Live in the present and make it so beautiful that it will be worth remembering.

As I hear Courtney tell of her journey, I have to weep. God sheltered me from much of this until the time Courtney could share it with me. I hope she knows how proud I am of her and how much I love her and appreciate her courage!

Courtney, just like those of you who are in the pit of emotional illness, is being equipped for greatness. The beauty God has given her is for a reason. Her temperament—tamed and under His control—can be used to bless the multitudes. And all those wasted years—"the years that the locusts have eaten"[16]—will be restored in the twinkling of an eye. For her, like all these other women, the best is truly yet to come! With God's help we can take lemons and make lemonade!

Let me just say this to hurting parents: Whatever the illness or problem you are facing, never give up on loving your child, but trust the heavenly Parent who understands all things. At times, you may feel you cannot endure any more pain, but you do. He will bring your precious one home—and the result will be a closer walk for you as well. It's out of your hands and into His, which is the best place for it to be.

The Pit of Premature Death

The most deadly dream-stealer of all is our final enemy. We will all face death at some point in our lives. But sometimes death snatches people before their time is up. "The days of our lives are seventy years; and if by reason of strength they are eighty years...So teach us to number our days, that we may gain a heart of wisdom" (Ps. 90:10,12). This sounds to me as though it's a promise with a condition—that if we use wisdom in making choices, our lives may be prolonged. Let me explain what I mean.

In a survey published by the Office of Disease Prevention and Health, all but one of the eight leading contributors to premature death are preventable. Tobacco is the top dream-stealer, followed by poor diet/lack of physical activity, consumption of alcohol, microbial agents, firearms, promiscuous sexual behavior, motor vehicles, and drug use.[17] Only a few diseases caused by germs—"microbial agents"—and accidents involving guns and motor vehicles are legitimate causes of premature death. The enemy, Satan, often uses these to snatch people away before their time. These and other kinds of early death may be his scheme to disrupt God's original dream for some people's lives.

But let me interject something right here and now: Only God knows the real truth and the length of our days. He says that they are numbered, just as He says that He counts the hairs on our heads.[18] Remember, the end of life is a season of life, but the length of days varies; it's not the same for everyone. Some "go home" earlier than others. The reasons why may be among our biggest surprises in heaven.

I still don't know why my beautiful sister, Mary Ashley, left us and went on to Glory when she was only 42 or why my sister-in-law, Danielle, died at 36. I don't know why the mother of a two-year-old could not be here to hold her baby in her arms and watch him grow to manhood. I only know that when I think of Mary Ashley, who loved digging in the earth and adorning spaces with flowers, tending her heavenly gardens, I am comforted. After twelve years, I can only imagine how glorious those gardens must be by now!

While it is sad to think of young mothers leaving their children too soon, we know that "...weeping may endure for a night, but joy comes in the morning" (Ps. 30:5). That word is for anyone who is still mourning "in the morning." Among those whose grief sometimes persists almost past endurance are parents who lose children. To me, this is perhaps the ultimate dream-stealer.

My friend Linda is still recovering from the loss of a beloved son. When she moved to Atlanta with her husband and three children from a small town in Ohio, she came under protest. Knowing her alcoholic husband's penchant for womanizing, she figured that there would be ten times as many temptations in the big city. Bracing herself, she clung to a verse of Scripture the Lord seemed to be showing her: "...See, I have set before you an open door, and no one can shut it..." (Rev. 3:8). With that verse, she made the move with a song in her heart.

Eleven months later, when Linda's youngest son was only ten years old and the older two boys were fifteen and sixteen, her husband left her for her next-door neighbor and new best friend. The song faded, but sustained by a little audiotape on which Scripture was set to music, she tried to help the boys work their way through the trauma. It was difficult to explain to them what had happened—or why. The middle child seemed to roll with the punches, but the other two suffered terribly. So much so that the youngest, Scott, began seeking validation from male friends.

"I didn't pick up on what was going on with him at first," Linda admits. "I was too busy juggling all the balls, keeping food on the table and peace at home. Besides, I didn't have words for my own anguish and felt pitifully inadequate in helping them articulate theirs.

"Scott was always such a delight. What a smart and creative kid he was and so good-looking—too good-looking maybe. He used his looks to win acceptance. And then one day he came to me with an expression on his face that broke my heart. Something told me that Scott needed to see a doctor—fast! The doctor told me what had happened. My son had been violently sexually assaulted and had contracted HIV. Yes, he was in the wrong place at the wrong time, but...this was *my* son!

"He lived for ten years after that, battling the illness, believing God for healing, praying the Scriptures, seeking the best medical care, changing his diet...we tried it all. And in the end, he lost his life. Not long ago, a grief counselor shared something that helped a little—a quote I keep on the fridge:

GOD did not take your loved one from you.
DEATH took your loved one from you.
But GOD took your loved one from death.

"Another fact that comforts me is that Scott was saved, and I know I'll see him again one day. We moved his hospital bed into the living room, where he could be a part of our family life as long as possible. Not long before Scott left us, I anointed him with oil and asked, 'Have you seen your angels yet?'

"'Yes,' he said.

"I was curious to know more. 'How big are they?'

"'Really big.'

"'What color is their hair?'

"'Blond. They're blonds.'

"'Have they said anything to you, honey?'

"His voice was weak, barely a whisper. 'No.'

"'They're here to comfort you, Scott.' Oh, I wish I could have seen them, could have gone with them when they escorted my boy home.

"My one regret is that I wasn't with him when he took his last breath. I had to work that day. But I have to believe this was the Lord's provision—the nurse who was with Scott at that time had red hair, just like me! Maybe God knew I couldn't handle it and sent in a sub.

"On the other hand, the Lord did tell me something so sweet one day. He said, 'I chose you to be Scott's mother—nobody else.' So I guess He must have thought I could handle this. With His help, I can. He knows me. He knows that when I've healed, I'll give everything I have to help other grieving mothers. I'll go where He wants me to go. There is 'a time to mourn,' but also 'a time to dance' (Ecc. 3:4). I'm almost there."

Linda and I connected several years ago and loved each other instantly. We have stayed in touch ever since. This is a woman who will use her pain to help the multitudes. What she has experienced, she will pass on to others. She is just about to step through that "open door." The dream will be reclaimed.

When you tell your story, one of the signs that you are well into your healing is that you will no longer feel the same intensity of pain. That pain is covered by the blood of Jesus, and you will begin to feel that this terrible tragedy happened to someone else. You will never return to that fearful place again, to the pit.

Linda tells of a powerfully encouraging word the Lord gave her one day not long after Scott's death. God said to her, "Now you know My heart.... My Son died too."

Those who mourn hear God's heartbeat. They feel the pulse of other suffering people. They know that there is "a time to weep, and a time to laugh" (Eccl. 3:4). It's time to be joyful!

Prayer of Release: Father of the fatherless, Father of the lost and lonely, Father of the destitute and suffering, Lord of life, we thank You that Your provision is plenty. We thank You that Your mercy is everlasting. We thank You that Your grace is sufficient, that Your cloak of love is our covering. And, Father, as we move out of this place of darkness and emptiness, we know that You are with us and that Your hand is extended to lead us out of the wilderness and into the joyous discovery of all that we will ever need to step through the open door of heaven when You call us home. In Jesus' name, amen.

Then Midianite traders passed by; so the brothers
pulled Joseph up and lifted him out of the pit,
and sold him to the Ishmaelites for twenty shekels
of silver. And they took Joseph to Egypt.

GENESIS 37:28

CHAPTER 7

The Kingdom of Darkness

But you are a chosen generation, a royal priesthood, a holy nation, His own special people, that you may proclaim the praises of Him who called you out of darkness into His marvelous light.

1 PETER 2:9

I am much more comfortable describing some lovely home I am currently decorating for a client than talking about the setting and atmosphere of the devil's dark domain. I'd rather tell you about the mingled bouquet of one of the gorgeous gardens I have visited in the world than to discuss Satan's wicked kingdom and his evil spiritual war tactics. It rankles me to think of wasting words on corruption when there is so much of truth and beauty begging to be enjoyed.

Needless to say, this will not be one of my favorite chapters. More than that, we are daring to step, deliberately, into the dominion of a tyrant who would make a terrorist look like Mr. Rogers. But we cannot stand on ceremony or social decorum—or fear. This is war (spiritually speaking), and war dictates that we know our enemy—his nature, his habitat, and his strategies. If I had learned earlier in life just how devious and diabolical Satan is and how he can slip up on your blind side with his cunning ways and his smooth talk, I could have avoided some pretty deep pits of my own. Thank God, He rescued me, just as He will rescue you!

Therefore, before writing this section, I contacted all my intercessors for prayer and covered this book project in the blood of Jesus.[1] We asked for a double portion of anointing and an extra measure of courage. Surfacing what has been buried in obscure passages of Scripture is one way to get Satan to tip his hand, but it can also stir up a hornet's nest. We are appropriately aware of the serpent's sting.

This chapter contains important material on the devil's attempts at stealing, killing, and destroying people's lives. He has had a heyday with many individuals, some of whose stories appear here, but God is still on His throne. He can reach to the bottom of the deepest pit or into the darkest part of Egypt and lead His people out!

Let me say in advance that you will read very little that is opinion-based. Everything in this chapter has been researched and documented, and lines up with God's Word or is taken directly from the Word. I would never dare to make an assault on enemy territory without the full armor of God—especially the Sword of the Spirit, (His Word), in hand![2]

Biography of the "Beast"

In my mind the term *Beast* is a perfect "nickname" for Satan,[3] the despicable and unrelenting enemy of our souls. We meet him first in the Garden of Eden disguised as a serpent. (Gen. 3:1.) I have never liked snakes. In fact, I loathe them! But how appropriate that Satan is forever associated with something that slinks around in the dirt on its belly. (v. 14.)

You will always find him wearing a mask. Although he was originally designed as a gorgeous creature with great eye appeal,[4] behind that deceptive exterior was a monster too hideous for words. Apparently he could speak, or at least communicate, because he soon struck up a conversation with the first lady of Paradise. His line has never changed. He caused Eve to question God, "...Has God indeed said, 'You shall not eat of every tree of the garden'?" (Gen. 3:1), and the rest is history.

Let's retrace the serpent's steps, back to his roots. Who was he? How did he slither into the Garden of Eden—that perfect setting created for the enjoyment of man and intimate fellowship with the Father? Satan was once an exalted angelic being, an angel named Lucifer who fell in love with his own beauty, and driven by selfish ambition, set out to overthrow the kingdom of God and take His throne for himself.[5]

Pride is the first and greatest sin. I believe that every other sin contains some element of pride. Greed, lust, murder, envy, covetousness, adultery, sexual perversion, you name it—all of these are wrapped up in "…inordinate self-esteem."[6]

God, of course, did not allow Lucifer to succeed, and in two passages from the Old Testament—Isaiah 14:12-15 and Ezekiel 28:11-19—the prophets record his fall from heaven. Some scholars believe that these words, directed to the kings of Babylon and Tyre, are also speaking of Lucifer, or Satan.[7]

In five defiant statements, found in Isaiah 14:13-14, Satan sealed his doom:

"I will ascend into heaven,

"I will exalt my throne above the stars of God;

"I will also sit on the mountain of the congregation…

"I will ascend above the heights of the clouds,

"I will be like the Most High."

In verses 15-20 the Most High has the final word, with five responses of His own:

"You will be brought down to the lowest depths of the Pit.

"You will be made a spectacle.

"You will be mocked and scorned.

"You will be cast out of your grave like a carcass.

"You will be alone."

God has given us a free will, but He always has the last word.

Revelation 12 lays out the rest of the story, how, in his rebellion, Satan persuaded a third of the angels to follow him. In verse 4, a "…third of the stars in heaven" has been interpreted by some scholars as being the angels who fell with Satan. The rest of the story includes how, once on earth, he repeatedly attempted to destroy the lineage of Jesus, His followers (the church), and ultimately Jesus Himself (vv. 13,17). But the tables were turned on Lucifer, and the cross, where Jesus voluntarily gave up His life for the sins of mankind, was his downfall (John 10:17,18). The devil has always been fighting a losing battle, but even more so since the Resurrection, Jesus' triumph over death. Eventually Satan will be bound for a thousand years and ultimately cast into the lake of fire, into outer darkness, forever—an endless end. (Rev. 20:2,10.)

Prince of Darkness

Our dreaded enemy is known by many titles and aliases. You have already observed that I have used several of them interchangeably—the enemy, Satan, the devil, Lucifer. Since names have significance, to know his name is to know a little more about him. God reveals these names to us in order to give us the advantage. While this may not be a very pleasant process, it is necessary to know what we're up against while we're living in his domain, the world. God's Word reminds us, "My people are destroyed for lack of knowledge…" (Hos. 4:6). What we don't know can hurt us.

These names and titles with a description of each are listed below in alphabetical order. It will then be easy to spot the copycat tactic Satan uses in imitating God and where the real power is.

- *accuser of the brethren*—"Now salvation, and strength, and the kingdom of our God, and the power of His Christ have come, for the *accuser of our brethren,* who accused them before our God day and night, has been cast down" (Rev. 12:10). I love beginning with this one. We see the enemy's fate right at the start—he "has been cast down." Note a favorite tactic of his: He accuses "day and night."

- *the adversary*—"…your *adversary* the devil walks about like a roaring lion, seeking whom he may devour" (1 Pet. 5:8). Don't let him deceive you, dear one; his bark is not necessarily worse than his bite.

- *Beelzebub,* prince of demons—"lord of the fly" was the Philistine "god of Ekron ['the name under which Baal' or Baal-zebub 'was worshiped at the Philistine city of Ekron']," used by the Jews to denote the devil.[8] "Now when the Pharisees heard it, they said, 'This fellow [Jesus] does not cast out demons except by *Beelzebub,* the *ruler of the demons*'" (Matt. 12:24). He's the lord of the flies. "Swat" him with the Word!

- *the deceiver*—"The devil, who *deceived* them, was cast into the lake of fire and brimstone where the beast and the false prophet are..." (Rev. 20:10). Deception is just part of his job description, so don't put anything past him. But one sure way to avoid his deceit is by staying in the Word and in a relationship with Jesus.

- *the destroyer*—"But with most of them [our fathers in the wilderness] God was not well pleased.... Now these things became our examples...that we should not...complain, as some of them also complained, and were destroyed by *the destroyer*" (1 Cor. 10:5,6,10). His mission is to seek and destroy, so don't be surprised at the devastation he can wreak. But remember that his power consists primarily of his power to deceive us.

- *the devil*—(This personal name of Satan, meaning "slanderer," is used 35 times in *The New King James Version* of the Bible.)[9] "Then He will also say to those on his left hand, 'Depart from Me, you cursed, into the everlasting fire prepared for *the devil* and his angels" (Matt. 25:41). This is just another reminder of the final "resting place" of our superhuman enemy and his minions. But it is also the place reserved for those who do not choose Jesus as Savior (more about that later).

- *the dragon*—a great, red monster with seven heads and ten horns.[10] "Then I saw an angel coming down from heaven, having the key to the bottomless pit and a great chain in his hand. He laid hold of the dragon, that serpent of old, who is the Devil and Satan, and bound him for a thousand years" (Rev. 20:1,2). Dragon is another figurative term for Satan, not a literal decription. Or does the devil have horns, after all?

- *the enemy*—"*The enemy* who sowed them [the tares among the wheat] is the devil" (Matt. 13:39). In this verse, Jesus reveals the meaning of a parable and unmasks the devil once again.

- *the evil one*—"...deliver us from *the evil one*..." (Matt. 6:13). This verse is from the Lord's Prayer. Jesus felt it necessary to include praying for deliverance in His instructions to the disciples on how to pray. His instructions were meant for us too.

- *father of lies*—"You are of your father the devil.... When he speaks a lie, he speaks from his own resources, for he is a liar and *the father of it*" (John 8:44). There's no such thing as a "little white lie" or "stretching the truth." It's all a lie from the father of lies.

- *god of this age*—"But even if our gospel is veiled, it is veiled to those who are perishing, whose minds the *god of this age* has blinded..." (2 Cor. 4:3,4). Remember that this "god's" power over believers is permissive and limited.[11] In the fullness of time, God will cut it off forever.

- *Lucifer* ("light bearer")[12]—"How you are fallen from heaven, O *Lucifer,* son of the morning! How you are cut down to the ground..." (Isa. 14:12). When Lucifer fell, his light went out.

- *murderer*—"...He was a *murderer* from the beginning..." (John 8:44). You may not consider yourself a murderer, but if you've gossiped, you've assassinated someone's character, and that makes you kin to someone we won't mention.

- *the prince of the power of the air*—"And you He made alive, who were dead in trespasses and sins, in which you once walked according to the course of this world, according to *the prince of the power of the air,* the spirit who now works in the sons of disobedience" (Eph. 2:1,2). No wonder our airwaves are bombarded with filth and all kinds of depraved music, visual images, and language. A considerable part of the Internet, movies, TV, and radio can and are being used as tools of the devil. We need to reclaim them for God![13]

- *the ruler of this world*—"Now is the judgment of this world; now *the ruler of this world* will be cast out" (John 12:31). He rules with an iron hand...but not for long!

- *the tempter*—"Now when *the tempter* came to Him, he said, 'If You are the Son of God, command that these stones become bread'" (Matt. 4:3). Have you ever noticed that the first temptation in the Garden and the first temptation of Jesus have to do with food? The tempter knows our weaknesses. That's why periods of fasting are so important. (Matt. 4:2; Mark 2:18; Luke 2:37.)

- *the wicked one*—"...the whole world lies under the sway of *the wicked one*" (1 John 5:19). This could be discouraging if we didn't know the end of the story.

I hope this little study will give you a more complete understanding of the archenemy of the Godhead; although not considering myself a Bible scholar, I may have overlooked some name or title. Just as we must be taught about God and learn His characteristics, so it pays to learn about the great deceiver—the exact opposite of everything that is good and holy. We can take comfort in the fact that the devil is a *fake*—a cheap imitation of the real thing.

Knowing the names and titles of "the real thing"—God the Father, God the Son, and God the Holy Spirit—can bring such peace. His names, which are numerous and are mentioned throughout the Bible, tell who He is and what He does for us. For example, He's the Alpha and Omega, the Beginning and the End, our Counselor, our Deliverer, El Shaddai—the God Who Is Enough, Everlasting Father, Faithful and True, Forgiver of Sin, our Healer, our Helper, our Protector, our Provider, our Shelter, our Shepherd, our High Tower, Triumphant One, the Word, and the Worthy One, to name a few.

Enemy Territory

When Joseph's brothers brought him out of the pit, he went from the frying pan into the fire. He was not set free to go back home, but was sold to passing traders on their way to Egypt. The name *Egypt* is generally regarded as symbolizing a place of darkness—a place without life, a place that deifies death and practices paganism. *Egypt* is often the term used to define the humanistic world and is the opposite of everything good and desirable.

Meanwhile, as citizens of the kingdom of heaven, we do not live in this type of Egypt, for we are not *of* the world, but we live *in* the world—enemy territory. When Adam and Eve sinned, they willfully walked away from God's calling as custodians and keepers of the earth. They abdicated their authority, and Satan slithered into the vacant space! (Eph. 4:27.) But even though God has permitted our enemy to hold the deed to this world, Satan's power is limited and his residence here is temporary: "Woe to the inhabitants of the earth and the sea! For the devil has come down to you, having great wrath, because he knows that he has a short time" (Rev. 12:12).

Satan was evicted from heaven, and this earth is not his home, just as it is not ours. But while we are living here together, we can and must protect ourselves from this evil deceiver who tries to come against people "...*as* a roaring lion,..." going about "...seeking whom he may devour" (1 Pet. 5:8 KJV). This is another of his attempts to imitate Jesus, who *is* "the lion of the tribe of Judah." However, Satan can be a very real threat to our well-being and our future security. He is enraged because his days are numbered, and he knows where he will be spending eternity. So he intends to make our lives as miserable as possible and take as many of us with him as he can lure into his web of deception.

We have already noted his wide circle of influence. Some of his titles— "ruler of this world," "the god of this age," and "the prince of the power of the air"—confirm the vast arena in which he operates. "This world" implies the system as well as the geographical boundaries.

Opinions vary on the location of Satan's headquarters, but whatever his official "address," we do know that he doesn't remain in residence for long. He is a "frequent flyer," roaming about continually, harassing the saints and wreaking havoc on the earth.

As for his permanent residence, that is easier to define. The Scriptures are full of references to "hell," "Hades," "Sheol," "the abode of the dead," "the bottomless pit," and the "Abyss." We know that hell is a place of punishment, both for the devil and his angels, and for the unrighteous who have rejected Jesus. But have you ever gathered all the Scriptures about hell in one place? I must admit that as I was researching this topic, I was overwhelmed by the evidence! I challenge anyone who is ministering to the unsaved to do a topical study and read these verses for yourself.

It might surprise those who question a literal hell to learn that Jesus had more to say about it than anyone in the Bible, usually in a forceful manner. At least ten times He mentioned "hell," so the fact that it exists is clear.[14] In fact, when He was describing hell, he often used the term *Gehenna,* meaning the Valley of Hinnom, or the garbage dump of Jerusalem.[15]

On trips to Israel, I have stood where Jesus walked, overlooking this valley and imagining what it must have been like in His day. I have a vivid imagination. When I read a book, I get a mental image of what is going on.

The movie is never as good as the book. When I read Jesus' description of hell in the Bible, I get the picture.

Into this place of desolation, this *Gehenna,* were placed the bodies of dead animals and executed criminals as well as all the refuse of the city. In Mark 9:44,46,48, Jesus says, "Their worm does not die, and the fire is not quenched." Over and over again, He speaks of outer darkness and a furnace of fire, where there will be wailing, weeping, and gnashing of teeth.[16] The book of Revelation adds a footnote: "...the lake of fire burning with brimstone" where the devil, his angels, and all whose names are not written in the Lamb's Book of Life will be "...tormented day and night forever and ever" (Rev. 19:20; 20:10,14,15; 21:8). I don't need a Steven Spielburg spectacular to make the point, do you?

As one biblical reference cites, "Because of the symbolic nature of the language, some people question whether hell consists of actual fire. Such reasoning should bring no comfort to the lost. The reality is greater than the symbol. The Bible exhausts human language in describing heaven and hell. The former is more glorious, and the latter more terrible, than language can express."[17]

Satan's Strategies

This smooth-talking devil was—and is—intelligent. He could outtalk Adam and Eve—so much so that he convinced them that he was right and that God was simply withholding something good from them. When they fell for his trickery, he took over the control of the world for himself. (Gen. 1:26; 2 Cor. 11:3.) How many times has that kind of scene been replayed in the dark corridors of our minds? Every sinful deed is first conceived in a thought contrary to God's will. And sin plays into the devil's schemes.

Satan is not only smart, he is powerful. This evil one who comes "as a roaring lion"[18] has such great strength and ability to deceive that he can negatively influence not only countries, but the thinking and imaginations of the people. He is active in the arts, in politics, in medicine and pharmacology, in finance, in business, especially in the entertainment world, and even in the church! I met a precious woman several years ago who knows what it is to be disappointed by a representative of God. (Fortunately this is not the norm in churches.)

Elaine learned early that Satan was out to kill, deceive, and destroy her. She grew up in poverty and violence, one of nine children whose father abused and abandoned them. When their sweet mother was too ill to mother them, they roamed the streets until the authorities took them away and separated Elaine from her siblings. One of the devil's most effective tactics is to divide and destroy.

She became the foster child of a preacher and his wife. Only twelve years old at the time, she had flowered early and looked much older. Elaine basically became their servant who did all the cooking and most of the cleaning. Soon her foster father tried to steal her innocence and purity, and the wife, who was mentally ill, did nothing to protect her. But her Father God was present. Once, when the preacher's wife was out of town overnight, the foster father tried to force his way into Elaine's room, only to be met by what Elaine describes as an invisible barrier that prevented him from reaching her.

Still, because of the abuse she had suffered all her life, Elaine battled feelings of uncleanness, unworthiness, and shame, but she never submitted to those spirits. That's how the enemy works. The roots of sin run deep and wide "unto the third and fourth generation" (Ex. 20:5). In spite of that, Elaine felt the wooing of the Holy Spirit. With not a single authority figure in her life that she could trust, with no family to mentor her, no ministers to disciple her, miraculously she found God's love through His Word. While living with another foster family in her high school years, she began to attend church and read the Bible. However, it was not until years later, through the baptism of the Holy Spirit, that God opened up the Bible to her and showed her that He had the most intimate love for her, that this Book was His personal love letter to her.

"Some people are healed and delivered instantly, but my healing and deliverance have come from the Lord inch by inch," Elaine confesses. "Through all the pain and trauma of my past, the seed of the Word slowly began to sprout. Through all the years of abuse, through all the shame and unworthiness, through all the lies and deception of the enemy, I am a testimony to the power of God's love—that even the most ravished soul can know purity again and that He can restore the most wayward sinner.

"Once when I was ill, I had to take a leave of absence from my job. The Lord met me every morning when I opened up His Word. He wrapped me in a blanket of love and poured in the oil and wine. As He opened my heart to receive the truth, He began to show me myself as a little girl sitting in a dank, dark corner of a room, sobbing my heart out. I wanted to hide, to stay hidden. The enemy works that way. He wants us to keep all our secrets to ourselves, to put on a false front and smile and say, 'I'm okay,' when really we aren't okay at all. But when the Lord Jesus entered that room, He turned my head around, and oh, He had made that room so beautiful—all bright, white light, and flowers everywhere! It was a radiant holy place. He showed me my finished soul, dressed in pure white. It was as if I had never ever sinned!

"I know the power of love to sustain and change. I know there is a Father and that He loves Elaine. I am His dearest treasure. He loves the ground I walk on. I am precious in His sight. I absolutely know beyond a shadow of a doubt that I am loved and adored. And now I am capable of love because He first loved me. He is my Dream. There is a Prince Charming, and His name is Jesus."

The enemy of our souls can prowl the earth, he can lie and deceive, he can con and connive, he can divide and attempt to destroy, but Elaine knows that God's power and love are greater and deeper and wider and higher than any scheme of the devil.

Satan's Sure Defeat

With all my heart, I believe that the Word of God is our greatest source of assurance as to Satan's destiny. Over and over again in the Scriptures—as in Luke 10:18, John 12:31, Romans 6:23, Revelation 12:9 and 20:1-15—we are reminded that, in this world, we are engaging a defeated foe.

Yet, as I have met people from every background and from every walk of life across the country, I am also reading the gospel according to Elaine—and Victoria and Jean and Sally, whom you will meet shortly. Their testimonies of deliverance from the deepest, darkest places are God's revelation of Satan's ultimate destination.

Not long ago I was having lunch with a group of "tea party ladies"—the ones who whirl about in all the right social circles. I decided to surprise them with a shift in the conversation. "I'd love to tell you about some of my closest friends," I began, watching as they perked up and turned their perfectly coiffed heads to hear more. "Some of my friends are former prostitutes. Some were drug addicts, and oh, yes—one of them was a member of the church of Satan."

The gasps were audible. "I...we're *shocked!*" one said. "Where do you find these people?"

"Oh, I don't go looking for them," I assured her with a little laugh. "*They* come to *me*. But let me tell you...they're my spiritual daughters, and I'm so proud of them! They're all heading national ministries now, taking the nations for Jesus Christ. But there isn't a one of them Satan hasn't tried to kill!"

The tea party ladies didn't budge. I had their complete attention, and they were about to hear the depths to which Satan will take us if we allow him a toehold. I hope that you are tuned in and listening too. Remember, these are candid testimonies, but they are going to make a point.

Victoria was a drug addict for eleven years and a stripper for four. Jean, who lived on a farm, was molested and sexually assaulted by her alcoholic father and others for years, beginning at an early age. Do you wonder, then, that she was fair game for a cult when she was older? Sally was lured into the church of Satan by a well-planted recruiter while she was sitting on a church pew!

"I knew *about* God, but I didn't know Him personally," Sally told me. "My mother and father never did get along and later were divorced. Once I got pregnant after being sexually assaulted, but I miscarried at four months. Finally one day I was so full of rage, I wanted to kill the man responsible, and I probably would have, too, if something hadn't stopped me."

What stopped her was God's hand on Sally's life—even then. She was in and out of correctional facilities many times because of her unrestrained "anger problem." If you ask me, it was probably righteous indignation, although she obviously didn't make wise choices in venting her anger. And the downward spiral had only begun.

"I started messing around with spell-casting at sixteen, sitting out in a shed with a friend of mine. The next thing I knew I was going to meetings off a Missouri highway and involved in animal sacrifice. When a strong masculine voice called to me, 'Come be with me,' I was tempted. Of course, I didn't know it was the devil. I tried to commit suicide three times and ended up in a psychiatric hospital. All I can say is that they replaced one set of addictions for another—prescription drugs. I was really in deep. Satanism teaches that Satan has control of the earth and that it's a lie that Jesus Christ will come back, regain the territory, and bind the devil. I bought it."

Things began to look up a little when Sally ran away at the age of seventeen and met a good-looking truck driver in an eighteen-wheeler. He got out of his rig, opened the door for her, and helped her in. It was the first time anyone had treated her like a lady. They were married three weeks later.

But Sally's old heroin addiction caught up with her, and three children later she left her family. Before long, she was so strung out that she wound up living under a bridge. "After my divorce, my ex-husband got custody of the kids. Guess I shouldn't have expected anything else. But it hurt. I loved those kids, and I wanted them back.

"Somehow I managed to get myself together long enough to get some decent work. I met Preacher Bob at the restaurant I was managing. I'd noticed him coming in a lot, but had avoided him. I was a mess! One night, though, I got cornered when I was short on help and had to wait on him. So just to be friendly, I struck up a conversation. 'I hear you're a preacher. Where's your church?'

"Right then he pointed his finger in my face and everything froze—like slow motion. The whole place went silent. 'Jesus loves you,' he said.

"It was the first time in my life anyone had ever told me that Jesus loved me. *How can He love me?* I was thinking. *I'm a Satanist, on heroin.* But Preacher Bob kept right on talking. 'God will set you free.' By the second 'service,' I denounced the devil and the power of drugs over my life, and I was free! That was 1998. I'm still free, married to Preacher Bob, and ordained to preach the gospel myself.

"It took me 35 years to realize that while I thought I was in control, I was playing right into the devil's hands. Now God has called me to root out and expose the dark stuff. I'm not afraid to get in the devil's face, call him what he is—a liar and a cheat—and slam the door in his face!"

By now the tea party ladies' eyes were wide. They'd never heard anything like this. But I wasn't through. I told them about my lovely friend Karen, who was in a satanic stranglehold for 45 years, although far more subtle than Sally's. Even as a child growing up in a denominational church, her brilliant mind was full of questions: *Why is anyone standing between the people and God? If we confess our sins to God, why do we have to turn around and tell them to a priest? Why do people carry Bibles around and never read them? Why am I to blame for Jesus' suffering on a cross?* These and many other unanswered questions drove her out of this church and into a quest to know the truth.

With no real foundation in the Word of God and an unguarded heart, Karen, then a clothing designer, and her musician husband moved to California, where they pursued their careers and explored various religions. Many successful people, including certain celebrities, were involved in a cult, which promised highly creative people like Karen and Peter an opportunity to expand their minds, build self-confidence, and tap into their true spiritual powers. This self-improvement approach seemed made to order, and they enrolled in the very expensive courses designed as a "pathway to spiritual enlightenment."

What Karen did not suspect was the entrapment of the next sixteen years of her life, during which she gave up her career and dedicated her life to this organization. For nine of those years, she was on staff at their base, located in a remote southern California desert valley, with little or no access to the outside world and little contact with her husband, who was working in another area. She was growing more and more suspicious that this was not the real answer to her lifelong questions. After two attempts to leave the enclave, then being found and forced to return and enter a "rehabilitation program," Karen was petrified. She was truly a prisoner of this group, yet her husband seemed content with his life there.

"What happened next was nothing short of a miracle," Karen says. "As I stood right there at my desk, surrounded by these busy people at their work, I heard within the depths of my soul a small, still voice totally foreign to me. I wondered if I were hearing things. Yet I felt as if all my fears were being washed away, as if someone were looking into my soul and just lifting my anxieties from me: *You need to be with God. You need to leave here...you'll be okay.* I didn't know God, wasn't looking for Him, yet I sensed that His loving hand had reached across a chasm and was pulling me to safety.

"The following day I escaped with a few things thrown into a laundry basket and $48 in my wallet. I still didn't know God, but it appeared He was taking care of all of the arrangements, and through a divine connection, I made it back to my mother's house in another state." There, Karen began attending a church, reading the Bible for the first time in her life, and perceiving that the pastor was filled with something—or Someone. It felt wonderful, warm, and safe. She wanted that.

As she listened to the account of how God brought His people out of bondage, her heart melted and she was gradually delivered from the bondage of the false doctrine she had been enslaved and deceived by. And on March 14, 1999, when she heard the words "Choose you this day whom you will serve," she chose to turn from her own, self-absorbed ways, ask forgiveness for her sins, and follow the one, true, Almighty God!

"The depth of the deception in this group is indescribable," Karen says, "but God's Word is truly a sword and cuts through all lies. I know now that my childhood questions and the disturbing unease I felt working with these people over the years was God at work in me to bring me to Himself. Even my mother, who accepted Christ and left the denominational church we used to attend, had been praying for my deliverance for a year!

"I believe it takes a miracle from God to cut through false doctrine that chokes so many people. But that's what God's Word is. There is wonder-working power in the blood of the Lamb! He has removed the scales from my eyes, and now I see the Truth! He has led me to a new life in Him, a new book that I am writing, a new husband who shares my passion for the Lord, and a new ministry, where I have been blessed with opportunities to share my testimony. My life now belongs to Jesus! The deceiver has failed!"

Do you see now why I'm so proud of my spiritual daughters? Elaine is a radiant witness for the Lord, whose husband calls her "the most exquisite woman I've ever known." Victoria, the ex-prostitute, has founded an organization called Victoria's Friends that goes into the strip joints and ministers to the prostitutes. Jean, who was abused sexually by her father, is now healed and whole and ministers on the Father's heart. Sally, the heroin addict and former Satan worshipper, is now a minister of the gospel of Jesus Christ. And

Karen, a speaker and author on the subject of the cult of which she was a part, is totally transformed by the Truth that overcomes every lie and deception of the enemy.

While these actions are certainly wrong, I don't care if you've had several abortions, have committed murder, have stolen a ton of money, have been a drug addict for years, or are living the homosexual lifestyle—every sin you have ever committed is rooted in deception and is a snare of the enemy to detour you from reclaiming your dream! Come to the Father through Jesus, His Son. Step out of the kingdom of darkness and into His marvelous light.

Prayer of Deliverance: Awesome God of all power and all kingdoms, we thank You for the revelation of who You are. You are the Author, the Creator, and the Architect of life, and beside You there is no other. Loving Father, we thank You that You reveal the adversary and his evil intent for mankind. We thank You for Your protection and wisdom, handed down in Your Holy Word that clearly separates the truth from the lie. We humbly and gratefully acknowledge that it is Your Presence in our lives that carries us through the darkest hours, out of the deepest pits, and beyond the desolate places where sin takes us when we disobey. Thank You for Your light that exposes darkness and for the sacrifice of Your Son, Jesus Christ, and His blood covenant that covers our sins through repentance and faith. We thank You for Your grace that leads us out, cleans us up, and sets us free. We bless You, and we thank You for all You are and all You will ever be to us, Your children. In Jesus' holy name we pray, amen.

Now the Midianites had sold him [Joseph]

in Egypt to Potiphar, an officer of Pharaoh

and captain of the guard.

...Joseph was handsome in form and appearance.

And it came to pass after these things that his

master's wife cast longing eyes on Joseph,

and she said, "Lie with me."

GENESIS 37:36; 39:6,7

CHAPTER 8

Resisting the Tempter

Finally, my brethren, be strong in the
Lord and in the power of His might.
Put on the whole armor of God, that you may
be able to stand against the wiles of the devil.

EPHESIANS 6:10,11

The devil doesn't play fair. Just about the time you think you have this life all figured out, he will throw you a curve, and you'll fall into a pit or wander in the wilderness for a while or end up in Egypt. That's what happened to Joseph, the favored son of his father, joint heir to the family holdings. Suddenly this young man from Canaan was a foreigner, thrust into a much more sophisticated culture, where he didn't know the language and the people worshiped creatures—cobras and vultures and scarabs—instead of the Creator. How very different from Joseph's rural roots back home. In Egypt, he was far from all that was familiar; far, it must have seemed at times, from the one true God.

I marvel at the wealth of knowledge and wisdom contained in the Word of God. I am just as amazed at the times in which the Bible is silent. All we know about Joseph's transition from the pit to the house of Potiphar is a few words in a couple of verses. So much is left to our imagination. What must this country boy have been thinking and feeling in those first days of captivity? Taken from the remote fields where a dysfunctional family and his father's flocks were his only companions and where his people dwelt in tents, Joseph had been thrust into a thriving civilization along the Nile, into the wealthy household of a high official of the realm. Talk about culture shock!

Where the Bible is mute, I think I can fill in the blanks for you. Oh, the treasures of ancient Egypt! The Egyptians were a sensual, materialistic people, fascinated by lovely objects of art, flamboyant color, and rich jewelry of hammered gold and carnelian[1] and turquoise and lapis lazuli.[2] The wealthy dressed to impress. Unveiled women flaunted their bodies. If the sights and sounds of "modern" Egypt were not enough of a challenge, then the women with their heavy makeup and wanton ways were a setup of Satan calculated to turn any young man's head.

Just watch as the story unfolds. There are lessons here for our own spiritual walk. Maybe you will even find yourself at some stopover in this segment of Joseph's journey.

Captain Potiphar

Some people are fascinated with the idea of peering into the lifestyles of the rich and famous. Our American media capitalized on this with a successful television program that ran for years. I can just imagine the script Robin Leach, who hosted that TV show, might have written about Potiphar, captain of Pharaoh's elite palace guard.

This was a man who, as a trusted officer, had been granted special privilege and great power by the king of Egypt. Potiphar commanded the soldiers charged with guarding the life of Pharaoh. Consequently, he was in the palace daily, issuing orders to secure the safety of the monarch of the most advanced civilization of the known world.

Typical of the Egyptian aristocracy of the day, the family probably resided in a house that would be considered a mansion by any standard. As an officer and a man of great wealth, Captain Potiphar's house was no doubt designed with columns and fountains and decorated with gilded furnishings of Lebanese cedar, Syrian conifers, ebony, and other fine woods.[3] This was the house where young Joseph was brought after he was purchased from the Midianite merchants. For a nomad accustomed to dwelling only in tents that could be rolled up and moved to pursue the choicest pastureland for their flocks and herds, this life must have seemed grand indeed.

And what about Joseph's new master? Potiphar himself must have made an imposing picture. A man of power and influence, he was not only captain of the palace guard but was "the chief executioner" for Pharaoh (Gen. 37:36 TLB). One wrong move, and off with your head! Yet there is no mention that Joseph was intimidated or awed. He had never been in any position but that of favored son. Now he is a servant, yet there is not a word about his being upset or disappointed that God had allowed this to happen to him. We are not told if Joseph even questioned God about what had happened to his dreams! Such staunch believers are few and far between. But my young friend Kimberly is one of them.

"My life has had its fair share of challenges," she writes. "There was a time in my early twenties where I truly had to make a choice between just doing enough to ensure my spot in heaven and jumping into the deep, the unknown, and trusting that God would complete the work that He had begun in me and fulfill His promises. I chose the deep. I had some very difficult experiences ranging from the loss of a dear friend to date rape, but any 'unknown' with God certainly beat my vain attempt to control a world that was crumbling around me."

With all the familiar things Joseph had known crumbling around him, he apparently chose to leap into the deep, to trust that God would somehow keep His promise and fulfill the dream. The very next verses are proof. "The Lord was with Joseph, and he was a successful man…in the house of his master the Egyptian. And his master saw that the Lord was with him and that the Lord made all he did to prosper in his hand. So Joseph found favor in his sight, and served him. Then he [Potiphar] made him [Joseph] overseer of his house, and all that he had he put under his [Joseph's] authority" (Gen. 39:2-4).

In fact, Potiphar so trusted Joseph that he turned absolutely everything he had over to the young foreigner and left him in complete control of the household, and "…the Lord blessed the Egyptian's house for Joseph's sake…" (Gen. 39:5). Again, we do not know just how long it took for Potiphar to recognize Joseph's integrity and leadership ability and elevate him within the ranks, but we do know that the captain acknowledged that it was the Lord who was with Joseph.

So, in spite of everything he could do to steal Joseph's dream, the enemy (Satan) had failed and would surely back off now, right? Oh, he doesn't give up that easily. Just wait until you meet Mrs. Potiphar! It is important that you get the picture of Satan's setup so as to learn how to avoid falling into the nearest pit.

The Temptress

Things were running smoothly in Potiphar's household. Joseph was in charge of the home front, so Potiphar was freed up to tend to his important responsibilities at the palace. All was well—or so it seemed.

Before continuing on with Joseph's story, let me tell you a bit more about the daily life of the wealthy Egyptians. These were a self-indulgent people, completely absorbed in accumulating treasures and entertaining themselves with games and lavish feasts and boating on the Nile. Mrs. Potiphar had a retinue of house servants and maids to care for her every need and to perform elaborate beauty rituals—bathe her with scented water; anoint her with exotic perfumes; clothe her in form-fitting gowns enhanced with golden necklaces, armlets, anklets, and earrings set with precious stones; make up her eyes and lips with kohl and paints; and dress her hair in elaborate coiffeurs. So there were many idle hours when she was free to roam about looking for her next distraction.

This distraction was not far away. It was Joseph, the good-looking young slave her husband had bought.

Not all temptations are right under our noses. Some people go looking for them. But giving in to temptation never satisfies. Marriages are often destroyed and lives are left in shambles. With this in mind, Mrs. Potiphar was Satan's setup to tempt Joseph and bring him down.

"And it came to pass after these things that his master's wife cast longing eyes on Joseph, and she said, 'Lie with me'" (Gen. 39:7). With no soap operas or cheap romance novels to titillate her mind, how did such a thought occur to Potiphar's wife? That's easy. The enemy was at work in her imagination—the devil's "playground"—setting up the scene for Joseph's downfall and using her as the bait.

Fatal Attraction

How could Joseph possibly resist Mrs. Potiphar's advances? After all, he was a single young man. He was probably lonely at times. He was far from anyone who knew him or would care if he had a brief fling. Besides, technically speaking, as the boss's wife, this woman represented some form of authority in the house. How dare he say no? "But he refused and said to his master's wife… 'There is no one greater in this house than I, nor has he [Potiphar] kept back anything from me but you, because you are his wife…'" (Gen. 39:8,9).

The battle is on. Of all the sins we can commit, I believe sexual sin is one that grieves the Lord most. Paul was quite clear about this: "Do you not know that your bodies are members of Christ? Shall I then take the members of Christ and make them members of a harlot? Certainly not! Or do you not know that he who is joined to a harlot is one body with her? For 'the two,' He says, 'shall become one flesh.' But he who is joined to the Lord is one spirit with Him" (1 Cor. 6:15-17). The opposite applies, ladies. Just substitute the word *lover* or the masculine equivalent of harlot, and you have the same strong warning. We can't play with fire and not be burned!

"For when we were in the flesh, the sinful passions which were aroused by the law were at work in our members to bear fruit to death" (Rom. 7:5). We're talking serious consequences here. Consider the "fruit" of David and Bathsheba's adultery. Wasn't it the death of their firstborn son? And what about Mother Eve? Her sin had far-reaching consequences. She, like Potiphar's wife, wanted what she wanted. Unlike Mrs. Potiphar, she took it, and now we, too, suffer the punishment for her disobedience: God said, "…I will greatly multiply your sorrow and your conception; in pain you shall bring forth children; your desire shall be for your husband, and he shall rule over you" (Gen. 3:16). Very interesting that there is a sexual consequence as a result of Eve's sin of rebellion.

As we just saw in Genesis 39, even in the face of almost overwhelming temptation, Joseph—a "CEO" with integrity—kept a cool head. He then asked Potiphar's wife a question that proved his deep commitment and faith: "How then can I do this great wickedness, and sin against God?" (v. 9). Whatever negative aspects Joseph's childhood might have contained, his family obviously had done some things right. He was taught about and highly esteemed the covenant God had made with his great-grandfather Abraham. Joseph called sin what it was and recognized that he would be offending God by his action. He was a rare breed—a man of honor and integrity who would not allow himself to grieve God's heart.

But the devil wasn't through with Joseph. This was more than a woman seducing a man. This was an evil plot of the enemy. The spirit of darkness in her recognized the Spirit of God in Joseph. The devil had been crouching at his door, just waiting for an opportune time, and he was relentless at it. Notice the phrase "day by day" in verse 10. This woman wouldn't quit! On and on she pursued Joseph with flattering words and coy looks: "How handsome you are, Joseph, how strong. Oh, but Potiphar makes too many demands on you. You should rest awhile." I can just picture her giving Joseph the subtle suggestion, the innuendo, and then finally, the outright invitation.

Joseph must have looked about and realized that no one was in the house but the two of them. The door of his lady's bedchamber was probably wide open, and her husband was off somewhere, maybe at the palace. How easy it would have been for him to succumb to her charms.

But Joseph refused her, and she was so insulted and desperate that she made her most aggressive move. She clutched at Joseph's garment. The Hebrew word for *garment* suggests that it was some kind of outer apparel or cover, as a robe,[4] which Joseph left "...in her hand and fled outside" (Gen. 39:13). Faced with this nearly irresistible invitation, he ran!

This was no cowardly act. Under the circumstances, it was the most courageous thing Joseph could have done. And it was entirely godly and biblical! Now, remember, Joseph had not read 2 Timothy 2:22 that tells us to flee youthful lusts. The New Testament had not yet been inspired by God; the writers were not even in existence. Nor had God given the Ten Commandments to Moses. But somehow Joseph knew the difference between right and wrong. I believe it was because the truth of God was written in his heart! By God's grace, Joseph resisted this devilish attempt to soil his reputation.

Some people are not always able to resist temptation as Joseph did. What about you? Have you been able to resist in times of temptation? One of the leading Bible teachers in this country, and a beloved friend of mine, speaks candidly about sexual immorality. "I know what it is to battle that 'inner man' in the area of sex, because I have been there. I know the pain, the regret that comes when sex takes place in a way that isn't according to God's plan.... I sinned. I broke God's commandments. That's what sin is—living independently of God. It's *you* acting like God, *you* deciding what is right and wrong.... I sinned, and it took me farther than I ever wanted to go and cost me more than I ever intended to pay...."[5]

If you've already committed some kind of sin (sexual or otherwise), whatever is your particular pit, it is not too late to change. You can begin by repenting and getting right with God. He alone can give you the help, strength, and will to overcome and walk in purity of thought and conduct. He has provided all the weapons of warfare necessary to be victorious over your own flesh as well as every "fiery dart" of the enemy. Joseph did not have the advantage of God's written Word when he was tempted by Potiphar's wife, but we do!

High Alert

Satan is after your character, and he'll stop at nothing to get it. Just as Captain Potiphar put on his armor each day—although it may have been ceremonial only—so you can "put on" the inner armor that fortifies you in times of temptation or when the battle heats up.

"Be strong in the Lord and in the power of His might.

Put on the whole armor of God, that you may be able to stand ["...vigorously opposing, bravely resisting, standing face-to-face against an adversary, standing your ground..."[6]] against the wiles of the devil....

"Stand therefore, having girded your waist with truth, having put on the breastplate of righteousness,

and having shod your feet with the preparation of the gospel of peace;

above all, taking the shield of faith with which you will be able to quench all the fiery darts of the wicked one. And take the helmet of salvation...."

Ephesians 6:10,11,14-17

Let's examine each piece of defensive armor with which God has equipped us and its significance for the kind of warfare we'll be engaging in as Christians.

Defensive Armor

The helmet of salvation—When the enemy is trying to bring you down, he will aim first for your mind—the computer center governing creativity, intellect, and memory, and the communication center directing your body to respond. He'll mess with your thought life, sometimes making such a logical argument for a certain decision or action that you'll be convinced it's the right thing to do!

It could start out as innocently as a business lunch with a married co-worker that develops into something you hadn't counted on. It could be a plan you thought was of God but was really rooted in selfish ambition. It could even be your "dream house" that occupies so much of your time and thought that there is nothing left for the Lord. "There is a way that seems right to a man [or woman], but its end is the way of death" (Prov. 14:12). This is deception at the highest level.

The best defense against attacks on the mind is to know who you are in Christ. If you have repented of your sins and received Jesus as your Lord and Savior, then you will be empowered to live this new life by the Holy Spirit. "For the weapons of our warfare are not carnal but mighty in God for pulling down strongholds, casting down arguments and every high thing that exalts itself against the knowledge of God, bringing every *thought* into captivity to the obedience of Christ" (2 Cor. 10:4,5).

My friend whom I quoted earlier on the subject of sexual impurity says that she "...battled continually with immoral thoughts and dreams. I cried, I prayed, I read before I went to sleep, but still my thoughts and dreams tormented me, leaving me feeling very unclean at times.... Then one day I realized these thoughts weren't coming from me but from the devil.... At that point, the devil was tangling with someone who had studied warfare, and I knew I wasn't to be ignorant of his tricks or devices.... You may need to do a study on warfare."[7] You can study spiritual warfare, too. We're learning at this very moment!

There is much more we can say about storing up God's Word for such times as this; we'll be covering some of it later in this chapter in "The Sword of the Spirit" section. But the Word tells us, "...whatever things are true, whatever things are noble, whatever things are just, whatever things are pure, whatever things are lovely, whatever things are of good report, if there is any virtue and if there is anything praiseworthy—meditate on these things" (Phil. 4:8). By meditating on the real—the true God and His infinitely beautiful character—you will develop such a sensitivity and discernment that you will be able to see right through Satan's disguises. You'll even learn his "lines." And you'll know when to run—as Joseph did—and when to stay put and stand firm.

The breastplate of righteousness—This piece of armor, one of the largest defensive garments of the early warrior, was made of thick leather or metal mail and covered the heart and other vital organs. The breastplate was protection against an arrow or dart that could penetrate and cause a fatal injury. In the case of a coat of mail, the construction was of small metal pieces that overlapped each other, not allowing for any crack or crevice through which the enemy's weapon could find its target.[8]

The enemy of our souls is looking for any small window of opportunity. He is not all-powerful, but he is plenty sneaky. So he watches for times when you are not dressed for battle, when your heart is unguarded.

How do we guard our hearts? The Word tells us that it is by "righeousness," or as Webster defines it, "acting in accord with divine or moral law...," which equals being "...free from guilt or sin"![9] Who wants to take a guilt trip, to feel the sticky slime of self-condemnation? "Righteous" living—doing what God says—will produce a freedom and lightness of heart that the world simply will not be able to understand. And it will stop the fiery darts of the enemy cold!

Remember, too, that we put on *Christ's* righteousness, not our own meager good deeds and charitable acts. "We are all like an unclean thing, and all our righteousnesses are like filthy rags..." (Isa. 64:6). Only as we are "dressed in His righteousness alone" will we be "faultless to stand before the throne."[10] It never ceases to stun me to silence when I consider that the Lord sees me as already perfected, already pure, dressed as a bride "...not having spot or wrinkle...but...holy and without blemish" (Eph. 5:27). And if you are submitted to Him, dear one, He sees you exactly the same way! Hallelujah!

The belt of truth—This is the first piece of armor mentioned in the Ephesians 6 passage, and it's first for a very good reason. Unless we know the Truth, Jesus Christ Himself, we will be powerless against the enemy.

Since this has come up again, now might be a good time to take spiritual inventory. Are you sure you know Jesus as Savior and Lord? If you died today, do you know that you would instantly be in His Presence forever? It is one thing to know somebody's name. You might even know his or her address, how many children there are in the family, and what that person does for a living. You could know many things *about* someone, but if you didn't have regular fellowship, you wouldn't really *know* that person.

The same is true for Jesus. You may know a great deal about Him, may even be able to quote His very own words from Scripture, but if you have not come under submission to His authority, it's time to give up, surrender, let Him become your Commander and direct your life. Only He has the real truth. Everything else is a lie or, at the very least, a distortion of the truth. Satan is extremely good at leading us down the wrong pathway and into a pit!

The shoes of peace—I'm not Imelda Marcos (the former "first lady" of the Philippines who is well-known for her huge shoe collection), but let's just say I am equipped to preach the gospel of peace on any occasion! In other words, I have no shortage of shoes, including some summer sandals.

The leather thong sandals of the biblical warrior were an important item of equipment. They had to be sturdy enough to cover the territory and flexible enough to provide comfort while engaging the enemy in warfare. The same is true today. Good, well-fitting footwear is still an essential part of one's wardrobe—especially our spiritual wardrobe. In Ephesians 6:15, *The Amplified Bible* says, "And having shod your feet in preparation [to face the enemy with the firm-footed stability, the promptness, and the readiness produced by the good news] of the Gospel of peace." You can't move forward and do a good job of representing the Lord in battle if your feet are killing you!

So, not only must you have the proper weapons, you must have on the right kind of shoes for each skirmish. Sometimes a soldier is called to run, sometimes to stand, and sometimes to dance! "I still dance with joy, but I dance with shoes that have been prepared," writes Shirley Arnold in the *Women of Destiny Bible.* "In a world of uncertainty and fear, everyone is searching for peace. We have good news to proclaim. God's peace surpasses all understanding. It is not dependent on circumstances or people. We are a part of an unshakable kingdom where peace is a person named

Jesus. The peace of God surrounds me; and everywhere I go, I leave a footprint of peace."[11]

The race is on, dear one. Put on your running shoes and don't lose your momentum. There's a battle to be won and a peace treaty that has already been signed in the blood of Jesus!

The shield of faith—The shield of the ancient soldier was made of leather stretched over wooden frames with handles on the inside.[12] Obviously shields made of leather did not offer as much protection as the metal shields that came later, but they were easier to handle.

In the Ephesians 6 passage, the shield that provided the most protection in spiritual warfare was the shield of faith. We must be able to handle this shield with skill and dexterity. Faith stands on "the substance of things hoped for, the evidence of things not seen" (Heb. 11:1). You can stand firm in the conviction that every promise of God—over 137,000—is true. You can say: *By faith, I believe that the Lord "will not leave [me] nor forsake [me]"* (Deut. 31:6). *By faith, I believe He will give me the desires of my heart when I seek Him with all my heart!* (Ps. 37:4; Deut. 4:29.) *I believe that Jesus Christ will provide all that I need for my earthly walk and will escort me to heaven when it's time to go home.*

You Go, Girl!

It is one thing to defend yourself when under attack by a hostile force. It's quite another to take the initiative in attempting to topple the evil regime of Satan when he comes against you. That takes real grit! Again, you are not left without all the resources necessary to win. At least three other offensive weapons are available to all believers in God through His Son and Holy Spirit.

Offensive Weapons

The sword of the Spirit—I have always been fascinated by both *swords* and *words*. That's why this phrase so intrigues me since "the sword of the Spirit," of course, is referring to the Word of God!

On trips abroad, John and I have visited many museums displaying weapons of warfare in various cultures, including elaborately embellished swords. Although this weapon is no longer useful in modern-day combat and has been replaced by long-range missiles and high-powered bombs, the sword is prized for its historic value and for the beauty of its craftsmanship.

This type of sword, however, is designed to *take* life; the sword of the Lord *gives* life! "This is my comfort in my affliction, for Your *word has given me life*" (Ps. 119:50). This "sword" also reveals our own spiritual condition: "For the word of God is *living* and powerful, and sharper than any two-edged sword, piercing even to the division of soul and spirit, and of joints and marrow, and is a discerner of the thoughts and intents of the heart" (Heb. 4:12). The razor-sharp blade of God's Word cuts through all the rubbish in our lives and exposes the truth. Then we are freed from our own sin to enter into hand-to-hand combat with the enemy and to aim God's Word directly at any plan or scheme designed to destroy us.

My Grandmother Williams, a staunch Southern Baptist, was adamant about her demand that all her grandchildren memorize Scripture. She assigned us a verse each week and frequently called on us to recite at a moment's notice. These were not one- or two-liners, either! They were deep passages that we were expected to know and be able to apply. I didn't appreciate my grandmother's expectations until my mid-twenties turnaround, after my divorce. Spinning and reeling from the devastation of that experience and fearing I was almost losing my sanity, I grabbed hold of the sure Word of God. Scriptures from childhood flooded my mind and heart, bringing comfort and stability. God's Word is solid ground.

Now that I have read the Bible through many times, it has become an old friend. I read and reread its pages, savoring this love letter from a Father to His daughter, the Bridegroom to His bride. Having hidden these precious words in my heart, the Spirit brings to my remembrance just the words that are needed for someone else's need in counseling or mentoring situations. I love this Book because I know the Author so well!

Prayer—Ephesians 6:18 gives us a strong exhortation to pray: "praying *always* with *all prayer* and supplication in the Spirit, being watchful to this end with all perseverance and supplication for all the saints." Notice the words *always* and *all* [kinds of] *prayer.* We are to pray all the time, "without ceasing." And we are to use more than one method of prayer. In other words, we should be in an attitude of prayer at all times, just as we would converse with a friend, a spouse, or a parent naturally throughout the day. Nothing is too small to bring to the Father's attention. I have to smile when I think of the little nuggets He drops into my mind at odd moments, sometimes in the midst of a conversation with a friend. He will remind me of some word of Scripture that applies to something my friend and I are saying, or He will even tip me off as to some insider information that only our mutual Father would know! But that's because the Lord and I have been sharing for so long.

My friend, Jean, whom you have met in a previous chapter, tells of a revelatory experience in prayer. "I thought I had a great relationship with God. We would sit together for hours in my quiet place—I, on one side of the room in my chair, He in another. At least, I could imagine Him sitting there. We would chat like old friends. It was beautiful and peaceful. The Presence of the Lord was so strong in that room that on the rare occasion when I would invite someone in to pray with me there, she would burst into tears. But something was missing.... And not until I heard a teaching on 'the orphan heart' did I understand what it was.

"Being the child of an abusive father, I had always inadvertently kept a certain distance between my heavenly Father and myself—the two chairs. But when I realized that I had really felt like an orphan since my childhood, abandoned and rejected, then it seemed that something broke inside and I allowed the Lord to reach out and touch me, intertwining my fingers in His! Now there is no sense of distance in my prayers. I love sitting in my Father's lap, His arms around me, holding me close and whispering healing words of love and comfort to my heart."

What a powerful testimony! In fact, I learned that Jean has an interesting take on spiritual warfare as a result of this breakthrough. She believes that we are often overly concerned with this aspect of our Christian life, putting too much emphasis on weapons and methods and making sure we are binding every demon. A vision she once had explains her position. "I was riding on a white horse, with Jesus behind me. On either side of the trail was inky darkness, although I could make out the figures of people wielding swords, fighting demons only half their size. In spite of that, the demons seemed to be winning. Hovering overhead were warrior angels, with bows drawn, ready to let their arrows fly.

"Only when one man glimpsed Jesus riding by did he cry out for help. An angel shot his arrow, and the demon fell dead. Yet the man didn't seem to notice that his enemy was no longer a danger to him. He just kept thrusting his sword and crying out for help. I believe that is the position of the church," Jean went on. "We seem to forget that we are fighting a defeated foe. A loving Father doesn't send His children out to fight a battle. We watch from the safe, secure haven of His arms."

I must admit that this is something to consider. But I do know that we are commanded to pray and that prayer is a huge threat to the enemy. Dr. Paul (David) Yonggi Cho's million-member church in Korea is built on continual twenty-four-hour-a-day prayer. He personally spends at least four hours on his knees daily and recommends the same for anyone in ministry. If you're too busy to pray, you're too busy!

I wish there could be national prayer each day at sundown, with bells chiming in every city and town in the country, calling God's people to pray, just as the church bells chimed in the historic district of Charleston where my Grandmother Winnie lived when I was a child. A nation on its knees is a force to be reckoned with. "If My people who are called by My name will humble themselves, and pray and seek My face, and turn from their wicked ways, then I will hear from heaven, and will forgive their sin and heal their land" (2 Chron. 7:14). That is just another powerful promise from the Covenant-Keeper.

The Authority of the Believer—When Jesus left this earth to return to heaven, He handed over His authority to His disciples: "Most assuredly, I say to you, he who believes in Me, the works that I do he will do also; and greater works than these he will do, because I go to My Father" (John 14:12). What an incredible promise! This was not mere idle conversation. Jesus used the term *most assuredly,* or "with the utmost assurance, absolutely, without question!" If we believe, we will do greater, or even more,[13] works than Jesus did while He was on this earth. Do you believe it? Then receive it! What did Jesus do? He ministered, He taught, He healed, He encouraged, He admonished, He set people free, He raised the dead, He loved the Father, He prayed, He gave His life for you and me.

Dear one, are you ready to do "greater works"? Is His dream burning in your heart? Are you willing to love as He loved? Are you able to step out of your comfort zone? Will you suffer with Him? Maybe die for Him? He has given you everything you need to follow Him all the way.

The Powerful Name of Jesus—"Jesus." There's just something about that name. "Therefore God also has highly exalted Him and given Him the name which is above every name, that at the name of Jesus every knee should bow, of those in heaven, and of those on earth, and of those under the earth, and that every tongue should confess that Jesus Christ is Lord, to the glory of God the Father" (Phil. 2:9-11). With every attack of the enemy come the resources and power, through Jesus' name (a name which means "salvation, sets free")[14] to turn the darkness into light, to transform tragedy into triumph. The enemy cannot hold the believer who trusts in God and calls upon the name of Jesus.

If you're going to name-drop, drop Jesus' name. Call Him Master, Redeemer, Savior, Friend, Captain of the Hosts of Heaven, Bright and Morning Star, Fairest of Ten Thousand, Beloved, Hope of Earth and Joy of Heaven, and a hundred more. That name opens doors that can never be closed and shuts the enemy's lying mouth. That name is your passport to heaven.

Commando With Boots On

Since I have been blessed with a ministry that often takes me into Satan's territory, my children have been a target of his attacks. They have been taunted and tormented so many times we have all lost count. They have been enticed into sin, have married the wrong men, and have sometimes called me up in the middle of the night, crying their hearts out.

It is then I take off the pearls and put on the whole armor of God. With my prayer room as the command center, I storm the gates of heaven on my face in intercession. I command Satan to loose my children. I command that his plans be dismantled in the powerful name of Jesus. I ask that Father God cover them with the blood of Jesus, dispatch angels to rescue them, minister to them, and guard them against future attack. I call upon the Lord to put this need on the hearts of intercessors beyond the walls of our house. At such times, I am no shrinking violet, no Southern belle sitting on my front porch sipping peach tea. I'm a warrior woman, shouting down the enemy!

But like my friend Jean, I intend to nestle in the Master's arms after the battle's over.

Warfare Prayer: Father God, Lord of all, Commanding General of the spiritual armies of heaven and earth, we praise You for Your awesome splendor, Your warfare strategies, the ability to command from Your throne room the answers to all our prayers sent up to You. We thank You for giving us the knowledge of the weapons of warfare to guard us from the enemy and to protect our rightful place as joint heirs with Your Son, Jesus Christ. Thank You for covering us with the cloak of Your Son's blood and for the anointed Scriptures that guide our every move throughout the ages. Thank You for protecting us when we didn't even know You were there. Thank You for the host of angels that surround us in our times of deepest need, when war is looming in the distance. Thank You for giving us the secrets of Your kingdom, internal strategy against the enemy of our souls, and for bringing peace through the Prince of Peace. In the powerful name that is above all names, Your Son, Jesus Christ, amen.

"Then Joseph's master took him and

put him into the prison....

But the Lord was with Joseph and showed

him mercy, and He gave him favor in

the sight of the keeper of the prison.

...and whatever he did, the Lord made it prosper."

GENESIS 39:20,21,23

CHAPTER 9

Hidden Destiny

*"The Spirit of the Lord God is upon Me, because the Lord has
anointed Me to preach good tidings to the poor; He has sent
Me to heal the brokenhearted, to proclaim liberty to the captives,
and the opening of the prison to those who are bound."*

ISAIAH 61:1

I have never done prison time. But I know something about solitary confinement. I have felt the sting of loneliness and rejection, and the pain of failure. I know what it means to be betrayed and the heartbreak of false accusation. I also know that it was during such times that God was doing His finest work in me. And He can do it in you.

There is something deep within us—the dream—placed there by the hand of God that requires the refiner's fire, the potter's wheel, the dormancy of winter, and sometimes the prison before it can burst forth free and full. But this doesn't mean that "the meanwhiles" are not long and tedious.

Meanwhile…someone has stolen Joseph's dream—a dream of greatness. He knows it is true. God has told him so.

Meanwhile…the dream-stealers—the ten bad brothers, the caravan of merchants on their way to Egypt, the alien culture with its false gods, the seductive woman—have snatched away all hope of the dream's fulfillment. Or so it seems.

Meanwhile…things are only getting worse. The master's wife, spurned and seething with rage, cries, "Rape!" and implicates Joseph with the evidence in hand—his outer garment. Her husband—whether he truly believes her or not—comes to her defense and ousts Joseph from the house where he has served so faithfully.

Meanwhile…Joseph is sentenced to prison.

When You're in a Prison

It's not fair! I didn't do it! Why did this happen to me? All perfectly natural reactions after a false accusation puts you behind bars. Yet we don't find Joseph complaining about his lot, although he must have felt the bitter sting of betrayal and wondered where God was keeping Himself these days.

Most people, however, especially when the charges are not true, experience a wide range of emotions when cast into a prison—be it steel bars or state of mind.

Denial and Defensiveness—In time of trauma, one's first response is usually shock—an instinctive knee-jerk mechanism, programmed into the mind by a loving Creator to cushion the blow. Denial is a gentle way of handling crises until you can learn to cope.

I remember well the moment I knew I had been betrayed and abandoned by my first husband, leaving me with our two little girls and no marketable skills that I was aware of. Any dreams or thoughts of destiny I had seemed lost. At 27, possibly the age of Joseph when he was falsely imprisoned, I felt the first real crushing of my life. Like Joseph, I had played by the rules. I considered myself a good and faithful wife and mother. I'd done it right. So what had gone wrong?

My husband had also emptied our bank account on the way out of town. How was I to buy groceries, make the house payment, pay bills? At the moment all I could see were prison walls closing in around me. If I had known then what I know now, if I could have felt God's loving arms cradling me, I would have been looking forward to the joy, the laughter, the love, the future ministry. I would have been excited about what He was going to do. But I was young and not yet fully trusting in His provision. I could not see any way out.

Being in some kind of prison—financially, in our health, or a relation-ship gone bad, for example—is often what it takes for some of us to come all the way to the end of ourselves and find God. Maybe that's one reason for my particular "prison." But I only know that the things that have hurt me the most are what have laid the foundation for my greatest blessings. Some of Joseph's greatest blessings started that way too.

Deferred Hope

Once a "prison door" has clanged shut in our life, all our dreams, all we've hoped for, seems to be on hold, or deferred. The word *deferred* means "put off, postponed, delayed, protracted, prolonged, held up."[1] Proverbs 13:12 (TLB) describes what that can do to us, saying, "Hope deferred makes the heart sick...." But the rest of that verse says, "...when dreams come true at last, there is life and joy." What a message of hope! The dream may be "postponed" or "held up," but it's not over until God says it's over. That means it can still come to pass.

Joseph's dream was postponed, first by his brothers' actions against him and then when he was thrown into prison for a crime he didn't commit, but he must have had hope. And since hope and faith are first cousins, I believe that he had faith. His freedom had been stolen, yet now he would have more free time than ever to meditate on the things of God. What else would have held him steady during those first long days and nights in captivity?

We are never told that he once faltered in his faith in God. He must have been praying. While all the others were bowing to idols, Joseph surely carried on intimate conversations with the only true God. How do we know? Four times in a single chapter the Bible says, "The Lord was with him" and "The Lord was with Joseph" (Gen. 39:2,3,21,23). Joseph may have been in a seemingly hopeless situation, but he was comforted because he knew that he wasn't alone; the Lord was with him.

What revelation knowledge comes as I write these words! "I Am With You" is actually a covenant name of God. It was spoken first to Abraham in Genesis 21:22: "...*God is with you* in all that you do" and again to Isaac: "I am the God of your father Abraham; do not fear, for *I am with you.* I will bless you and multiply your descendants..." (Gen. 26:24). Later, God said it to Joseph's father, Jacob: "*I am with you* and will keep you wherever you go" (Gen. 28:15). But that isn't all. God spoke to me from His Word when I was a young woman, desperately needing to know that He would not leave me after my first husband had: "...Be strong and of good courage; do not be afraid, nor be dismayed, *for the Lord your God is with you* wherever you go" (Josh. 1:9). Needless to say, this has become my life verse.

To me, the most incredible reference of all is the New Testament version of the name *Immanuel:* "Behold, the virgin shall be with child, and bear a Son, and they shall call His name Immanuel, which is translated, *'God with us'*" (Matt. 1:23). Imagine, the incarnate God would live on earth *with* us as tangible proof of His reality and would die on the cross *for* us as proof of His unconditional love. Then He would arise from the dead and send us His Holy Spirit to accompany and empower us on the journey of life.[2] Praise God from whom all blessings flow!

In his confinement, Joseph had a lot of quiet time to meditate on his limited knowledge of God and to practice His Presence. Joseph had solitude, and he used it well. *Solitude* can be a lovely word. It can suggest the image of still waters and green pastures, a picture of peace in the midst of frantic activity. In Joseph's solitude, he sought the Lord and found that He was already there.

Look for the Good

Being of the choleric temperament, I did not waste much time crying over spilt milk after my first husband left us. I set about to assess the situation, look for solutions, and come up with a strategy for making the best of a bad situation. Joseph obviously did the same thing, because in no time his leadership abilities were recognized by the prison guard, and he was "promoted" to overseer of all the other prisoners.

What you don't want to do when you are in some kind of prison is to become ingrown and self-absorbed. You'll be eaten up with self-pity. So no pity parties; no woe-is-me's; no more questioning God and shaking your fist in His face. He doesn't cause negative circumstances, but He has something good for you in them if you'll only open your eyes and behold it. After looking *up* to receive wisdom from above, you need to look *around* and see who else is in there with you. It's time to get busy and minister to those in the same boat—even before you've reached the other shore!

The only thing Joseph had to do in prison was to use the gift God had given him, his gift of interpreting dreams. And before long, although we are not told how long, the opportunity came. One of the dreamers was a fellow inmate, the butler, Pharaoh's cupbearer.

The Butler's Dream

The butler of ancient times ("cupbearer" in some versions)[3] was the Oriental potentate's right-hand man. In fact, he was such a trusted servant that the king literally placed his life in his butler's hands at each meal, expecting him to sip from the royal cup to test the wine for its excellence and to rule out assassination by poisoning.

For some reason the Bible does not consider important enough to mention, the butler in Joseph's story had offended Pharaoh and was thrown into jail—the same prison where Joseph was serving time for a crime he had not committed. It was here that Joseph and the butler had an encounter that would change history.

You never know when you get up in the morning at what moment God may intersect your life with a divine appointment. It pays to be ready, as Joseph was. He was gifted, he was in the right place at the right time, and he was more than willing to be used by God.

Even though Joseph's circumstances made him appear to be an unlikely vessel, the original vision for his life was still in effect. God does not withdraw the dream. Joseph's leadership style—authority with humility—was evident to all. Even the prison guard recognized it, along with Joseph's fellow inmates, and they began seeking him out when they had questions for which there were no answers.

The butler's dream was brief, but significant: A vine and three budding branches that ripened into grapes, which the butler squeezed into Pharaoh's cup. When Joseph was asked to explain what this dream meant, his reply was good news for the butler, but it also revealed Joseph's utter reliance on the Lord. He began by declaring: "Do not interpretations belong to God?" (Gen. 40:8-13), and went on to tell the butler that he'd be restored to his position in the royal household in three days. Joseph could have taken credit for the answer, thus exalting himself in the eyes of the prisoners. But he chose to give all glory to the Dream-Maker.

Like the apostle Paul, Joseph prospered in prison. So did Chuck Colson, former President Richard Nixon's hatchet man and founder of Prison Fellowship Ministries. "People think the White House is where the power is," he writes. "It's not. I saw in prison, where people were powerless, that the only power that really mattered was the kind that changes a human heart. And that can only happen through Jesus Christ, the Son of the living God.

"The other important lesson I learned was that all I had invested in striving to get to the top, to achieve success, power, money, fame—I found it meaningless. In prison, with all those things gone, I found that the only identity, security, and meaning a person ever has is when he or she is at peace with God and knows Him personally.

"I identify with Alexander Solzhenitsyn, one of my heroes, who spent years in a Soviet gulag. From the gulag he wrote…'Bless you, prison. Bless you for being in my life. For there, lying on the rotting prison straw, I came to realize that the object of life is not prosperity as we are made to believe, but the maturing of the soul.'"[4]

Joseph, too, learned what real life is all about while in prison. The false accusation that banished him to a jail cell during some of the best years of his life—his prime time—could have made him bitter. Instead, it made him better. Among all those inmates, he stood out. He gained the respect and the trust of the prison official, who placed him in charge of the other prisoners.[5]

Joseph was not only a leader, he was a prophet. The sign of a godly prophet is that the prophecy comes true. When you have this gift,[6] you are able to see clearly what the answers are. But it is best to remember that the answers come from God, the Revealer of secret things. Those who come claiming to be prophets must be tested against the Word of God. Just as there is a Holy Spirit, there is also an unholy spirit who masks and imitates but can never love or accomplish. Only God can do that.

When the butler was released from prison three days later and reinstated in the palace as Joseph had prophesied, Joseph's credibility as a true prophet was established, and the chief butler reclaimed his dream. Everyone was impressed, especially the chief baker who also had dreamed a dream and needed an interpretation from someone he could trust.

The Baker's Dream

The baker's dream was another story. This time there was no good report, no restoration to anticipate. He dreamed of three baskets carried on his head. From the third basket, filled with all kinds of baked delicacies, the birds ate their fill. Joseph's interpretation was this: In three days the chief baker would be hanged from a tree, and the birds would pluck off his flesh. How awful! But God had a plan in revealing this and the earlier intepretation to Joseph.

One would think that Joseph might have been reluctant to share such a grim prophecy, but there is no indication in the Word that he shrank back from his obligation. A true prophet of God tells the truth as God reveals it to him, and Joseph was a man of rare integrity and truthfulness.

What was the difference in these two dreamers? Both were trusted employees, with direct access to the food and drink served at the king's table each day. Yet one was condemned to death and the other set free. There must have been some character flaw, some significant discrepancy in the baker that caught the king's eye. Perhaps this servant did not guard well those things that were entrusted to him. Whatever the reason for Pharaoh's judgment, Joseph simply told, with accuracy and courage, what God had revealed to him.

At this point in Joseph's life, he had won the trust of everyone within his sphere of influence. John Maxwell calls this "The Law of Solid Ground": Each setback is followed by a comeback.[7] Let's leap ahead in Joseph's story and get the big picture:

Setback:
1. Joseph sold into Egyptian slavery.
2. Framed as an adulterer.
3. Forgotten in prison.
4. Endured seven years of famine.
5. Faced the return of his brothers.

Comeback:
1. Developed competence and organization.
2. Used his ability to discern dreams.
3. Interpreted Pharaoh's dream.
4. Saved Egypt and Pharaoh's wealth.
5. Showed patience and integrity.

At this stage in Joseph's journey, however, he was still in prison, with the greatest test yet to come. He couldn't see the triumphant end from the beginning. He didn't have divine perspective. Meanwhile, there would be more delays, more hurdles before Joseph could begin to reclaim his dream.

Ladder of Favor

When Joseph's father, Jacob, dreamed of a ladder whose top was propped against the gate of heaven, he recognized that he was standing on holy ground and, appropriately, built an altar as a memorial. Joseph, too, knew the sanctity of the sacred and feared (or reverenced) God from an early age. Because of this, he began climbing another kind of ladder—the ladder of favor.

The Favor of the Father—As we say in the South, Joseph was born with a silver spoon in his mouth. According to God's covenant with his great-grandfather Abraham, which was restated to his father Jacob, this family would "spread abroad to the west and the east, to the north and the south; and in you and in your seed all the families of the earth shall be blessed" (Gen. 28:14). Joseph was a rich kid, even though he didn't know it at the time!

Besides this lavish inheritance, we know that Joseph was his father's favorite son. Jacob made no bones about it. He was crazy about the boy, a fact that drove the other sons to distraction and gave Joseph no end of trouble, as we have observed.

There is no doubt that we are the products of our environment. How we are regarded at home often sets us up for success or failure later in life; although when we are born again, God, our heavenly Father, has the final say. I was blessed with a father who adored me. What this means is that I was always welcome in his presence, never a bother or a nuisance. I'd crawl up in his lap, knowing that place was reserved for me, and be privy to much confidential information—counsel he passed on to clients or advice he offered his employees on the farm. He withheld nothing from me. Even when I was in sin or making some unwise decision (I was not a perfect angel), he was *for* me. He believed in me, and he taught me by example how to live and how to die.

The greatest blessing I ever received from my father was on the day he died. Hovering near his bedside, I leaned near to catch his words, whispered through the tubing that snaked around his head to provide him with oxygen.

"You have been a blessing to me your entire life," he managed, then waved away my offer to pray for his healing. "No, honey, don't do that. I'm going home." I knew what he meant. Home was not Orangeburg or even "Willbrook." Home was where God is.

I am aware, even as I write these words, that Joseph and I are privileged characters. Unfortunately, our fathers are a rare breed. So many people can't relate to that kind of relationship with their father. There are horrible atrocities that go on in homes. I know that. If that has happened to you, let me remind you of a Father who does love you unconditionally, who will be there for you whenever you need Him, a Father who will never betray your trust or hurt you in any way, a Father who can help guide your steps through the wilderness and bring you out safely on the other side. My new son-in-law, Nelson McDonald, is a perfect example of how God loves and cares for His children.

Nelson is a love! I believe I was almost as thrilled about his marriage to my daughter Margo as he was! He tells of a moving moment in his life when the Lord spoke clearly to him—as a Father. Nelson had been rereading that wonderful passage from 1 Kings 19, after the prophet Elijah had taken on the prophets of Baal on Mt. Carmel and won. Despite that victory, though, the old prophet was fearful of Queen Jezebel's wrath and ran until he was completely exhausted. The Lord sent an angel to prepare lunch and to instruct him to move on to Mt. Horeb. There he hid in a cave. A great wind blew across the mountain, so savage that it broke off chunks of rock, but the Lord was not in the wind. Then an earthquake rumbled through, but the Lord was not there either. Finally, fire, but the Lord was not in the fire. He came, instead, in a still, small voice.

Elijah wrapped his mantle—symbolic of his calling, his purpose—over his face and crept out into the mouth of the cave. The still, small voice proceeded to tell him what he was to do with the rest of his life and ministry. Nelson says that recently, the Lord did that for him. He said to Nelson, "I am going to so make you My son that when all else fails, when everything changes—through the wind, earthquake, or fire—you won't even ask Me what I'm doing. You will just trust Me!" This is the favor of the Father.

Joseph and I were blessed with the favor of our earthly fathers. Nelson is coming into another dimension of favor, just as Joseph did.

The Favor of Potiphar

Having been sold to the captain of Pharaoh's guard, Joseph's innate trustworthiness and integrity soon won him favor in the workplace. As you already know, the keys to the household were turned over to him. He had the run of the place. Potiphar so trusted Joseph that he didn't concern himself with anything that went on at home but pursued his business in Pharaoh's palace.

My son-in-law Nelson, who came to know the Lord as a child, reminds me of Joseph. In business, he has the Midas touch. Straight out of college with a degree in accounting, he soared quickly to the top of his field and was looking for new worlds to conquer.

"It's the Lord," Nelson is quick to confess.

"After my accounting days, the Lord opened up a door for me as head of sales and marketing for the large concern where I had been head controller. The sales reps knew I didn't have any experience in marketing, but when the Lord opens the door, no man can close it. After calling a staff meeting, I decided to put all my cards on the table right up front.

"'I know what you're thinking,' I told them. 'You're thinking this guy doesn't have any experience, and he's going to tell us how to run our lives. Right on the first count; wrong on the second. I don't have any experience in sales, but I do know how to get the job done. Here's the plan: I'll go to bat for you with management. I'll be your advocate and take care of the stuff that keeps you from doing what you do best. I will not tell you how to do your job.' Long story short: We went from 25 million in sales to 55 million—in the middle of a recession! When God provides the favor, He also provides the plan!"

Nelson continued, "In 1995, I was sitting at the top of the heap. I was number-one guy at the number-one golf community in the Southeast, making big bucks. But something was missing. On vacation in Hawaii in 1995, I was watching a sailboat sailing out to a distant island and found myself praying a life-changing prayer: 'Lord, I want to do something that has significance and meaning. But I don't have a clue as to how to get from here to there. You do it; I can't imagine how.' I came home from that vacation to the news that I was being replaced in the job. Instead of feeling like the sky had fallen, I was overjoyed! Because of the nice severance package they gave me, I would have the rest of the year to find out how the Lord was going to take me to the next level.

"I didn't have to wait that long. I was sitting at home—no résumés out, no frantic phone calls to former bosses, no networking of old friends—when I got the call to become a consultant. I would never have thought of that. But it was a huge lesson in trusting God. When you get your heart in the right place and stay open before Him, He'll extend favor and do it in ways you could never ask or imagine!"

Joseph's heart was right, so he was ready for the next step when it came. But who would ever have thought that the future prime minister of Egypt was on his way to prison?

The Favor of the Prison Guard

I love the covertness of God. Jesus, born in a stable; Jesus, riding on a donkey; Jesus, the Son of the God of all creation, dying on a cross. We have to have new eyes (spiritual eyes) to see the hidden things of God, His secret agenda. So when Potiphar's wife accused Joseph of rape and he was sentenced to jail, what appeared to be the worst possible scenario was just another example of God's covert operation.

We certainly don't think of prison as a place of favor. But it wasn't any time before Joseph was once more practically handed the keys and given authority over all the prisoners. Call it a choleric temperament. Call it natural leadership. Call it anything you want, but what it was, was the favor of God.

There was always something different about Joseph that others noticed and respected. He didn't have that prison attitude. He didn't whine or complain. He didn't have a chip on his shoulder. What he had was trust in God and belief in the dream. Whatever happened, it would turn out all right. While he was hidden away in prison, Joseph was becoming all that God had dreamed for him to be. God can use a man even while he is in prison—and doesn't that make the jailhouse rock!

Joseph's attitude in prison reminds me of a story my friend David Harbuck told me. He has founded a mission called In His Steps, ministering to prisoners and their families. From his years of ministry, David has learned to distinguish "jailhouse religion" from the real thing. Some inmates, hoping to curry favor from those who come there to be a blessing, say all the right words, but their hearts are not in it. Others refuse to be resentful of the authority that sent them up, but are grateful for this time to learn about true freedom in Christ. Johnny is one of the latter.

A "lifer" in prison for murder, Johnny stands out from all the rest. Johnny's mother had spent everything she had trying to buy him a reprieve. After exhausting every human avenue, they turned to the only One who could help them. Jesus set Johnny free inwardly, and now he testifies, "I may still be in prison, but I'm out on the inside!" Now Johnny is learning and growing in Christ and has been granted favor with the prison authorities as a trustee. David says, "You will never see Johnny without a big grin on his face!"

You'll have to forgive me, but there's one more thing I must share with you about my son-in-law Nelson that is along these lines. I know I may appear to be a typical proud mother-in-law. After all, I think that he's the answer to every mother's dream for her daughter. But right now, he is just like Joseph; the world would say he's been "in prison" since recently he, along with many other Americans, lost a lot of money. The significant thing about that is not the loss, but the spirit in which he is accepting it. Is he worried? Absolutely not! As Nelson says, "We are only imprisoned by our mindset. Nothing is impossible with God."

Even with the latest downturn in the economy, Nelson recently gave away three cars—one to his mother. It was something the Lord prompted him to do around Mother's Day. Nelson himself didn't understand why. It wasn't that his parents couldn't have afforded new cars. They are affluent people and have invested wisely. It's just that he heard God's "still, small voice" in his heart, and so he obeyed without further question.

He tells how he called his mother one day to take her out for a ride, with the idea of surprising her by pulling into the car dealership. He wasn't sure she would go. She had not been getting out much recently. She surprised him by accepting. And when she saw the Land Rover "Discovery" in the lot, and Nelson handed her the keys, she wept.

"I think this means the Lord's not through with me yet. I must have places to go." Only then did Nelson understand God's secret. His mother, too, has a hidden destiny!

Who can tell what layers of purpose and worth are written in invisible ink in the pages of Joseph's story (or Nelson's, or yours)? What goes on while we are in prison—whether it is financial reversal, illness, or any other setback—is often the catalyst for some of life's most meaningful moments. And the best is yet to come.

A Prayer for Favor: Father God, God of the lonely, the lost, and the imprisoned, thank You for Your gifts of mercy and forgiveness and for Your Son, Jesus Christ, who sets every prisoner free. Thank You that He is entrusted with the keys to heaven and is the door through which all must enter to come into Your Presence. Thank You for being the God of hidden destiny and for having invited us to abide with You so that You can tell us Your secrets. Thank You for releasing Your anointing on those of us who deserve it least. Thank You for Your favor that takes us into unlikely settings and allows us to become Your ambassadors. And thank You for the example of Joseph, who never gave up but rested in Your favor and trusted in You for the dream You had birthed in his heart to become a reality. In Jesus' name, amen.

"But remember me when it is well with you,
and please show kindness to me; make mention of
me to Pharaoh, and get me out of this house."
Yet the chief butler did not remember
Joseph, but forgot him.

GENESIS 40:14,23

CHAPTER 10

When the Dream Dies

*"...forgetting those things which are behind and
reaching forward to those things which are ahead,
I press toward the goal for the prize of the
upward call of God in Christ Jesus."*

PHILIPPIANS 3:13,14

Forgotten! Is any word in the English language more heart-wrenching than this one, more poignant, more piercing? Even after Joseph's faithful service in prison, even after his exemplary conduct, even after he had blessed his fellow inmates by interpreting their dreams, with only one small request—that he be remembered when they gained their freedom—he was forgotten!

How discouraged Joseph must have been when the chief butler returned to his duties in the palace, daily working in the king's presence, yet never whispering a word in his ear about Joseph's plight. How hopeless he must have felt when two more long years passed with no sign that God had heard his cry. How forsaken (or so it seemed)—even by the One he had always trusted.

If anyone ever had a right to feel sorry for himself, it is Joseph—and maybe my son-in-law, who has also seemingly been imprisoned in a season of stretching. Like Joseph, Nelson has been stripped of many of his material possessions, his position in the business community, and some of his former relationships—but never his faith in God! In fact, with every loss in the natural, he is growing exponentially in the supernatural.

Could this be part of the divine holding pattern, that with so much more to learn, God needs our undivided attention, no distractions? Could it be that the best classroom for some lessons is a pit or a prison cell, that sometimes it's a good thing to be left behind?

Coping When You Can't!

When a person feels forgotten, the dream dies. That's when doubt can enter in and cause you to wonder if you ever really heard from the Lord in the first place. At this point it would be easy to give up, to forget all about trying, to quit.

That must have been a temptation for Joseph. After he had interpreted the chief butler's dream, the interpretation proved accurate soon afterward, and the butler was set free. All he had asked of the man in return was this: "Please remember me when things have settled down...and put in a good word for me with Pharaoh." But the butler forgot and Joseph remained in prison.

Sometimes, just when you think things could not get any worse, sure enough they do! My dear friend Karen Hayter tells of a single year in her life when she suffered one devastating setback after another, each with its own mind-boggling story:

1. *Divorced by her husband of thirty years!* At 55, Karen's husband, a pastor, told her he had never loved her, should not have married her, and wanted a divorce.

2. *Shunned by the church!* Instead of receiving comfort and consolation from her friends in the church, they sided with her husband, and she was rejected. One minute she was the pastor's wife and the next, a visitor in another church! The chasm was vast—she was stunned by the depth and breadth of it.

3. *Near death of her mother on not one but several occasions!* As an only child, Karen is close to her mother, often a girl's best friend when walking through any kind of ordeal. But just when she needed most to confide in someone she could trust, her mother became gravely ill and almost died—several times!

4. *Death of two beloved pets!* Not even the animals in her life survived to provide companionship.

5. *A major move!* With the death of her marriage, Karen was forced to sell her home and move in with her mother.

6. *Loss of job!* The position that had brought much meaning to Karen's life experienced deep budget cuts, and she was offered early retirement.

May I say that this is not just any woman simultaneously experiencing several of life's most serious setbacks, which on the stress Richter scale, would be out the top! This is a woman of God who has been consistently faithful. As a licensed professional counselor, Karen was in private practice in Fort Worth, Texas, before being invited to become the producer and host of a television show called COPE, which she describes as "a kinder, gentler Dr. Laura" type of program. Before this job was deleted, Karen was responsible for the production of 5,000 live shows, with approximately 50,000 callers and their 50,000 problems discussed on-air.

"During my own series of crises, I would counsel for seven minutes of live programming," she says, "then cry for the two-and-a-half-minute commercial break, praying the whole time that I would not be bitter and that I would not be angry. Counsel for seven minutes, cry for two and a half. When we'd go back on the air, I would often not have a clue as to how to respond to the next caller. In those times I leaned hard on the Holy Spirit and shared what He was directing me to say. Sometimes the caller would reply, 'I can't believe you said that! How did you know that? I've never told anybody!' I can only tell you that this ministry saved my life. If I had not been able to give to others during my season of greatest need, I could not have made it."

What Karen is saying is that even during the pit and the prison times, we are to continue being servants. We can always find someone else whose suffering is worse than ours—and serve them. That's what Joseph was doing all those years in prison. He was using his unique gift—interpretation of dreams—to bless those around him. But he was also anticipating his release, and when he was not freed as soon as he had hoped, time must have hung heavy on his hands, and his heart must have been broken again.

Karen tells of one guest on COPE who demonstrated the art of pottery making. The potter threw some clay on the wheel, skillfully turning and shaping, but keeping her eye on the "heart" of the clay. I was surprised to learn that clay has a heart!

"Yes," she said, "and the potter has to be very careful with that heart. It's the most vulnerable spot. When the potter takes the piece off the wheel, it has to be set up to dry, or it's useless. This time of drying is essential to the finished product. I think that's what was happening with me during my setbacks and what might have been happening in Joseph's life—it was the drying time.

"He had to be wondering the same thing many of us are wondering: *Why me, Lord? I'm a good person,* or *I've been falsely accused,* or *Why is this happening to me?* I think it's all right to be honest with God. It's not irreverent to be real. He knows what you're thinking anyway.

"One of my favorite stories is an incident in which St. Teresa of Avila was riding in a donkey cart when it hit a huge rut and bounced her out. She landed on the hard ground and immediately asked the Lord why He had allowed such a thing to happen to her. 'This is how I treat all my saints,' He explained, whereupon she replied, 'Then no wonder You have so few of them!'"

Karen goes on to explain that while we're being honest with God, He will quickly remind us of His sovereignty. We may be "good people," but we are good only by Jesus' stripes. If we hope to share in His glory, we must expect to share in His suffering. In fact, instead of asking "Why me?" we should be asking, "Why *not* me?"

Broken Vessels

Actually, Karen and I, along with many other people, are broken. But we're in good company. "For...time would fail me to tell of Gideon and Barak and Samson and Jephthah, also of David and Samuel and the prophets: who through faith subdued kingdoms, worked righteousness, obtained promises, stopped the mouths of lions, quenched the violence of fire, escaped the edge of the sword, *out of weakness were made strong,* became valiant in battle....were tortured, not accepting deliverance, that they might obtain a better resurrection...had trial of mockings and scourgings, yes, and of chains and imprisonment....were stoned...sawn in two...tempted...slain with the sword—of whom the world was not worthy" (Heb. 11:32-38). In all our broken places, we can actually emerge from the ordeal stronger and ready to be more useful in His service.

Most of what I have in my house—furnishings and accessories—has been put back together. Therefore, it doesn't bother me at all when a grandchild breaks something. I'm much more concerned about a little heart that is less easily mended than some object made by man. I, too, am a broken vessel that has been put back together better than before.

I deal with a vendor in Atlanta who sells some of the finest porcelains in the city. In one area of this shop is a section where items have been so meticulously repaired and repainted that you can't tell they were ever broken. These are great bargains! I once delivered some of them to a client whose housekeeper was appalled at the idea. I could hear her muttering to my client, "Miss Patricia, that lady brought you some busted-up stuff!" But that "busted-up stuff" was as good as new. One would never notice the gluing or stitching or bracing on the back of a fine plate displayed on a mantel or bookshelf.

Most of us are scarred in some way. I happen to have two C-section scars left over from the birth of my two children. I have never disliked those scars because of what they represent—the gift of the lives of my precious daughters. And what about the scars Jesus bore for us? It took His nail-scarred hands to convince Thomas that Jesus was truly his Lord, risen from the dead.[1] Resurrection scars! What power triumphed over the grave!

I love this passage of Scripture. A framed version, written in beautiful calligraphy, was given to me by my friend Kay Arthur and is hanging on a prominent wall in my design studio office. I often read and digest these words because they are so true. His grace is sufficient for every need!

> …"My grace is sufficient for you, for My strength is made perfect in weakness." Therefore most gladly I will rather boast in my infirmities, that the power of Christ may rest upon me.
>
> 2 Corinthians 12:9

Although far from a popular theory, some believe that suffering is not merely the result of living in a fallen world. This theory holds that only very special people are "chosen" to experience great suffering, that, to tell the truth, it's a compliment from God to be entrusted with infirmities of various kinds.

I'm not sure what I feel about this theory, but I do know what the Word says: "The Spirit Himself bears witness with our spirit that we are children of

God, and if children, then heirs—heirs of God and joint heirs with Christ, if indeed we *suffer* with Him, that we may also *be glorified* together. For I consider that the *sufferings* of this present time are not worthy to be compared with the *glory* which shall be revealed in us" (Rom. 8:16-18). *Sufferings...glory.* There does seem to be a direct connection between these two opposite extremes. From suffering to glory—but how long is the in between?

God's Waiting Room

In suffering, there is usually some kind of waiting period. Generally, a person is confronted with some horrific circumstance—a terminal illness, a grim diagnosis, a sentence to some term of duty—with little or no idea of how long the ordeal will last. Almost anything is made more bearable if we know the length of time before the end comes. Every pregnant woman lives in expectation of the baby's delivery after nine months. Students expect to graduate high school after twelve years, or college in four. Soldiers join the Army, believing they are signing up for a certain period of time, except during wartime, and then the enlistment may be "for the duration."

In researching this book, I have pondered Joseph's situation in that prison. Day after day, he is waiting out the news that might come at any moment—that he has not been forgotten after all, but summoned by Pharaoh for release. But the call never comes. No doubt he is crying out in prayer to God, if silently, about his plight, possibly saying something similar to this: "How long, O Lord? Will You forget me forever? How long will You hide Your face from me? How long shall I take counsel in my soul, having sorrow in my heart daily? How long will my enemy be exalted over me?" (Ps. 13:1,2). The psalmist David wrote this plaintive cry hundreds of years later, but Joseph could have penned those very words.

Sometimes, for whatever His reasons, God puts us on hold. Perhaps the question then becomes, "How can we make the waiting time productive?"

I wish you could know a new friend of mine, Thelma Wells, a darling African-American woman crowned with silvery hair. Despite being abused and neglected as a child, often hiding in a dark closet, Thelma came to know the Lord as her personal Savior at the age of four. She has walked with Him ever since. I love talking with Thelma and dipping into her vast reservoir of wisdom.

For example, recently she spoke of a seven-year financial "drought" that took place in the mid-80's. "When we're striving to become more like Jesus, God will test us in the meantime—which can be a 'mean' time," she said with her irrepressible humor and a twinkle in her eye.

"My dream appeared to have died about 1986. I went from megabucks to nothing. During that period, the question kept coming up, *Is this really how the Lord wants me to live?* One day I was having a major pity party, driving up and down the streets of my town, looking for work. In front of me was a truck. The bumper sticker read: 'LIFE IS TOUGH, AND THEN YOU DIE.' For a minute I bought into that negative thought. *Why are You allowing me to suffer like this?* I whined to the Lord. *Why do I have to go without money?* Oh, my! God is so awesome!"

A beautiful smile lit her face. "I turned around and drove in the opposite direction. Ahead of me was a flashing sign at the Ford dealership. On that sign was a quote I'd heard Dr. Schuller speak many times—the Dr. Schuller from the Crystal Cathedral in California: 'TOUGH TIMES DON'T LAST, BUT TOUGH PEOPLE DO!' O, Lord! You're talkin' to *me!* O, Lord, I thank You that I'm not dying. I thank You that I've got You on my side!

"As I praised Him more and more every day, something began to happen. Oh, I didn't land a million-dollar job. No, my circumstances didn't change, but something in my spirit started to change. I began to be able to see some things He was doing. The Lord started sending blessings—a little blessing here, a little blessing there...."

Thelma's story offers a powerful lesson in how to make it through the "dry spells" of life.

Praise—the first step in waiting out a dry spell. "Enter into His gates with thanksgiving, and into His courts with praise. Be thankful to Him, and bless His name. For the Lord is good; His mercy is everlasting, and His truth endures to all generations" (Ps. 100:4,5). When Thelma's perspective changed, she developed a thankful heart. That's when her spiritual eyes opened to see the abundant blessings of God on every side.

"I have learned to praise God as much as pray to Him," she says. "It's important to pray. We're told to pray, but prayer is for us—God already knows what we need before we open our mouths. It's our praise He inhabits. When we praise Him, we please Him, and He responds in incredible ways.

According to the prophet Zephaniah, as I worship and sing to the Lord, He sings back to me! He loves me so much that as I dance, He dances with me! He rejoices over me! He spins like a top! (Zeph. 3:17.) What revelation!"

I'm sure Joseph was spending his days in praise to the only living God. In spite of his prolonged prison sentence and his disappointment when the butler let him down, Joseph must have been grateful for the Presence of God in his life, for the Lord was "with him." And I'm guessing that on many a long night, gazing out through the bars into the inky black Egyptian sky, he and God were singing a divine duet.

Prayer—conversations with God. I know exactly what Thelma is talking about when she says, "God already knows what we need before we open our mouths." In fact, I'd go so far as to say that in my heart, I know that any prayer I pray in agreement with God's will is answered the minute I pray it. It's on the way. For example, I've already told you that just as soon as I had prayed for a godly husband after my divorce, I knew it was a sealed deal. That's the way God does things. His signature was on the deed to my future husband's heart. I could get on with my life and not worry about how God was going to answer my prayer—or when.

Joseph knew the Lord and probably talked with Him more than with anyone on earth. In the first year of his servanthood to Potiphar, of course, Joseph didn't know the language, although later he was sure to have become fairly fluent, especially during his imprisonment as he interacted with the prison guard and the other prisoners. Still, in his off-hours, I feel sure that he was communicating with God in the language of prayer—a language that does not necessarily require words. The more time we spend with Him, the more intimate the relationship becomes.

Obedience—doing things God's way. Thelma and I have learned, and the Lord doesn't keep it a secret from anyone, that "To do what is right and just is more acceptable to the Lord than sacrifice" (Prov. 21:3 NIV).

She goes on to share more of the rules of God's waiting room—and it's all about obedience. "In due season, the Lord will bring another step. That's when He begins cleaning up your life, cutting away some things that don't belong—like my obsession with the Publishers' Clearing House. I used to fill that thing out every time it came, just sure I'd win. Then I heard the voice of the Lord (in my heart), 'You will not get yours like that.' I put it in the trash.

"I had a little problem with tithing, too. 'How do You expect me to give when I don't even have a job?' I complained. So to teach me a valuable lesson, not only did the Lord instruct me to tithe what I did have, He had me give several people $2.60 each. Now don't ask me why that particular amount. I only know God told me to, and I did it. I could tell He wasn't pleased with me, and I desperately wanted to please Him.

"And there was the matter of my wardrobe. Three times He had me clean out my closet and pile everything on the bed. 'You want me to do *what,* Sir? Give my things away? But I *love* my clothes!' That still, small, but unmistakable Voice came again. 'Oh, and You want me to do it *cheerfully?*' I mustered up my good graces and called some folks, who promptly came and carried away armloads of my worldly goods. In return, what did I have? Joy unspeakable!" I'd say that's a great exchange.

God's Precious Word—all the solutions to all the problems. Of course, Joseph didn't have the written Word of God to pore over and study in his lonely moments. There were no scrolls in Joseph's day. The children of Israel (his father) were only in the embryonic stage as a people. Their stories of faith were still fresh from God, imprinted in the memory, no doubt, but not on parchment.

But Joseph did have the living Word. I believe—and it's only conjecture—that the Holy Spirit hovered over Joseph in that prison. How else could he have survived this "second sentence"—a stretch of time that must have been worse than the first?

So many Scriptures flood my mind as I recall the various prisons of my life and how I was equipped to become more than a survivor. Each one of them is like a lifesaver that sustained me through the waiting time.

> Trust in the Lord with all your heart, and lean not on your own understanding;
> In all your ways acknowledge Him, and He shall direct your paths
>
> Proverbs 3:5,6

> Delight yourself also in the Lord, and He shall give you the desires of your heart.
> Rest in the Lord, and wait patiently for Him....
>
> Psalm 37:4,7

"The Spirit of the Lord God is upon me...

"...to give them beauty for ashes, the oil of joy for mourning, the garment of praise for the spirit of heaviness...."

Isaiah 61:1,3

Regardless of the prison I was in at the time, I knew that I knew that I knew that God was in control and that His way was the right way. If I would be patient, He would work out all things for my good and His glory. I chose to believe Him fully, and He has yet to fail me. Through prayer, praise, obedience, and resting in the strong Word of God, I have received the blessing of peace in the midst of every trial.

A Matter of Time

When you persevere as Joseph did, as so many of our wonderful friends have, God not only provides, He promotes. It is only a matter of time. Yet before the promotion, there is still plenty to learn. There are things to be done. There are places to go in the Spirit—even when all it appears we are doing is waiting on the Lord.

Several years after John and I married and before we were launched into full ministry, we were living in a house we built our first year together. Because we had lots of room, ours was one of the designated host homes for Bible study groups in our church. Our meetings were always well attended, some coming from as far as ninety miles away. But one particular Friday night stands out.

Over a covered dish supper, we met a guest of one of the regular attendants and learned that this young African was involved in the ministry of Reinhard Bonnke, a world-famous German evangelist. According to the young missionary, he had even witnessed resurrections from the dead in some of Bonnke's huge evangelistic campaigns. As a gifted storyteller, painting word pictures of the crusades and the country in his distinctive accent, this young man had me literally sitting on the edge of my seat. I could *see* Africa, could *smell* it, *taste* it! I was *there!* And when the group leader called us together for the study, I was actually disappointed. I could have literally listened all night to the amazing testimonies of God's miraculous power operating on the continent of Africa today.

After everyone left and with my two daughters—then teenagers—away for the night, John and I were alone in the house. Something in the atmosphere had shifted. Even the very air was charged with energy. We tidied up in tandem, putting dishes in the dishwasher, fluffing pillows, straightening magazines on the coffee table—stunned to silence by the things we had heard.

John stepped to the front door, still open to admit any cooling breeze on this late spring evening. Outside, the night was moonless and still. Not a leaf stirred in the branches of the trees, now lush with May foliage. With no near neighbors and no street lamps, the total blackness was intrusive, like an unwelcome guest. John closed the huge steel door, checked the double lock, and turned out the lights.

On the way upstairs to our bedroom, I finally spoke. "That was powerful tonight, wasn't it?" John murmured in agreement. We made short work of our nightly bedtime ritual, than sank into our four-poster bed and stretched out, still not yet ready for sleep.

In the hushed silence, I spoke again, unwilling to disturb this moment with much more than a whisper. "There is such a Presence of the Lord here, John…like I've never felt before. I think we've gone beyond the veil."

"I agree."

"Let's pray and worship the Lord," I suggested.

I was about to get out of bed and fall on my knees when I felt John's hand in the darkness, gripping mine, and he began to pray aloud. Suddenly, before he had uttered more than a few phrases, we were startled by a whirring sound, like a ceiling fan on high speed…but there was no fan in this room! I was compelled to open my eyes. What I saw next defies human description. Somehow, nestled in the folds of the canopy covering our bed, were thirty-six angels—I counted them!

I blinked and looked again. They were still there! Not wanting John to think that his wife had lost her mind, I asked him to tell me if he saw anything unusual. "Yes," he said, "it seems we have company." When he described exactly what I was seeing, I sighed, overwhelmed by the phenomenal manifestation above our heads.

As a designer, scouting the world for unusual finds for my clients, I have seen many marvelous sights—the finest paintings, the richest tapestries, rare and beautiful treasures—but *never* anything like this. Feeling somewhat like John the apostle in describing his vision of heaven in the book of Revelation, I can only make a feeble attempt to translate into human terms the glorious sight that appeared before our eyes that night.

Fluttering in perfect precision and rhythm, neither overlapping nor bumping into each other, were seventy-two wings...layer upon layer upon layer of thin, translucent, iridescent, pearlized material not of this world...shimmering...glimmering...brilliant white...a white so white it transcended light...transcended sound...a celestial symphony of angels! Then, just as suddenly as they had appeared, they flew out from under the canopy en masse and vanished with a whoosh, similar to what "the rushing mighty wind" of Pentecost must have sounded like when the Holy Spirit was poured out on the disciples in the Upper Room (Acts 2:2).

John and I lay there, hands still clasped, breathless with wonder. What had just transpired in our bedroom? We fumbled for words, ideas, some understanding of what had taken place.

It was years later before the Lord revealed more fully the kind of visitation we had been granted. In conversation with some good friends at dinner one evening, we heard of a supernatural episode (as was ours) experienced by our friend's father-in-law when he was called into the ministry. Later still, I found words in the Bible that confirmed that John and I, too, had been tapped for kingdom service. "For the eyes of the Lord run to and fro throughout the whole earth, to show Himself strong on behalf of those whose heart is loyal to Him..." (2 Chron. 16:9).

God doesn't always use signs like this to let people know they're called into ministry. He is not limited to a certain method or formula. There are many other ways, such as hearing His still, small voice and having a knowing in your heart or through a prophetic word spoken to you by another believer or by revelation knowledge God gives you of a Scripture. But for some reason He had chosen to use signs with my friend's father-in-law and with us.

God had certainly shown Himself strong to John and me in the angelic manifestation that night! It would be four more years before we would enter into the fullness of the ministry God had planned for us, but that night marked a turning point that neither of us would ever forget.

You Will Never Be Forgotten

There are some things God chooses to forget. "I, even I, am He who blots out your transgressions for My own sake; and I will not remember your sins" (Isa. 43:25). "...they all shall know Me, from the least of them to the greatest of them, says the Lord. For I will forgive their iniquity, and their sin I will remember no more" (Jer. 31:34). "I will be merciful to their unrighteousness, and their sins and their lawless deeds I will remember no more" (Heb. 8:12). God says that He will forget your sins, your iniquity, your unrighteousness, and your lawless deeds! What incredibly good news!

What He chooses to remember is equally encouraging.

- He remembers that you are dust. (Ps. 103:14.)
- He remembers your name. (Isa. 49:16 NLT; Rev. 21:27.)
- He remembers His covenant. (Ps. 105:8.)
- He remembers His mercy toward you forever. (Ps. 136:1.)

In other words, God has no intention of forgetting you, forsaking you, or leaving you behind.

As a believer, these kinds of precious promises may have comforted Pfc. Jessica Lynch during her term of duty in the war with Iraq that began in March, 2003, including nine days she spent as an injured POW—days which probably seemed unending, days when she surely wondered if she would ever get out alive. But our military performed a successful daring rescue, intent on not leaving her behind in the hands of the enemy.

How important you are, dear one! God sees your need. He knows your pain—the torture and torment you are experiencing at the hands of the enemy of your soul—and His heart is "cut." Wherever your prison, whatever your pain, there is absolutely no limit to the lengths to which God will go to reclaim your soul—or your dream.

A Prayer for Steadfastness: Heavenly Father, thank You for catching our dreams and holding them close to Your heart while we wait on You. Teach us Your timing. Show us how to be thankful for the pauses by allowing us to see that these can be times of great personal growth. Thank You for stretching us when we thought we could not be stretched any further. Thank You for granting us more faith when we were barely able to believe at all. Thank You for holding our dreams in Your hands when the dream almost died and breathing on us once again the breath of life. Thank You for sending those who could aid in our rescue and deliverance and for sending the One who not only risked His life, but willingly gave it to take us Home. In the name that is above all other names, the holy name of Jesus, amen.

PART III

Recovering the Dream

*"But don't be angry with yourselves that
you did this to me, for God did it!...
"Yes, it was God who sent me here, not you!
And He has made me a counselor to Pharaoh,
and...ruler of all the land of Egypt."*

GENESIS 45:5,8 TLB

Then it came to pass, at the end of

two full years, that Pharaoh....

...sent and called Joseph...out of the dungeon....

And...said to Joseph, "I have dreamed a dream,

and there is no one who can interpret it.

But I have heard it said of you that you

can understand a dream, to interpret it."

GENESIS 41:1,14,15

CHAPTER 11

Counselor to the King

"A man's gift makes room for him, and brings him before great men."

PROVERBS 18:16

"Two full years"—that interminable period when Joseph waited to be remembered by the chief butler—must have felt like an eternity. But Joseph was not forgotten, after all. In the fullness of time, when God deemed that the wait was over, Pharaoh had a dream. This dream required more than all the Egyptian mystics and magicians could fathom. Inspired by the only true and living God, this dream required God's man, a man who at the time was confined to prison. What an unlikely vessel. What a strange and surprising outcome. What an unusual pulpit—Pharaoh's palace!

If you have traveled to Egypt or visited a museum displaying Egyptian artifacts, you have some idea of the splendor of this ancient civilization. Nothing in Joseph's experience could have possibly prepared him for the magnificence of the palace to which he would be escorted when the pharaoh, reigning and absolute monarch of all Egypt, would summon him to interpret the dream.

Since I have never visited Egypt, let me paint the picture for you from material gathered from an old interior design textbook.[1] Inside the massive stone structure with its spacious throne room was row upon row of columns, brilliantly decorated with color, their capitals carved to look like lotus blossoms. The walls were covered with elaborate murals—figures of humans or animals, patterns, and hieroglyphics—arranged to chronicle a story or to record a progression of historical events. Tile friezes—floral bands of lotus and fruit clusters—also embellished the walls. Furnishings were of fine woods inlaid with ebony and ivory and often enhanced by symbolic gold ornaments—lion, swan, and duck heads. Instead of the dirt floors of Joseph's tent at home, he would walk on colorful glazed tile and sit on soft cushions. Such luxury was unknown by the nomads of Canaan who lived a simple lifestyle, and surely Joseph's eyes would be wide with wonder when he beheld the beauty and pageantry of Pharaoh's court.

All this—and much more—was awaiting Joseph the instant he left the prison.

"All this—and much more"—awaits you, dear one, when your long "prison sentence" ends, and you are free at last!

Hold Fast the Dream

A successful businesswoman in the Atlanta area tells of a dream she had 25 years ago that has directed the course of her life ever since. Left with two small sons and a huge debt, Jackie was plowing her way through a bitter divorce when she cried out to the Lord, "If You don't do something, I'm going to die!" That night God sent her a dream.

"In the dream, I had stepped out onto a lovely balcony," she begins, "when I was supernaturally prevented from turning around to look at the double French doors through which I had come. I got the distinct impression that I was never to look back again. As I kept my gaze directed forward and relaxed into that pose, I became aware of water coming up to the floor, with not a drop spilling over onto the balcony.

"Suddenly, with every sense heightened to a degree I had never before experienced, I looked out over the water. Only about eighteen inches deep, it sparkled clear and pure as the finest crystal. What first appeared to be rocks embedded in the stream were dazzling jewels—diamonds, pearls, rubies, amethysts. Arched in a leafy canopy overhead were trees bearing every kind of fruit I had ever seen or imagined! In the trees birds were singing—heart-piercingly beautiful melodies no ear had heard. The soft breeze that sprang up to caress my cheek was the perfect temperature—neither too hot nor too cold—and carried a distinct but delicate fragrance unlike anything I had ever smelled.

"When I awoke the next morning, I was refreshed and energized—no more thought of hopelessness or despair. It took several weeks to receive the interpretation of the dream. What I had seen was the River of Life flowing from God's throne. Now, knowing what is ahead of me, I will never again fear what is between here and there!"

Joseph has been tested and tried time and time again. He is about to step through the prison doors onto a balcony overlooking his indescribable destiny. The long wait—with its pits and its prison time and its wilderness wanderings—is almost over.

Come Quickly!

After waiting forever, it seems, some truth comes to light, some prayers are answered, some needs are met in the twinkling of an eye. Like the Berlin Wall and Jackie's experience, some regimes are ended and some dreams are reclaimed almost overnight.

When Pharaoh's top advisors—his wise men and magicians—were unable to shed any light on his disturbing dreams, it was time to look elsewhere. And Pharaoh was too desperate to be choosy. He had heard of a prisoner with rare discernment and an understanding of dreams, so he sent for the incarcerated foreigner.

As soon as the prison guard got the word from the palace, Joseph was brought "quickly out of the dungeon" (Gen. 41:14). For Joseph, this was the day of deliverance. Yet, upon hearing that he had been summoned to the court to appear before Pharaoh, Joseph must have had at least a passing qualm. *What does the king want of me? I could easily lose my head over this, or at the very least, be hanged like the chief baker!*

There was little time for speculation, however. He must prepare for his audience with the king, so "he shaved, changed his clothing, and came to Pharaoh" (v. 14). What rich treasure is hidden in these few words. Joseph shaved—leaving behind his Semitic beard for the clean-shaven appearance of the Egyptian, symbolic of his coming promotion to ruler of the land. He changed his clothes—exchanging his prison garb for something more befitting a man who would soon be counseling a king. And he "came to Pharaoh." He answered the call ASAP!

You may be in some kind of prison right now—a miserable marriage, a dead-end job, a besetting sin—thinking there is no way out. But God will give you a way out, dear one. You must simply listen for His call and be sensitive to the moment of opportunity. You could waste a season or a lifetime by not responding quickly to the King when He summons you for service. Don't miss a moment He has for you!

Joseph hadn't missed it. In fact, he had been preparing for this very encounter all his life. And now his time of reflection, of wondering why, of pondering God's purpose, was almost over.

Purpose in Pain

Tracy, one of my Margo's best friends and a businesswoman with a double master's degree in counseling, tells of the "pit part" of her life that eventually brought her into the Presence of the King. "My parents divorced before I was a year old. After that was a succession of marriages for my mom, who was desperately trying to find happiness to ease her pain, but left me feeling abandoned and displaced. I was a disaster waiting to happen.

"In my teens I went Gothic—the white pale face, the black makeup, the dark clothing. I hung out with the drug crowd when homosexuality came out of the closet. I remember being so miserable in the early 90s, lying in bed and crying out to God or the devil, anyone who could help me. Everyone else had rejected me. As my most recent stepdad became more and more abusive, even threatening my life at one point, I called my birth father and told him, 'If you don't come get me, I'm going to kill myself!'

"He did come to the rescue and took me home to live with him and his wife. That living situation was a little better in that my dad was a Christian by this time, but my stepmom had a problem with me. I think it was because of some unresolved issues with my real mom. Still, despite the fact that this was another kind of pit in a way, I found the Lord as my personal Savior while I was there. What a huge turning point!

"Sometime, too, during all this confusion, I sought counseling. I remember feeling disappointed with the way things were handled and thinking, 'I believe God is calling me to be a counselor, but I want to be a *good* one.' Later, alone with Him, I heard Him say, 'Tracy, you're going to bring *Me* into the counseling room.' After that, I never doubted my calling, but because of my fractured past, the reaction of everyone around me was: 'Yeah, right!' Like Joseph, I was a pretty unlikely candidate."

Tracy is thirty years old—exactly Joseph's age when he was summoned before Pharaoh. The parallels with his life don't stop there. She, too, was in a holding pattern for a time. She attended a Christian college after high school, away from "Joseph's brothers," the critical people who had tried to steal her dream, still completely confident of the calling God had planted in her heart. There she developed leadership skills, becoming head of student government and president of her class, and working in church ministry.

One day, while lying on the lush green grass of the Asbury College campus, with her Bible open on her lap, Tracy distinctly heard the Lord speaking to her. "Tracy, you have been through much pain. All the tears you have sown, you will reap in joy." At the time, she didn't realize that she could have flipped a few more pages and found those very words in Psalm 126:5!

That confirmation held her steady through several setbacks planned by the enemy to discourage her—a serious illness in her senior year of college and a job as a nanny that seemingly had no end. Every day she was in this position, she was dreaming of being in graduate school.

In retrospect, Tracy can see the hand of God in all of it. Her illness caused her to rely totally on the Lord for her strength. And just as Joseph used his gift of the interpretation of dreams to help two fellow prisoners, so Tracy was able to help the family for which she was a nanny for their children. Before she finally left to enter grad school to pursue her calling as a counselor, she led all of them to faith in Christ and counseled their mom through the death of their grandmother. In fact, they considered her "an angel sent from heaven."

Like Joseph's "two full years," maybe Tracy's illness in college and her job as nanny for the three years immediately following was her final surrender, the ultimate test of her commitment to the call before her promotion. Today, Tracy is in full-time private practice with names of clients on a waiting list. Parents are bringing teenagers from out of state to her office, where she is able to connect with so many through the details of her painful past. She is featured on Moody radio as host, co-host, and frequent speaker on the program "Marriage and the Family Today." After struggling with an obvious inability to trust men for a while, she is happily married to a godly husband, and they joyfully serve the Lord together. She has moved from the pit through the prison to the palace! She is reaping joy from the tears she has sown. And there is more to come!

Being Obedient to the Call

When the King calls, will we recognize His voice above the clamor of so many conflicting voices in the world? And how do we walk out our calling to restore the dream? With great wisdom, Tracy points out the path:

- *Welcome opposition.* Ironically, when opposition comes, when there is a struggle to reach your destiny, this is usually a confirmation of the call. Every opposite spirit must be overcome by God's Spirit, and you must battle through.

All the opposition Tracy encountered only made her more confident that she was on the right track, and she was determined to stick it out, no matter what. God allows these tests to build character, to strengthen our resolve, and to prove—usually to ourselves—that we are serious about reclaiming His dream for our lives.

- *Proclaim the dream out loud.* Tell "safe" people, people you trust. But don't tell "Joseph's brothers"—the critical people in your life, the dream-stealers.

Speaking the truth not only seals it in your spirit, but actually releases it into the atmosphere. And what God has spoken to you will not return void. Developing a support system of intercessors and friends you love and trust is also foundational to pursuing or reclaiming your dream. We will discuss this at length in a later chapter.

- *Rejoice in closed doors.* Tracy was met with yet another delay after she moved to Atlanta to pursue graduate school. "Only one point away from the scores I needed for my GRE," she says, "I pouted and whined, kicked and screamed. I threw a tantrum because I knew God had called me here. But I wouldn't be where I am today if it had not been for that closed door. Another master's program opened up that allowed me to work in ministry, to meet my husband, and to work in a church. God is not a taker. When He closes a door, He is only setting you up for a greater blessing!"

If Joseph had any last-minute doubts about meeting Pharaoh, I believe that they would have been laid to rest by the same or similar words that Tracy heard from the Lord: "Joseph, all the tears you have sown, you will reap in joy." When God calls, you will know it. When God clears your name, no one can corrupt it. When you stand in His Presence, all of the pain will suddenly have purpose.

Joseph was about to find out for himself.

Pharaoh's Predicament

Pharaoh of Egypt—"...supreme commander of the armies, chief justice of the royal court, and high priest of all religions...."[2] Perceived to be a god, the pharaoh's power was absolute. Evidence of this "power" was an early-morning ritual in which he supposedly awoke the sun god Re by breaking the seal to his statue and saying a prayer, ostensibly causing the sun to rise and start the day for all the people.[3] Their world revolved around a single word from Pharaoh, a command, an action.

Yet this particular unnamed pharaoh of Joseph's day was not altogether typical of other more dictatorial tyrants the people had come to expect of their rulers. God had strategically positioned him in this particular historical era to set the stage for the coming of His Son in a future millennium—the ultimate Dream for mankind. While many Egyptian kings were savage and barbaric, here was a humble man, one who listened and learned, who sought the counsel of others, who admitted that someone else might have answers he did not have. John Maxwell, author, lecturer, and respected authority on management and leadership, writes, "This pharaoh showed remarkable wisdom and insight, as well as a heart receptive to truth...as a strong leader he acknowledged his sense of unease, but as a humble leader, he enlisted the advice of others."[4]

When Pharaoh dreamed some most unusual dreams, he turned first to his own well-trained wise men and magicians.[5] These men had been instructed in dream interpretation, using the ritual books of magic of that time. But they were not truly wise men; they didn't have a clue what the dreams meant. So heavily did these dreams weigh on Pharaoh that he could think of little else. He knew there was something extremely significant about them. Some calamity was looming on the horizon—but what?

Just as nothing in Joseph's background as a shepherd boy in the hills of Canaan had prepared him to behold such splendor in the court, nothing in Pharaoh's pagan background had given him the ability to discern the deep things of the Spirit. Uncharacteristically, the great monarch of the land was perplexed. So he must have been relieved and hopeful when he learned of Joseph's proven ability—somewhat curious, too, to hear what this foreign prisoner might make of these night visions that had left him so unsettled.

Joseph had no sooner appeared before Pharaoh than he laid out the troubling dreams. Pharaoh had seen seven lean cows eating seven fat ones and seven thin heads of grain devouring seven thin ones. What was even more disturbing was that these dreams occurred not once, but twice! What could they possibly mean?

Joseph's Gift

What does one give a pharaoh—the man who has everything: incredible wealth, the top position in the realm, worldwide renown? Joseph was poor, a prisoner for years in the king's own prison. He had absolutely nothing of this world's goods to offer. Just as it is appropriate to take a thoughtful gift to your hostess when you are invited to her home for dinner or as an overnight guest, it was customary in that society to bring something wonderful to present to the king. Later, the Queen of Sheba would astonish King Solomon with her fabulous gifts: camels bearing more spices than had ever been seen in Jerusalem, much gold, and precious stones. (1 Kings 10:2.) The wise men of the New Testament laid gold, frankincense, and myrrh at the feet of King Jesus to celebrate His birthday. (Matt. 2:11.) And now here is Joseph coming before the king of all Egypt with nothing in hand.

Fortunately, there was much in his heart, placed there long ago as a boy by God—the dream of greatness and a gift of interpretation of dreams. All those years in prison Joseph had stayed in close touch with the Dream-Maker.

By the time he reached the palace, I suspect he walked into that courtroom with no fear and a sense of great dignity based on faith. He knew the God who was "with him." That was all he needed to know. God had sent him on assignment as ambassador from the kingdom of heaven to the Egyptian pharaoh with a gift that no one but God Himself could give.

Joseph was the only man with the message for the hour. God trusted him to deliver it. His first words are eloquent in their humility: "...It is not in me; *God* will give Pharaoh an answer of peace [those things necessary for his *shalom,* a Hebrew word for peace and 'welfare']"[6] (Gen. 41:16). Can you believe it, dear one? When Joseph is asked to interpret the strange dreams, he does not suddenly feel proud and important. He doesn't use this time to plead his case and beg for clemency. He doesn't even remind the pharaoh that he has been sitting in prison all those years on false charges! Rather, he humbly diverts attention from himself to the Lord.

I have known very few truly humble people in my life. Those in places of prominence—whether secular or spiritual—are tempted to think of themselves more highly than they ought to. (Rom. 12:3.) One man of true humility who comes immediately to mind is Dr. Billy Graham, who, in person, is exactly the same as he appears in public—modest, gentle, genuinely interested in others, kind, and on assignment from God. It was once my pleasure to have breakfast with him and an "intimate" group of about forty others. When he walked into the room to join us, he was alone. No entourage of assistants or bodyguards accompanied him, although we sensed the presence of angelic escorts. Instinctively, all of us rose to greet him, clapping out of our great respect for his time-tested walk. But he put up both hands and shook his head, signaling by that, that he was on the Lord's business. This was not a Billy Graham moment.

Nor, in the court of Pharaoh, was this a "Joseph moment." Joseph was there to represent the King of kings, to do His business. And His business that day was to confront this pagan king with the power of His might and to pave the way for the preservation of His people. God had been refining this young man in prison, honing his gift and building his credibility as an interpreter of dreams. Now the gift had brought him before the king.

Joseph listened to Pharaoh tell about his dreams, and when he was finished, Joseph gave him God's interpretation. It was so simple, as God's dreams usually are: Seven years of plenty, followed by seven years of famine. But do you see that, dear one? Do you see that God warned Pharaoh before disaster befell them? How good and merciful, how loving and compassionate He is! He so often warns us before calamity strikes—to give us time to prepare!

Counseling the King

The prophetic dream demands a prophetic plan—one that covers both feast and famine. God used Joseph to deliver the blueprint that would save not only Egypt but future Israel and every other nation on earth from extinction when blight struck the land. It was a brilliant plan, but nothing conceived in the minds of brilliant men. This was a God-thing, orchestrated by the Creator Himself. He who creates also preserves.

In a way Joseph's response was a state of the union address before he was even sworn in to office. "...God has shown Pharaoh what He is about to do" (Gen. 41:28). Can't you just imagine that the king and all his courtiers were all ears, ready to hear whatever this man would say next?

Joseph went on to interpret the dream, and he spoke with the authority of God: There would be seven years of plenty, followed by seven years of famine. The dream was repeated for emphasis—like a splash of color in an otherwise monochromatic room or an exclamation point at the end of a sentence! God had "established" it (v. 32)—from the Hebrew word *kuwn,* meaning accomplished, confirmed, ordained, fixed.[7] In other words, it was a sure thing! God had also warned that it would come to pass "shortly"—from another Hebrew word *mahar,* meaning promptly, hurriedly, quickly, hastily, suddenly.[8] Or, in the Ann Platz translation, "You'd better get busy; there's no time to lose! Stop whatever you are doing, and get over there right now!"

Joseph wasn't through. He recommended the appointment of "a discerning and wise man" (v. 33) to oversee the collection and storage of grain during the years of plenty, to be distributed during the lean years. The plan was sound. But where was the man to carry out the plan? "...Can we find such a one as this," Pharaoh wanted to know, "a man in whom is the Spirit of God?" (v. 38).

How interesting that this pagan king should acknowledge that the new leader should be filled with the Spirit! All the idols of Egypt—including the sun god Re—could not accomplish the monumental task before them. It seemed obvious, even to Pharaoh, that the man for the job was standing right in front of his eyes. "...Inasmuch as God has shown you all this, there is no one as discerning and wise as you. You shall be over my house, and all my people shall be ruled according to your word; only in regard to the throne will I be greater than you" (vv. 39,40).

Instant promotion. "Humble yourselves in the sight of the Lord, and *He* will lift you up" (James 4:7). Joseph's humility and integrity were the keys to his promotion—a promotion not from Pharaoh, but from God.

Exalted by God

When God moves you into place to reclaim your dream, it can happen quickly. All the years of waiting will now seem like a dim, distant memory. As the plan unfolds, you will walk under His covering of protection and His mantle of authority. "Humble yourselves under the mighty hand of God, that He may exalt you in due time" (1 Peter 5:6). Being "exalted" by God often carries a manifestation in the natural world that brings glory to Himself and shouts of His provision to a watching world.

Joseph received at least five manifestations of God's grace and favor.

1. *The fulfillment of his dream of greatness*—second in command over all the land of Egypt; prime minister. When you are promoted, you will also be a *prime minister.* Your ministry will carry a huge responsibility. People will be looking to you for wisdom that comes only from God. This means you have to walk more closely with Him than ever, listen more carefully for His next instruction, and obey instantly and in every detail. This will not be merely a job with great perks. It will stretch you, challenge you, and complete the good work begun in you. But you will accomplish all things while resting in the Father's arms. You will do only what He says; He will do the rest.

2. *The signet ring*—the mark of highest authority. Pharaoh stripped off his own ring and put it on Joseph's finger. This ring, with a seal crafted into it, was used much like a signature on a document today.[9] It stamped the

person as authentic and his word as true. You will carry God's signature written on your heart as you work under His authority.

3. *The garments of fine linen*—proper apparel for a person on business with the King. Linen was a common fabric used in the Ancient Near East, but fine linen—"...cloth woven so finely that it cannot be distinguished from silk..."[10]—was reserved for priests and the aristocracy. As a believer and a person whose rank has been raised to a position of new authority, you will wear Christ's own robe of righteousness. He sees you as His beautiful bride, in a bridal gown without spot or blemish. This gown was not cheap, purchased on sale at Bargain Boutique, but at the cross at great expense—the precious blood of Jesus.

4. *The gold chain*—another symbol of authority. Although gold was relatively plentiful in Egypt, this chain was taken from the pharaoh's own neck and placed around Joseph's to mark his new position. In the same way, you may wear a gold cross that represents your position with Jesus, your Bridegroom, who delights in giving His bride lovely ornaments. (Ezek. 16:8-13; Rev. 21:2.) He is the King who has conquered death and has risen to guarantee your place with Him in heaven forever!

5. *A new name*—signifying an elite membership. Pharaoh changed Joseph's tribal name to an Egyptian name, *Zaphnath-Paaneah,* meaning "the God has said, He will live."[11] His new name promised life! Your new name—Christian (encompassing interpreter of dreams, healer, counselor, encourager)—promises not only eternal life, but a partnership with God in ministry. But remember, He guides you through His Spirit—the same Spirit that enabled Joseph to carry an entire nation through turbulent times and ensured the future of God's people.

From Feed Sacks to Fine Linen

If ever a person went from rags to riches overnight, it was Joseph. From the goat-hair tents of Canaan, and later an Egyptian prison, to the lavishly appointed palace of Pharaoh, the young Hebrew was suddenly lifted out of poverty and into plenty—just the opposite of the grim forecast prophesied for Egypt. God's hand was on his life. Joseph's gifts of leadership and interpretation of dreams were given for a purpose greater than his own prosperity. That is always the case. Spiritual gifts are bestowed by God for the benefit of others.

I would love for you to meet my good friend Anne. Next to Joseph's comeback story, hers is one of the most compelling I have ever heard. She is a woman who, by the grace of God, has risen above childhood adversity to prosper in every way "…just as [her] soul prospers" (3 John 2). I adore Anne! She is so real. I have tried hard to condense her testimony, but just read on. Every paragraph is a jewel, and you are sure to find yourself somewhere in this story.

"My earliest memory is trying to survive as the seventh of nine children growing up in a log cabin with no indoor plumbing, no running water, and no electricity. Life was difficult, and I just knew there had to be something out there better than this. Being curious and adventurous by nature, I suppose my 'dream' was to get out and explore the world.

"I wore out the Sears & Roebuck catalogue, dreaming of all the beautiful clothes I would have. Back then, Mother and Grandmother made our clothes out of colorful printed feed sacks. My first 'store-boughten' outfit was a pink pinafore with a frilly white blouse, purchased for me by my Aunt Patsy, who lived in the big city. The outfit came with a little straw hat with pink ribbons. Aunt Patsy had no children of her own and seemed to enjoy doing for us. She was a big influence in our lives, teaching us proper English and encouraging us to make something of ourselves.

"Living under those conditions, I suppose faith and hope almost came naturally. In addition to this teaching, Mother taught us to hold our heads high, keep a smile on our faces, and offer a word of encouragement to those around us. My father, who was a good man when he was sober, worked hard but gambled away his money. The day of my graduation, Mother was sick in bed, my father was drunk, and my aunt and uncle had to take me to the ceremony. Immediately afterward, I decided to leave the farm and go live with my older sister and her husband to make a new life for myself.

"While working in a bank in Nashville, I met my future husband. He was the all-American college boy—handsome, charming, and rich—and I fell for him hook, line, and sinker. With wealthy family connections and a mother who had been a Mardi Gras queen, it was high society all the way. Not knowing much about real love, this little country girl thought she'd hit the jackpot! My sister tried to warn me, but I did not have ears to hear. It was much later before I learned that his family was as dysfunctional as ours and that both parents were well on their way to becoming alcoholics.

"Shortly after the birth of our first child, my husband began running around, but we managed to have two more beautiful children and work together in his quest to become one of the youngest bank presidents in the country. During that time we sat on the front pew of the church, although ours was certainly not what you would call a Christian home—appearances only. You know what I mean.

"Many dream-stealers along the way tried to sabotage my dream. Along with my early environment and the people who said I would never amount to anything, the most devastating dream-stealers were my husband's infidelity and drinking problem. These were challenges I hadn't counted on, and I didn't know where to turn. I was working in the rose garden one day—a favorite diversion of mine—when I heard an inner voice say, *You have always wanted a Christian home. Let's start with you.* Wow! Although I didn't know Him well, I recognized the voice of God speaking to me!

"Thus began a search that led me to mutual friends who had found Jesus. I knew they had something I wanted, but I was defensive about my own understanding of the Lord. When they prayed for me, though, it was like nothing I had ever heard, and the dam broke. I poured out all my childhood hurts and unrealized dreams—the poverty, embarrassment, and shame—and I was taken back to those days on the farm. With tears flowing from the depths of my soul, all of the past left me, and the blinders came off my eyes. I could see things I had never seen before.

"When I started going to a Spirit-filled Bible class and digging into Scripture, my family, especially my husband, noticed the dramatic change. God began to give me insight into all things that concerned me. In seven days He restored 'the years the locusts had eaten,' stolen by my father. Later, when he suffered a massive stroke and was not expected to live, I spent hours singing to him about how much Jesus loved him and rubbing his bald head. He began to rally and came to accept the Lord. On the seventh day, the doctor came in, shaking his head. 'Mr. Morris, you are a miracle, and I'm sending you home today.' The next week he was back on the farm, working, and lived another seven years!

"Life was sweet. I even had hope that my husband would repent, be healed of his addictions, and become the man of my dreams. Like Joseph, I was soon to be tested. One day, when my husband came home, he asked me to go for a walk on the beach. So *this* would be the time he would beg my forgiveness, and a breakthrough would occur! But what he had to say caused as much pain as if he had slapped me in the face: 'I know you have the key to life,' he said, 'but I don't want it. I'm a Judas and I'm leaving you and the children. I purchased a condo on the beach and will be moving out next Wednesday morning. All I want is my desk.'

"The day the divorce was final, I fell to the floor weeping and screaming. Afterward, a peace settled over me, and I began to be honest with God. 'Lord,' I prayed, 'I don't want to be alone for the rest of my life. I've asked Your forgiveness for any wrong I've done. I'm asking You now to heal me and the children and give me someone to love us. You know I enjoy material things, but You can take this beautiful home and everything in it. All I want is to serve You.' With my wobbly knees and feeble hands, I rose to accept that which I could not change and found my daughter Linda entering the room with a small bouquet of flowers in her hand. 'Mama, God speaks to me, too. You are going to be a very happy woman.'

"I came alone with the Lord and grew in my intimacy with Him. It was as though He were physically walking beside me every step of the way. I resigned all the boards on which I served and got an unlisted phone number. I knew my source was in Him alone. He gave me seven things to do, and I did them. Out of one act of obedience—going to work in a small gift shop in an exclusive shopping area—I met the man I was to marry and his very ill wife. Later, after her death, we married.

"God gave me the dream of my youth and answered my prayer at the hour of my deepest grief. He gave me a precious man who had lost his wife and been good to her. Not only did I receive the material things I had once known and enjoyed, but a new son and daughter to love and guide. Our family, deeply hurt by the divorce, reconciled, and my husband and I walk hand in hand with

Jesus. I have been restored…to serve Him for the rest of my life. Only in Him will our dreams come to fruition. Only in Him are we complete."

Anne is living out her dream, a true picture of transformation and restoration. She has gone from poverty to plenty—both in the natural and in the supernatural. She wears the ring of God's authority, the robe of His righteousness, and the gold chain of His favor. All of this is available to you when you become born again; the moment you begin reclaiming your dream you can have a fresh awareness of all that is yours as a child of God.

Prayer for Humility: Father, we come before You—King of kings, Lord of lords, our Maker and Creator. We acknowledge the famine of our hearts and Your vast ability to supply our need—in abundance. We praise You today as You lead us to the palace of the King to present the gift that only You can give. Father, we thank You that You provide wisdom, knowledge, peace, and grace to Your people, that You provide counsel and give discernment. We thank You for the portrait of Joseph as counselor to the king, recognizing this humble, Christlike example of Your man for his time. Father, we are amazed that You have stripped us of our old prison garments, re-clothed us in Your righteousness, cleared our names, and given us a new one—"Redeemed." Thank You for the journey, sometimes so painful and dark, that has brought us to this place of honor. In the name of Your Son, our King, amen.

Now Joseph was governor over the land; and it was

he who sold [grain] to all the people of the land.

And Joseph's brothers came and bowed

down before him with their faces to the earth.

So Joseph recognized his brothers,

but they did not recognize him.

And he turned himself away from them and wept....

GENESIS 42:6,8,24

CHAPTER 12

Mending the Broken Dreamer

He heals the brokenhearted and binds up their wounds.

PSALM 147:3

A spouse from an impeccable family background, two beautiful children, a palatial "dream house" with fashionable Egyptian decor, seven years of plenty, great wealth, power, prestige, the respect of an entire nation, and most of all the favor of God—what more could a person possibly want in this life?

Even when the promotion comes and things begin to look up, there are always loose ends dangling from the past. Just because Joseph is now prime minister of Egypt, enjoying the perks of that position, does not mean that suddenly all of his dreams have come true. What about his family in Canaan, who are suffering from the predicted global famine; what about his jealous brothers; what about his beloved father, Jacob, and his younger brother, Benjamin? Oh, it's not over yet. God's dream for Joseph has only begun.

What about you, dear one? Have you been released from the pit and the prison, only to find another kind of bondage staring you in the face? You have climbed Jacob's ladder—godly steps to success—to encounter yet another kind of snare. You're learning that dream recovery comes in stages, and you aren't there yet.

Don't despair! This is not the time to throw in the towel or rest on your laurels. Now is the time for the real work to begin.

What It Takes To Break

Remember those ten bad brothers and their flawed characters, examined under a microscope in an earlier chapter—their murderous hearts, their immoral conduct, all the bitterness and jealousy and betrayal? Who would have thought that they would have ever humbled themselves enough to beg? But there is something about hunger and the need to provide for one's family, and there was the dream that God had dreamed for Joseph before the foundations of the world and planted in his heart. It was time for that prophetic dream to come to pass.

When the party of ten arrived in Egypt to buy grain for their aging father and the rest of the family back home, and were escorted into Joseph's presence, they didn't recognize him. This could not possibly be the bratty little brother who once boasted about his dreams of "making it big." Besides, the last place they would have expected to find him was in the Egyptian prime minister's office! As a matter of fact, they had forgotten all about him and considered him gone and out of the way.

Joseph, clean-shaven and dressed in fine linen and gold, was virtually in disguise. He was now a grown man, approaching forty, and people change with time. To further confuse his brothers, he was not speaking in Hebrew, but was using an interpreter. Joseph was not ready to reveal his identity. His brothers had to prove themselves first. But he didn't plan to make it easy for them—not because he had revenge in his heart, but because he was interested in discovering what was in theirs!

Chapters 42-45 of the book of Genesis give a fascinating account of the brothers' journey—not only from Canaan to Egypt, but from the kingdom of spiritual darkness to the kingdom of "unapproachable light." When you make this journey, you have to be "hungry" enough to:

- *Acknowledge your spiritual famine.* Joseph's brothers' original plan was to fulfill their basic need for survival by traveling to Egypt to buy grain from the vast storehouses there. They received so much more from the rich reservoirs of God's provision (*pro* meaning "for,"[1] and *provision* referring to support of the vision)! God wanted to bless the entire world through these ten men plus Joseph's two sons, Ephraim and Manassah. To do so, they must acknowledge how much they needed Him. For some, like Betty, whom you met earlier in this book, it takes a lifetime of running before we run into the arms of the only One who can fulfill the dream.

- *Admit it when you're wrong.* The first inkling Joseph had that his brothers had begun to change occurred when he demanded that they go home and bring back their youngest brother, Benjamin, to prove that they were who they said they were. In those days, before passport photos, drivers' licenses, and Social Security numbers, the evidence of one's identity was more difficult to come by.

Now, confronted with the thought of possibly breaking their father's heart if he lost yet another beloved son, they began to lament their sinful past (in Hebrew, not knowing that Joseph is overhearing every word they are saying!): "…We are truly guilty concerning our brother [meaning Joseph], for we saw the anguish of his soul when he pleaded with us, and we would not hear…Therefore behold, his blood is now required of us" (Gen. 42:21,22). This confession must have been music to Joseph's ears! No one was blaming anyone else. All were sharing the guilt. Maybe there was hope for them, after all!

- *See with new eyes.* One setback after another for Joseph's brothers: falsely accused of being spies; imprisoned for three days; Simeon held hostage until the other brothers returned with Benjamin; their money returned to them in their grain sacks. More trouble? Just a small taste of the suffering Joseph had endured for the past thirteen years. By now the brothers' "…hearts sank and they turned to each other trembling and said, 'What is this that God has done to us?'" (Gen. 42:28 NIV).

As Charles Swindoll writes in his contemporary classic, *Joseph: A Man of Integrity and Forgiveness,* "Instead of being happy about this surprise, however, they were frightened…. The original word that is translated 'trembling' is the same word used in 1 Samuel 14:15 to describe a giant earthquake…Joseph's brothers began to shake…. Not only are they now feeling the full brunt of their own guilt, they are also sensing God's hand in this."[2] The best sign, so far. They are finally beginning to fear God.

- *Make an offer God cannot refuse—yourself.* Again Joseph tests his brothers by placing his own silver cup in Benjamin's grain sack. Will they defend the youngest when Joseph accuses him of thievery or turn against him, too, to save their own necks?

Then comes that moving plea from Judah, the same Judah who committed incest in his younger days: "...His brother is dead, and he alone is left of his mother's children, and his father loves him.... Now therefore, please let your servant remain instead of the lad as a slave to my lord, and let the lad go..." (Gen. 44:20,33). The ultimate offer—to lay down his life for his brother and become a servant.

The great breakthrough! Joseph is convinced now. His brothers' hearts have softened. They are broken men, and he can no longer hide his identity from them. He bursts into tears and says, "Please come near to me.... I am Joseph your brother, whom you sold into Egypt" (Gen. 45:3,4).

When you come to the Lord again and again in confession and repentance, and lay down your own life, your own agenda, your Father will reveal Himself to you: "Come near to me. I am the light of the world.... I am the door of the sheep...I am the good shepherd...I am the Son of God...I am the resurrection...I am the way, the truth, and the life...I am the vine, you are the branches. He who abides in Me, and I in him, bears much fruit.... If you abide in Me, and My words abide in you, you will ask what you desire, and it shall be done for you" (John 9:5; 10:7,14,36; 11:25; 14:6; 15:5,7).

He sees your tears, and He is moved to supply your need.

A Time To Weep

Even strong men cry. Let's replay a few of those scenes we have just skimmed by. Joseph, mightiest in the land of Egypt and second only to Pharaoh himself, was not ashamed to shed a few tears. He wept when he recognized his brothers for the first time in thirteen years as they came to buy food during the early years of the famine. (Gen. 42:24.) He wept again when they brought his younger brother, Benjamin, to see him: "Now his heart yearned for his brother; so Joseph made haste and sought somewhere to weep. And he went into his chamber and wept there" (Gen. 43:30). What a poignant picture—Joseph, so moved by this reunion that he slipped into his private chamber to hide his tears so he would not betray his true identity too soon!

He wept a third time when he finally revealed himself to his brothers on that third historic buying trip: "Then Joseph could not restrain himself...and he cried out, 'Make everyone go out from me!' So no one stood with him while Joseph made himself known to his brothers. And he wept aloud, and the Egyptians and the house of Pharaoh heard it" (Gen. 45:1,2). He wailed so loudly that everyone in the palace heard him!

There is a time to weep. And one of those times is when you come into a place of discovery, only to learn that you have more to learn. My friend Martha Wolfe, one of the most respected counselors in Atlanta, conducts grief recovery seminars for her clients. In the first session, she assures them that tears are God's way of handling grief and that these counseling sessions will provide a safe environment to vent their emotions.

Whatever the source of one's grief, tears are a healing agent. When grief becomes locked up, this "frozen grief," as Martha calls it, can affect the immune system and cause all kinds of ailments. She encourages her clients to let their grief out. No more buried pain!

Martha also wants to dispel some of the myths that have become associated with grief:

- *Myth #1: Suck it up and don't cry at all.* That's exactly what the enemy wants you to believe. Crying "like a baby" does not mean you are emotionally immature. God gave us tears, and if you need further proof, just look at John 11:35: "Jesus wept." Those tears fell because of the death of His friend Lazarus, even when Jesus knew that in the next few minutes, He would be calling Lazarus out of the tomb to strengthen the faith of those who were mourning!

- *Myth #2: Time heals all wounds.* Ridiculous! If that is true, what do we make of the survivors of the German concentration camps during World War II, for whom some sound or smell can still bring pain? Or a mother who lost a child years ago, yet at the sight of a curly-haired toddler, feels anguish so fresh it is as if she is grieving all over again? *Time* does not heal all wounds. Only God is the Healer.

- *Myth #3: Anesthetize your grief.* Go shopping! Or drown your troubles in alcohol or sleep it off or give in to some other addiction. Escapism in any form is not the answer. Escapism is a delay in the remedy for grief. Grief is meant to be experienced. We cannot get to the joy God intends for His children if we do not first experience the suffering, not deaden ourselves to it. As Martha says, "We don't get the joy without going through the pain—not under it, around it, or over it, but through it!"

- *Myth #4: Everyone must transition through the five stages of grief in sequence: denial and isolation, anger, bargaining, depression, acceptance.*[3] Dr. Elisabeth Kübler-Ross, pioneer in the field of death and dying and author of the award-winning book by that title, has helped us take an honest look at a difficult subject. But she did not intend for her groundbreaking research to be misunderstood.

Every human being created in the image of God is unique and special. And each person who suffers loss grieves uniquely. We do not move neatly from grief to joyful acceptance in five easy steps. There is no pat formula for achieving peace and acceptance of loss except through the knowledge that it is God who heals our hurts and binds up our wounds.

When Martha's niece was heartbroken over a long-desired marriage that didn't happen and was letting go of all her pain in her upstairs bedroom, Martha marched up the steps, put aside all her fancy professional training, and kept it short and simple. "You may not feel like hearing from me, but I want to speak to your spirit. In all my counseling, I have found that there is really only one thing a person needs to know," she told her teary-eyed niece. "I have seen Jesus heal more broken hearts than anything else. That's the second thing He came to do!" referring to Isaiah 61:1-2: "The Lord has anointed me to preach good tidings to the poor; *He has sent Me to heal the brokenhearted*...to comfort all who mourn"!

People who have been "broken" are then in a position to help others patch up their lives and put the pieces back together. The incredible result is found later in that passage in Isaiah: "They shall *rebuild* the old ruins, they shall *raise up* the former desolation, and they shall *repair* the ruined cities, the desolations of many generations.... Instead of your shame you shall have *double honor*" (vv. 4,7). "Rebuild, raise up, and repair"—that's what God's broken people do best, and for their efforts, they are sometimes rewarded with "double honor."

Beauty in Brokenness

Betty is a beautifully broken woman who has achieved "double honor" and is helping others create a stunning mosaic of all the shattered pieces of their lives. A friend for whom I prayed and prophesied before I even knew her, Betty was born in "Pharaoh's palace"! She is the daughter of a former Southern governor, during whose administration the state prospered. Her mother, a fine artist and a phenomenal woman who was way ahead of her time, oversaw the building, design, and furnishing of the governor's mansion. No wonder Betty has the combined giftings of leadership skills and art. Now, after a shaky start and a few "pit" stops along the way in her own version of Joseph's journey, Betty is making progress toward her destiny in the Lord.

"As a child, I really didn't like all the attention I got," she confesses. "Having to be escorted by the highway patrol everywhere we went, all the little boys wanting to be my boyfriend, never knowing who my real friends were. Being in the public eye can make you distrustful of people's intentions. So, for years, I ran.

"When I gave my heart to the Lord in 1991, I had been having severe anxiety attacks and was in a desperate place. I was instantly delivered from fear and have never had another attack, but I had no idea how much work there was yet to be done in my life!"

In some ways Betty started at the top, both in the natural—her charming, accomplished family background—and spiritually—her immediate transformation after her conversion. Like so many others, though, she soon learned that her life was fertile ground for the Lord to do some further refining. Others were watching to see how this "model citizen" of the kingdom would fare and whether her brand of Christianity was authentic.

"My friends, who have known me at my worst—when I was living for myself, for fleshly pleasures—can now see the difference. I have definitely made some changes. For some reason, they haven't written me off as a hopeless lunatic or a Jesus freak. The fact is, I have learned who my real friends are, and we love each other. I also love sharing what I'm learning, helping other people get free. Even Christians can be so beaten down and overwhelmed. It's exciting to invite them to my house, along with others who can instruct us and pray over us, and watch my old friends break out of their prisons."

Pretty, feminine, and well-connected, Betty is just the kind of bait the Lord loves to use. She has the rope—the Word of God and the power of the Holy Spirit—and she is reeling in her friends, hauling them up from their own individual pits as quickly as possible. They adore Betty and flock around her at these Bible studies in her home and in the inner city arts program where she volunteers regularly.

"The truth is, I have always been drawn to the blue-collar people—the ones who are real and unpretentious. Even in the governor's mansion, I loved being back in the kitchen talking to the cooks. So it was perfectly natural, after I was saved, to reach out to the needy people in our city—the down-trodden, the ones caught up in drugs and alcohol. They know me, and they trust me down there because I've walked where some of them are walking. And I can help. I have…Connections. I can tell them about the only One who can really meet their needs.

"I also have a heart to serve. The Lord has taken my gifting in art, has handed me the mantle of my father's leadership, and has placed me where I can be a blessing, broken as I am. Now I am mature enough to appreciate what my parents have done, and I enjoy the doors it opens for me. Because of my wide exposure in all levels of society, the broad expanse of individuals I touch, I know the Lord is preparing a place for me that will benefit other broken people. I want to give them something that no one can take away—first, the Lord, and then, a sense of their own accomplishment. So maybe it will be founding a Center for the Arts for the homeless, who knows? I've stopped reading my horoscope and now look to God's Word to reveal the future.

"And then there's Ann Platz. I met Ann a couple of years ago and instantly wanted more of what she has! I wanted to get to know her, to grow in the Lord through her teaching. She has added a whole new dimension to my awareness of life in the Spirit and has brought to me areas I had not released to the Lord. It's time now to take the next step and move into greater commitment to Him. I have an idea that the best is yet to come."

It is such a joy for me to have connected with Betty. That is what God does when He reclaims your dream: He places you as a vital part of the pipeline to feed the hungry—physically and spiritually—wherever they are found. I love Betty—her spirit, her heart, her sisterhood. She is someone who is going to do something monumental for the Lord!

"It's so much more than being some famous artist," Betty insists. "It's not about me. God has expanded my vision to see with His eyes. Maybe I can explain it this way. Not long ago, I was down at a church were people from many other churches in the city volunteer to feed the hungry. Now the Lord was leading me to go further in ministry and stay for fellowship afterwards. I was talking to some people, encouraging them to express their own thoughts and bring forward their gifts and talents.

"One man, who is mute and without a penny to his name, was writing a poem. I asked to see it and was astonished when I read the words on the page! Even though he cannot speak, he had written an eloquent piece that began: 'When the Lord holds the pen....'

"I knew instantly what he meant! It's the same with me. When the Lord holds the paintbrush, I can express myself in ways that surpass my natural gift. These people need to be heard. How can they be discarded? They are precious in God's sight, and He has given them a gift, a dream that should not die. Perhaps my dream will prepare the way for their dreams."

That's right, Betty. That's the way God works. He planted the dream in you, lifted you out of the pit, helped you to hang in there when your dream was delayed, renewed your vision, and restored you to Himself. Now it's your turn to ignite the fire in others and pass the torch.

The Oil of Joy

When brokenness comes, you will know it, as did Betty. Only then will you be able to minister fully and effectively. When I had tried everything, when I finally realized that all of my efforts had come to naught, I waved the white hanky of surrender. That's when the Healer comes to pour in the oil of joy.

"Joy" is more than an expensive perfume, my mother's signature scent. Joy is the essence of the sweet aroma of the Lord. Tuck that one away in your heart. And here's another: "...the Lord has anointed me...to give them beauty for ashes, the oil of joy for mourning, the garment of praise for the spirit of heaviness" (Isa. 61:1,3). Write that verse on something huge and frame it. Then put it where you can see it often. Healing is one of God's greatest promises.

Joseph was able to speak to his brothers from a healed heart, a godly response that comes only through brokenness. When he named his first son Manasseh and stated the reason— "...God has made me forget all my toil and all my father's house" (Gen. 41:51)—he didn't mean he couldn't remember his trials and how his brothers had treated him. He was saying that the pain associated with his pit and prison time was over, and he was emotionally healed.

I love Martha Wolfe! She is a no-nonsense, practical woman and one of the wittiest people I know. Martha, as a counselor, pours in the oil of joy from her own mended vessel every day. "I came to the Lord so broken myself," she admits. "I had consulted three psychiatrists. I quit the first one because he fell asleep during our sessions and the second because he prescribed Valium. The third gave up on me when I became suicidal!

"After I was born again, I didn't want others to hurt like I had hurt. As I received healing from the Lord, I gave it away. God would give me some more healing, and I would give that away. Light obeyed brings more light. Light disobeyed brings darkness. Little by little, there was more of the Lord and less of me. When you have a broken heart, the anointing leaks out, but as that heart is healed, then your container is fuller and you can pour out more joy.

"I tell my clients that it honors God when they laugh. I tell them to ask Him to increase their sense of humor. As the Bible says, 'A merry heart makes a cheerful countenance...' (Prov. 15:13), or in the Martha Wolfe translation: 'For heaven's sake, lighten up!'"

Martha is right. I'll leave you with this hilarious incident on what was otherwise a solemn occasion—the funeral of my beloved younger sister, Mary Ashley. Being a part of a prominent political family, our family occasions are usually well attended. Mary Ashley's funeral was no exception. The church, sitting majestically front and center on the town's central square, was filled to capacity with her friends, my parents' friends, people from all walks of life, and statewide dignitaries. The sanctuary was overflowing with floral displays and love for our family. The eulogy was stirring, personal, and powerful—a tribute to a life well lived and too soon over.

After the service, as we were leaving the church to form the funeral procession to the cemetery, we went to our respective limousines, provided to accommodate the large entourage. I was in the second limo with my husband, two brothers, and their wives. As is the custom in South Carolina, all the limousines were lined up, waiting for the passengers to get in before proceeding in formation to the gravesite.

When it was time to leave, our driver turned the ignition key, and to his complete astonishment, the engine backfired loudly, three times in a row—bam...bam...bam—leaving a cloud of black smoke in the air. Startled, we sat frozen, casting a sidelong glance at each other, not daring to speak. Embarrassed, the driver turned the key and we sat in silence for a few long moments. He restarted the engine. Again, the shocking sounds: bam...bam...bam! More black smoke!

Whether the moment was all that funny or whether we just needed an excuse to release the tension, the six of us began to laugh hysterically, doubling over in merriment. We could not stop. It was a Mary Ashley moment! There had been no reason to smile for weeks preceding her death, and here we were, at her funeral, convulsed in hysterics.

Mary Ashley had a dynamic personality and a great sense of humor. She even invited friends in for "slumber parties" when she was receiving chemotherapy during her illness and wore fashionable cocktail dresses to doctors' appointments. When she got really excited about something, she would say, "Bus up, everybody, bus up!"

I could see Mother in the limousine directly in front of us, peering around to see what had caused all the racket. Catching our eye, she gave that look that only a mother can give that clearly said: *You children, behave yourselves!*

When we finally got started, trailing black smoke in front of the First Baptist Church and all over the vehicles of the dignitaries to the rear of us, we were still laughing. By now, we were also yelling, "Bus up! Bus up!" Mary Ashley was, no doubt, cheering us on, pleased as punch that we were enjoying her funeral so much. She always loved a good party.

We arrived at Memorial Gardens and left our limousine to take our places beside Mother. "What were y'all doing back there at the church with all that smoke and noise?" she asked in a stage whisper.

Leaning over, I said the first thing that occurred to me, "We were giving Mary Ashley a twenty-one gun salute!"

Learning to laugh after brokenness is one of the most healing things we can do. Martha…and Mary Ashley agree. As we are led out of pain, we come into the season of plenty.

Prayer of Hilarious, Outrageous Jubilation: Father God, awesome Protector and Mender of Broken Dreams, we come before You in pieces and fragments and tears and rips and splinters, needing the glue that only You can apply to our hearts and minds. Thank You, Father, for the net You place under us, for the people You position around us, for the Word that abides within us. I thank You for the promises that are true, for the healing that is forever available to us, for the laughter and the tears. With outrageous jubilation and wonderment, we receive Your joy that fills us and spills over into a river of living water to bless all who mourn. In the jubilant joy of Jesus, I pray, amen.

"Do not...be grieved or angry with yourselves

because you sold me here; for God sent me

before you to preserve life.

"...to preserve a posterity for you in the earth,

and to save your lives by a great deliverance.

"So now it was not you who sent me here, but God...."

GENESIS 45:5,7,8

CHAPTER 13

Forgiveness: Patient Love

"Love suffers long and is kind....bears all things,
believes all things, hopes all things, endures all things.
Love never fails...."

1 CORINTHIANS 13:4,7,8

Being the type-A personality and the strong, take-charge Choleric that I am, my biggest challenge has been learning to wait on the Lord. It has never been a problem for me to trust Him or to depend upon Him, but to wait on Him? I am not the most patient person God ever created. I'm the one who's sitting at the red light, tapping her foot and racing her engine, anxious to be off!

Part of the creative drive is getting things in order quickly and efficiently. I love that phase of a design project or a book—dreaming up the vision, getting the big picture, finding the parts of the whole, seeing the streams of concept flow into one rushing river. So when it comes to living my life, the Lord has had His hands full teaching me to listen until He says it's time to go!

I have become aware, however, that God is not going to stamp my passport and send me on my way without instructing me in basic protocol. Before I could move on to the next level in Him, I had to learn to forgive. Like Joseph, I felt I had every reason *not* to forgive—abandonment, rejection, being stripped of funds as Joseph was stripped of his beautiful coat. *Unlike* Joseph, as the "innocent" victim, I was enraged by the injustice of it all! Nor did I fare as well in the pit or the prison as he did. My prison term was not spent in quiet contemplation. I was snorting and pawing the ground, eager to get on with it and disliking every moment of the delay.

Patience, Ann. And while you're at it, have some faith, hope, and love, forgiveness, mercy, and grace. These traits are all tightly intertwined like the tendrils of a vine, growing toward God. When God saved my soul in response to my repentance through faith, He mercifully did not hold my sins against me, but forgave me, canceling my debt. Joseph is a near perfect portrait of God's forgiveness. In no other character in the Old Testament are these virtues more beautifully displayed on the canvas of a life than when Joseph forgave his brothers. Only Jesus in the New Testament is the mirror image of His Father. How interesting that the last act of Jesus' earthly life was also an act of forgiveness: "...Father, forgive them, for they do not know what they do..." (Luke 23:34).

I can hear Him saying, "Ann, go and do thou likewise."

Reluctant Forgiveness

Forgiveness has to start somewhere. So often the feeling just isn't there. But feelings are never as important as facts. And the fact is, as believers saved by grace, we are to extend that same grace to others.

You are not going to believe this story. Yet it happened. And because it happened, one woman's life was forever changed, and the ripple effect of her powerful testimony will continue to impact generations to come.

She was a professional dancer and model, born in Florida. There, she competed in dance contests and often won—*so* often, that she and her partner attracted the attention of Atlanta's *Creative Magazine,* which dispatched a journalist to cover the story, complete with photos and multiple interviews.

During one of the interviews, an unseen observer stood watching. He was still watching when she got in her car to leave for home around 1 A.M. She soon noticed a vehicle following, the lights blinking. Not having been warned that it is never a good idea for a lone woman to stop her car without being sure who is making the request, she pulled over. Thinking nothing of it, she smiled at the nicely dressed man who got out of his car and approached her, saying he had noticed some trouble with a rear tire and wanted to know if he could help. Still trustful, she opened her door.

The next thing she knew she was being lifted off her feet and tossed inside his vehicle with the threat that if she screamed or tried to get away, he would kill her. "But my car is still running and my purse is on the front seat," she argued, thinking fast and stalling for time. She could tell she had caught him off guard. Holding a gun to her throat, he warned her again, then sprinted for the other car.

In those few seconds she was off, running for her life toward an apartment complex, with the gunman closing in on her. A couple, out on their deck, noticed the commotion as she literally flew over a six-foot cyclone fence. But the assailant grabbed her by her ankles and slammed her onto the ground, breaking both knees. With the adrenaline flowing, she felt no pain. As he choked her, she was forced to look into his crazed, demonic face and thought, *I am going to die, and I am going to hell.* In nanoseconds, her mind was flooded with the images of Campus Crusade kids, who covered the beach at spring break, preaching Jesus to the sun-worshippers soaking up the rays. Now it was too late.

In that instant she looked into the would-be rapist's eyes and said a simple prayer, *Jesus, if You are real, save me!*

Later she would learn that, at that instant, the Lord sent an angel who spoke in an audible voice to a hunter, lying asleep inside the apartment complex. The voice said, *Take your gun and go outside.* With no more direction than that, the man rose and quickly obeyed. Seeing the struggle on the parking lot, he fired a warning shot that sent the assailant fleeing into the night, but not before pursuing him and taking down his license number.

The young woman was able to pick the man out of the police lineup. Despite her positive identification and the witnesses to the incident, they didn't have sufficient evidence to charge him at that time so the case was not closed, and thus began a five-year court battle. The Lord chose to use these "pit" years as a time to redeem her soul from eternal destruction. Not coincidentally, the two detectives assigned to the case were Christians and "tricked" her into attending a church service, where the pastor led her to the Lord. She was soon baptized and filled with the Spirit.

Several years later, she received a call from the District Attorney. They had finally caught the man, who was identified as the River Bend Rapist, near the very church where John and I attend every Sunday!

In the meantime, the woman was invited to a Bible study where she knew not a single person there. The evangelist who was speaking looked directly at her, and under the anointing, spoke a word of knowledge to her, saying, "You must forgive that man for what he has done. If you don't, I can't forgive you for your sins."

Although time had passed, she was still feeling the pain of her violation and honestly wanted the man dead. Yet the Holy Spirit was convicting her, and she felt as if her heart were being ripped apart. She began to cry, lying prostrate on the floor before the Lord. "I forgive him. I forgive him," she said, as the realization broke that her attacker was a tormented soul himself, in bondage to the spirits who controlled him. Now it would be up to the Lord to bring him to ultimate justice—or to save him, too.

Although hers had been a reluctant forgiveness, mumbled through cold lips, she actually spoke with her attacker in court and told him that she had forgiven him. Not only was her news *not* received with gratitude, but she was ridiculed for her faith. The Lord was testing her forgiveness. Would it stand, or would she revert to hatred and blame?

Thus began a series of harassments, carried out by "connections" her attacker still maintained with the underworld. The woman had to go before the Lord for emotional healing to hold on to her forgiveness. The final test was a bomb, planted in her car parked in the garage of her apartment while she was away from home on business. Had it not been discovered by the observant police detectives, she would have been murdered by a man in confinement!

Eventually the rapist was sent to prison. "In my humanness, I wanted the man dead," she says, "but we all deserve death. Every one of us has fallen short of the glory of God. None is worthy of God's grace. My attacker is where he needs to be, a place where I firmly believe he will have an opportunity to repent. And I am where I'm supposed to be."

Where she's "supposed to be" is serving as the wife of the pastor of one of the most outstanding churches in the nation—my pastor's wife and an outstanding leader in her own right! What began as an attempted rape resulted in a transformed life and a ministry of forgiveness to other hurting souls. What the enemy intended for evil, God meant for good.

Barbie's "reluctant forgiveness" was tested and proven—and it held firm. While her heart might not have been in it at the beginning, she now realizes that she, too, has been forgiven much, and she has no choice but to forgive in return.

$\mathcal{F}$orgiveness $\mathcal{I}$s $\mathcal{N}$ot an $\mathcal{O}$ption

It really isn't! Forgiveness is not merely a suggestion or the proper, polite thing to do. We are commanded to forgive: "...forgiving one another... even as Christ forgave you..." (Col. 3:13).

But what about my rights? you may argue. *I didn't do anything. Somebody (or something) stole my dream. I was the victim of _____* (sexual abuse, lies, gossip, slander, verbal abuse, mistreatment, rejection, abandonment, etc.), and the list goes on. You fill in the blank!

The Word of God is very clear. There is no room for misinterpretation or misunderstanding when He says: "Whenever you stand praying, if you have *anything* against *anyone,* forgive him, that your Father in heaven may also forgive you.... But if you do not forgive, neither will your Father in heaven forgive your trespasses" (Mark 11:25). Forgive...what? *Anything.* Forgive...whom? *Anyone.* No exceptions. No exclusions. Forgive everyone for everything—all the time! Why? So God will forgive you!

In Beth Moore's incredibly rich Bible study *Living Beyond Yourself: Exploring the Fruit of the Spirit,* she points out that the Greek word for patience—*makrothumia* (listed as one of the fruit of the Spirit)—is actually related to forgiveness. This word means "the quality of a person who is able to avenge himself yet refrains from doing so."[1]

Isn't Joseph a classic picture of forgiveness—a man who had the power to avenge himself, yet "refrained from doing so"? Can't you see Joseph's patience as he waits out his pit and prison years—thirteen altogether—and then for a time longer until his brothers appear to him in Egypt, literally begging for bread? It is only then that he is able to see the fulfillment of his boyhood dreams of greatness. Remember those dreams—how the sheaf of wheat arose in the field, while his brothers' sheaves bowed down to his; how the sun, moon, and eleven stars bowed down to him (Gen. 37:7,9)? "...And they bowed their heads down and prostrated themselves" (Gen. 43:28). It has all come to pass—but not because of Joseph's selfish ambition or greed. No, because God planted that dream for His own purposes: to bring about the deliverance of His people who would then become the nation of Israel!

Still, Joseph might have refused his brothers. Apparently, they were terrified that he would! He had every right and all power in the land to reject them, to imprison them, to send them home empty-handed, even to take their lives. He could have had his revenge. But he chose to forgive.

Even hearing this powerful story, you might say, "But, Ann, that was long ago in another time. You have no idea what I've been through. God surely doesn't expect me to forgive *that*."

Forgiving Those Who Have Abused You

Some of the most heart-wrenching stories I hear are those in which wounds were inflicted in childhood, when little ones are purest and most innocent. A new friend, but one whom I greatly admire, is Laura, who was physically and emotionally abused by a stepmother. Food was withheld and sleep prevented, sometimes for several days, until she "confessed" to taking whatever she was accused of stealing. The problem was, she never knew what it was supposed to be and had to guess until something sounded good to her stepmother. Following this "confession" was punishment, which included being beaten with a belt and locked in an attic for a prolonged time without food or access to the bathroom, or being ordered to do excessive cleaning chores, with her stepmother looking on and beating her if she missed a spot. Laura never knew when the cycle would begin or what would trigger it.

And there is the question of sexual abuse for some. Many atrocities committed against innocent children are almost too awful to be imagined. So what do we do when the unthinkable happens?

Laura speaks openly about her experience. "I struggled with anger and grief for a long time. My mother died when I was four, and much began to surface when my stepmother came into the picture. My father was always the passive one, escaping into alcoholism and turning over his parenting responsibilities to my stepmother. So I put up walls to protect myself and wouldn't let anyone near me emotionally.

"My family background is liberal atheism, but somehow I became a Christian when I was 22, and God began to deal with my issues. I went for counseling but didn't make much progress until one day Jesus showed me a picture of a little girl holding her father's hand and looking up at him in total trust. Jesus told me that I was that little girl and that He would be holding my hand all the way through the process. Since Jesus was with me, I could tell my story to a counselor I learned to trust.

"Slowly, I began to see God as my Father. As I did so, He revealed the root of many of my issues. My earthly father was acting out of his own woundedness. He couldn't bear losing my mother, and with no strong model in his own life as to how to handle loss, he used alcohol to escape his pain and abdicated his role as head of our household. My stepmother resented her new husband's grief over his first wife and took out her frustration and anger on the children. Consequently, as I began to heal, I learned to see my family as people who, without God, could not help themselves.

"Oh, don't get me wrong. It wasn't easy to forgive. It was really hard to let the anger go, especially with my father since he had stood by and allowed the abuse, so there was always a dark cloud hovering over me. But one day, a wonderful woman who was standing in as a mother figure led me in a simple prayer of forgiveness, and the cloud broke. There was a tremendous release of joy again, just as there had been when I was first saved.

Two years later I married, and my husband and I now lead a healing and deliverance ministry in our church, bringing others out of bondage. When people ask us why we had to go through 'all that,' we can tell them from our experience: God doesn't desire adversity for us; in fact, it grieves Him. But 'He comforts us so we can comfort others.'"

What a breakthrough for Laura, one that led naturally to a desire to help others escape their prisons of mistrust and anger. And it all began with a simple concept, one I first heard from Evelyn Hamon, the wife of Bishop Bill Hamon: "Hurting people hurt people." When you gain an understanding of why people act as they do, it is easier to forgive even the most heinous of crimes against you.

Laura outlines seven steps to forgiveness:

1. Acknowledge your pain and anger and recognize the need to forgive.

2. Deal with the anger and hurt by pouring it all out to God and turning it over to Him.

3. Forgive those who have hurt you. (Recognizing the root causes of their behavior, which is hurt, can help.) Ask God to forgive you for your responses to the anger and hurt.

4. Forgive yourself.

5. Begin to walk in the healing and restoration of your dream.

6. Allow God to continue His healing and address the various levels of forgiveness.

7. Forgive again and again as the healing goes deeper. This is an ongoing process.

"An ongoing process"—I'm glad Laura reminded us of that last point. We may not be finished when we forgive someone once...or even seven times. We may be required to forgive, as Jesus told Peter, "seventy times seven" (Matt. 18:22)!

God does take us step by step, but he is pleased with every step we take. For example, Laura has had to let go of her expectations of who her father should be. God is now her Father, and she gets her hugs and her approval from him. She had to stop expecting her dad to give her love in the way she wanted it to be given and accept the love he was giving in the only way he knew how to give it.

In our conversation, Laura mentioned another matter that needs to be addressed. With abuse so prevalent in our society today, we need to be careful not to become co-dependent with the abuser. You can and should forgive, but you need to test the heart of the abuser before letting that person back into your life. Again, Joseph showed us how that looks when he did not reveal himself to his brothers right away. Each of the three times they appeared before him, he devised a test to take their spiritual temperature. When he was convinced that they had "changed," he declared his kinship with them: "...I am Joseph your brother, whom you sold into Egypt" (Gen. 45:4).

Because Laura has experienced the healing which began with forgiving her father, she is now able to let him into her life more than ever before. They are no longer antagonistic toward one another; they are able to share and enjoy a loving, caring relationship. He has recently been genuinely repentant over what happened in the past, acknowledging the abuse for the first time and expressing sorrow and regret for his part in it. Just like Joseph with his brothers, Laura has allowed her father back into her heart little by little. The more healed she has become, the more she is able to let him in. Forgiveness is key to spiritual growth.

ℱorgiving the Dream-Stealers

Through the teaching and case studies in this book, we have "witnessed" many occasions on which the dream-stealers did their dirty work. Such incidents leave either open wounds or thick scars that must be healed or removed by forgiveness before the dream can be fully restored. Even our prayers and our gifts are hindered if we fail to forgive. Jesus said so: "If you bring your gift to the altar, and there remember that your brother has something against you, leave your gift there before the altar, and go your way. First be reconciled to your brother, and then come and offer your gift" (Matt. 5:23).

My ministry took on a facelift after forgiveness settled an old, old hurt. After my divorce and subsequent move to Atlanta, I looked for a church home for myself and my two little daughters. We chose a denominational church where some good friends of my parents were members. The little girls quickly found their place in Sunday school and made new friends. I, on the other hand, had an entirely different experience.

When I asked the woman in charge of placing newcomers, I was met with a broad, fake smile and a puzzled look in her big, brown eyes. "Well, dear," she fumbled, "we only have the married class and the singles class, and I'm not sure you'd fit in either one, so I'm not quite sure what to do with you!" I so needed to fit, and you can not imagine my pain when it appeared that there was not a place for me. I visited both classes, but decided she had uttered a prophetic word. There truly was not a good fit anywhere in the church.

After much prayer, I met with her again and suggested that I teach a children's Sunday school class. A look of alarm registered on the dimpled face, and I could practically read her mind: *A divorced woman—teaching in our Sunday school!* But she murmured something soothing and a few days later called with an assignment—the fifth grade girls.

I enjoyed the girls, but what I really needed was to be nurtured and restored, surrounded by a loving circle of women who would encourage me and mentor me and strengthen me for the place God intended. I stayed in that church—dry and unfulfilled—often tearful by the end of the service but not because of the message. The church should be an oasis for the hurting, a place of refuge for the weary, and a way station for women without husbands. But it was none of those for me at that tender time in my life.

God at last heard my cry and sent a remarkable woman from another denomination, Eliza MacLemore, to rescue me. Eliza was my "Moses." I met her in my wilderness time, and she led me into the promised land of spiritual grace. I loved her the moment we met; her grace, her love, and her true concern for me to grow spiritually were so evident. It was she who suggested I try Mount Paran Church—a place where many had been restored and recharged.

I will never forget the feeling of love and grace I felt as I experienced the Presence of God in that body of Christ for the first time. The praise music and worship time filled my heart with such emotion that I could not hold back the tears, and the message that night was directed to me! When the altar call was given for healing and prayer, I went forward, drawn by the lyrics of that beautiful old hymn "Come Home,"[2] which says for everyone who is weary to come home (or come to the Lord). I was so weary...and I needed to come home.

The fit was perfect as the girls and I settled into our new church home, and my faith soared to new heights. In the next decades, God sent my true husband and a new calling, greater and grander than any dream I had ever asked for or imagined. Eventually I began telling my story through the lecture circuit and in print.

While sharing my testimony with a large gathering of women one day, I wept as I told of being redeemed and restored, of coming into a "significant place of service," how the Lord led me every step of the way...providing people and resources...opening and closing doors...shielding me from hurt and filling me with His truth...and so much more. By the time I finished my talk, every person in the room was wiping her eyes.

Afterward, I was sitting at a table signing books when I was approached by a woman who looked vaguely familiar. Then it dawned on me! This was the woman from the church in Atlanta, the one who had said I "didn't fit." I braced myself, but I was totally unprepared for what she was about to say.

"Can you ever forgive me?" she began, speaking softly. "I did not know who you would become when I met you. I just didn't know where to place you, and I'm so sorry if I hurt you or hindered you in any way in our church. Please say you forgive me."

I smiled, flinching a little at the wording of her apology, but I meant it when I said, "I forgive you." I also shot up a little prayer of thanks to the Lord that I had been on the receiving end of her rejection years ago, and not some other woman who might have felt terribly wounded and left the church forever. God knew this incident would simply guide me to the place where I could recover my dream…His dream for my life! He brought closure that day to what had been a painful episode, as He always brings closure to hurtful things.

Forgiveness asked, forgiveness granted. That's the way it should always be—as many times as necessary.

ℱorgiving Others in Ministry

One of the most painful kinds of betrayal sometimes comes from others who are called to kingdom ministry. It's the unkindest cut of all. "If an enemy were insulting me, I could endure it; if a foe were raising himself against me, I could hide from him. But it is you, a man like myself, my companion, my close friend, with whom I once enjoyed sweet fellowship…" (Ps. 55:12-14 NIV).

My precious friend Evelyn Hamon, a highly respected bishop's wife, speaks on this subject. "More than most anyone I know, Joseph had the opportunity to feel sorry for himself, to feel like he may have missed God. Maybe he was imagining things. After all, his dreams had gotten him nothing but a desert pit and a prison cell.

"I can't envision being sold as a slave on the auction block. But I do know something about being sold out by your brethren. Some people see the favor of God on your life—your anointing, your coat of many colors—and they're fearful or maybe a little jealous, and they turn away. My husband and I had each other during our early ministry days, but Joseph didn't have a living soul. He had nobody who understood his God or his way of life or his family. Actually, he had come from an important family, one where his father and mother loved him and waited on him, in spite of those mean old brothers. Suddenly he went from everything to nothing…to everything!

"If Joseph hadn't gone through all those hard times, all those testing times, he wouldn't have had the training to be the ambassador God intended him to be. And if my husband and I hadn't gone through our pit and prison terms, we wouldn't be where God intended us to be. Let me tell you a little story. My husband—the bishop—and I taught in a Bible school in the early years of our ministry. It was a great time. The children were small and in school, and life was good. Then, through a circumstance that caused the president to become uneasy about my husband's anointing, we were released at the end of the school year, with nowhere to go. Since we were living on campus at the time, we also no longer had a home! No job, no home, and nobody to turn to. It was a horrible time!

"But we had to forgive. One day the bishop was feeling so bad about the situation as he drove down the road that he had to pull over and cry out to the Lord. God spoke in that still, small voice and said, *What do you want Me to do about it?* My husband had the distinct impression that whatever he had asked at that moment, God would have done it for him. I suppose the bishop might have been a little reluctant when he sighed and said, 'Bless them, Lord, and we'll do whatever it is we're supposed to do.' We really didn't desire for them to hurt as we were hurt. There was no vindictiveness there. So Bishop just let it be.

"When we look back on that time, we can see the hand of God. If Joseph hadn't forgiven his brothers who had thrown him in that pit, he would not have become Prime Minister of Egypt. If we hadn't forgiven and moved on, we wouldn't have founded Christian International. That's God."

If you're in prison and can't get out, then get over it! Don't give up; get over it. The Lord wants us to learn that He is in every circumstance, and we have to do the best we can where we are.

Even when you make a total mistake, like David did when he committed adultery with Bathsheba, you ask for forgiveness and go on. You can't keep blaming yourself, saying. "I'm not worthy, just look at what I did." He has made you worthy. If you're born again, you're standing tall in the Lord, and you go forth in the knowledge that you have a destiny and a dream. As long as you allow God to work, you can be "prime minister" of the land. No matter what is going on in your life, God isn't going to change His mind about your destiny. Only you can change your destiny by not receiving God's love and forgiveness or not forgiving yourself. Nothing can separate you from the love of God—except you.

ℱorgiving ℐourself

Joseph knew God like few people do. I doubt if he ever felt completely separated from God's love, even when the years passed by and his prayers appeared to go unanswered. He was so sure of that love that he could find it in himself to reassure his brothers when they began to berate themselves for doing their dastardly deed. He could say with true compassion and mercy, "Don't blame yourselves. God had a better plan for me, and you're included in that plan. He sent me ahead of you to save your lives. So, you see, it was really not your idea when you threw me into that pit, but God's" (Gen. 45:5,7,8, author's paraphrase).

How awesome! What a picture of God's grace, His patient love. He "suffers long." He waits on us to come to Him in the first place. He waits for us to work up the nerve to forgive others. He waits until we get around to forgiving ourselves.

Pamela is a daughter of my heart who didn't know for the longest time that she needed to forgive herself. She was brought up in a church-going home, acknowledged Jesus as her Savior early—with no intention of declaring Him her Lord—and proceeded to live life her way. As a result she conceived a baby out of wedlock, then married before the baby was born. By the time she got pregnant again, she had a job, was trying hard to make a "perfect" home for her little family "like Mom did," and burning the candle at both ends. "I couldn't take on one more thing!"

Abortion was "in," the socially accepted solution for an untimely pregnancy. Without a second thought and after consulting with her husband, Pam went to her physician who referred her to another doctor for the procedure. "I feel like the Maytag repairman," the first doctor said, shaking his head sadly. "I'm always available, but no one wants to see me."

Still, Pam had not a twinge of conscience. With the passage of Roe vs. Wade,[3] it was a pivotal time in our nation. Liberal abortions became the way out for so many women who felt overburdened by an unwanted pregnancy. That's what people did when another baby was out of the question, she reasoned. She handled everything matter-of-factly, even going to church the day after the abortion. No one would ever have known. No one would ever have suspected what had gone on just the day before. The second abortion, several years later, was even easier.

After going through "Healing Streams," a twelve-week restoration course at her church, Pam realized what she had done and was even led to give the aborted babies a name. It was not until September 11, 2001, however, after the terrorist attack on the Twin Towers, that Pam came face to face with the reality of it all. At church that night, she heard her pastor's wife bring up a topic that seemingly had nothing to do with terrorism in America. She connected the terrorist activities of the day to the millions who are being killed every year…the subject was abortion. Although thousands had been killed by terrorists in airplanes, millions are being put to death—with our nation's approval!

The pastor's wife talked about abortion as sin. Startled, Pam sat up and listened carefully. "The Word of God says in 2 Chronicles 7:14, 'If my people who are called by My name will humble themselves, and pray and seek My face, and turn from their wicked ways, then I will hear from heaven, and will forgive their sin and heal their land.' People don't want to humble themselves. They don't want to know how God sees abortion—how much it grieves His heart."

"That night it hit me," Pam says. "I was weeping like I had never wept before. All the emotions of that terrible day and all the other emotions I had stifled until that moment…grieving the loss of my babies and all the ones that had gone before…understanding, for the first time, how we have stood by and let this nation walk away from God. I found myself having to forgive America for putting those laws in place so that abortion is so easy and accepted. I found myself having to forgive…myself.

"Still, my emotions are intact. God has given me great strength so I can tell my story without breaking down. I can talk about the whole incident with grace. I take full responsibility for those abortions."

Praise God! Another breakthrough for Pam! She has climbed another rung in the ladder to recovering her dream. I can't wait to see what God has for the rest of her life!

Passionate Mercy

Other insults and injuries are more easily overlooked or forgiven than the ultimate betrayal of a spouse. So I have saved this story for last only because it represents a quantum leap in my own story of reclaiming my dream.

Several years after my first husband abandoned my two young daughters and me—seven years in which he made very few attempts to see the girls and no offer of any child support—I came to a place where I knew I could not go on to the next level in my spiritual journey until I moved in forgiveness. Still, I was angry every time I thought of him. I could get so worked up at the mention of his name. For five years, I had held bitter resentment toward a man whom once I had loved and promised to cherish all the days of my life.

I was angry, too, every time one of the little girls would come to me with some question or childish observation. "My friend told me I can't be in the Brownies 'cause I don't have a daddy," one of them said one day.

"What?" I shot back, fire in my eyes. "Who said that?" My anger had turned to hatred. How could he do this to his own darling little girls? He had no idea what a vacuum he had left in their hearts. I could justify hanging on to all the hurt because it was being inflicted on my beautiful little daughters.

As I studied the Scriptures, one message was clear: "You must forgive," and it pierced my heart. Somewhere, sometime, I would. But not now. Still, God kept prodding me, and I kept arguing with Him. "Lord, You know how I feel! I hate what he's done to my little girls and to me! I hate him!"

The still, small voice came again. *Write him. I'll partner with you.*

"Lord, You know You are asking me to do something I'm not capable of doing."

But I will be there with you, and I will tell you what to say. I will guide your pen.

Well, I guess that was an offer I couldn't refuse. I sat down at my dining room table, but not before setting the stage, being the decorator that I am. I placed a bouquet of flowers on the table, found my best stationery—lots of it—an ink pen, a box of Kleenex. I even pulled up a chair for the Lord! After all, He was my writing Partner.

This would not be just any letter.

"Dear...."

As I wrote his name, I honestly wanted to stab it! "Oh, Lord, just look at me!" I cried out to Him, plucking out a tissue and dabbing at my tears. "I'm pitiful! Look at me. I have such a black heart. I will never get through this!"

I finished the salutation, took a deep breath, exhaled, and began to write: "I'm writing you today because I have had a change in my life, a powerful experience with the Lord...." At that moment the Spirit of the Lord fell, and I felt His sweet Presence flooding my cold, dead heart. Love—the love of God—stirred in me for this man that I hated. I began to experience a melt-down of the anger and resentment I had held for him.

My pen raced across the paper from the anointing that was present. "I know now that I can't move any further in my life without coming to you and asking you to forgive me." What was I saying!

All of a sudden my heart opened up and filled with love to set this man free. I went on to write the strangest things: "You see, I'm just as guilty as you. I moved ahead of the Lord when I married you. I didn't wait for what He had for my life. I now see that I had a rebellious heart. I was not willing to trust Him. No offense, but you were not God's utmost for His highest for me...but I'll have to admit I was no prize for you, either." I wrote and cried...cried and wrote. Words poured from my heart onto the pages as I cleaned up and cleared out the past hurt.

Six pages later, I ended: "I forgive you, and now I'm asking you to forgive me. Even if you choose not to answer this letter, I forgive you. Just know that I'll be praying for God to bless you. Love, Ann."

I couldn't believe what I had written! More than that, I couldn't believe how free I felt. Writing that letter liberated me, and God graciously cata-pulted me to a higher level in my Christian walk. I think my forgiveness blew the doors open to my healing, and the feeling of this freedom has never left me.

That's what happens when you partner with God. He shows you such revelation. He removes bondages from the past, takes your broken dreams and the broken dreamer, and puts it all back together. Patient love...passion-ate mercy...I love those words. I have experienced this spiritual grace—and you can, too, when you forgive!

Prayer for Patient Love: Father God, Patient One, we come before You as impatient as we can be, seeking Your answers, when all You're asking us to do is wait. Thank You for Your written Word that over and over again instructs us in the wisdom of the wait. And thank You, Father, that during this waiting time You are working—arranging and orchestrating the path of blessing. Thank You, Father, for making forgiveness so available to all of us and teaching us that it is by walking in forgiveness, we are healed. Thank You for the person reading this book at this crucial point. May they examine their lives and lay before You the deepest places that need forgiveness. Thank You for Your patient love, Your passionate mercy. And thank You that in Your time, You will bring beauty from ashes. In Jesus' name, amen.

"You shall dwell in the land of Goshen,

and you shall be near to me, you and your

children, your children's children, your flocks

and your herds, and all that you have.

"There I will provide for you...."

GENESIS 45:10,11

CHAPTER 14

Restoration: Taking Back Territory

"I will restore to you the years that the...locust has eaten....
And it shall come to pass afterward that I will pour out My Spirit
on all flesh; your sons and your daughters shall prophesy, your
old men shall dream dreams, your young men shall see visions."

JOEL 2:25,28

When I think of Joseph's brothers, now forgiven, hearing of the provision made for them in Goshen—a place of plenty, "the best of the land"[1]—I can only wonder what they must have been thinking. *Do you suppose Joseph is going to kill us at sunrise?* they might have asked one another. *Maybe he will invite us to a feast and poison our food!* They're so horribly guilty, and they know it. Yet, instead of the death they deserve, they are receiving life in the lap of luxury! It must have seemed too good to be true.

Is this not the very picture of God's gracious redemption and restoration? We stand before Him, as guilty as can be, and we're offered life—in the high-rent district! Or, just when we think it's all over, He takes us beyond our wildest dreams to a place of fulfillment that only gets better as we learn to lean on Him. Let me remind you that nothing is impossible with God, dear one. He is capable of fully restoring you and enabling you to reclaim your dream.

There are some things you need to know about restoration. The word *restore,* in Webster's dictionary, means "to bring back or return to a former or original state."[2] In other words, the craftsman takes what is there and reworks it to its greatest potential. I am reminded of a process used in restoring fine antiques to their former brilliance, called French polishing. An abrasive agent and a cloth are used to rub and rub, in a swirling, rounded motion, until the dull finish is removed and the piece, with application of stains and wax, is transformed to a gleaming patina. In a sense, that is what God does with lives dulled by sin. He "roughs" us up a bit through adversity, applies the stain of His Son's blood to cover our flaws, then polishes us to a high luster to reflect His image.

Another form of restoration is brought about by the application of heat. One of my hobbies is observing people under pressure, the ones who are in hot water. You see the true essence of character when the heat is turned up!

Our friend Terre, who has been helping us mine for gold in the Scriptures during this project, once worked as a metallurgical lab assistant with the Federal Bureau of Mines. Day by day, in the pilot plant where he worked, he ran experiments and watched as men in asbestos suits heated iron ore to a high temperature so that the impurities could rise to the surface and be skimmed off. This is also the process used for refining precious metals— silver and gold—as well as the symbol used in the Bible for bringing God's people to a restored state with Him. "For You, O God, have tested us; You have refined us as silver is refined. You brought us into the net; You laid affliction on our backs...we went through fire and through water; but You brought us out to rich fulfillment" (Ps. 66:10-12).

Did you notice the end result of all that refining and restoring? "Rich fulfillment." Or, as the *King James Version* translates: "wealthy place." The Hebrew word for wealthy, *ravayh,* means "satisfaction:—runneth over," as in Psalm 23:5 that says, "...my cup runs over."[3] God brings us through the painful process of refining and restoration into a place of such supreme abundance that we can't even contain it!

In the *Spirit-Filled Life Bible,* James Robison comments, "When something is restored... it is always increased, multiplied or improved so that its latter state is significantly better than its original state.... For example, under the Law of Moses, if someone stole an ox or a sheep, it was not sufficient for him simply to restore the animal he had taken. He had to pay back five oxen or four sheep (Ex. 22:1). When God restored Job after the terrible trials he endured, He gave him twice what he had lost and blessed him more in his latter days than in the beginning (Job 42:10-12).... God multiplies when He restores...."[4]

Will you take time to look with me at some precious promises? These words of life should motivate and inspire you to press through any trials you may be experiencing right now.

He Restores Your Soul
(Psalm 23:3)

How precious of God, when in the very process of creating you, He "...breathed into [your] nostrils the breath of life; and [you] became a living being [soul]" (Gen. 2:7). What an intimate moment—the Lord getting right in your face and blowing His own breath into you! And that which He creates, He can restore—by the same process!

How often we need the breath of God—*ruwach* in the Hebrew, meaning the Holy Spirit[5]—to come and powerfully blow away the cobwebs and stir the downcast heart, to walk with us "...beside the still waters" and to make us "...lie down in green pastures..." (Ps. 23:2).

The word *soul* implies the mind, will, and emotions. Here is the storehouse of memory, thought, and heart attitudes. You may need healing of your memories. You may need to change your mind. You may need a heart transplant. But if you are weary or wounded, you definitely need to be refreshed, to be healed.

Sometimes, however, the wounds go very deep.

During a particularly trying time in my friend Audra's life, it seemed that everything was conspiring against her. The loving church that had nurtured her for the past fifteen years took a dramatic turn, and the pastors started to make unreasonable demands of those in leadership. As Audra resisted, knowing this was not God's way, her children, who were attending the church school, showed symptoms of stress and began to "get into trouble." At one point, an insider informed Audra that her young daughter was being held in a storage area like a caged animal and was being harassed by two teachers, under orders by the pastors. Of course, my friend rushed to the rescue.

As this kind of outrageous treatment continued, Audra, although unskilled in such things, began to suspect witchcraft. Each day was worse than the day before, and soon she was at her wit's end. Nor could her unsaved husband offer any real support.

Having managed to break away from the nightmare for a few days, Audra and her husband and children set out on a trip to Washington, D.C. On the way up, they stopped off at Virginia Beach, site of Pat Robertson's CBN ministry. There in the lovely inn, she felt such liberty. She didn't have to report to anyone where she was going or what she was doing with her time. At lunch, the food was exquisite, and the peaceful surroundings were enhanced by the music of a pianist, playing hymns of faith.

Later, still in their street clothes, the family visited the beach. While Audra's husband took the children to explore a nearby jetty, she paused along the seashore, gazing out over the vast, endless ocean where heaven met earth. There was no one else around at the moment. Small boats dotted the horizon like a child's toys strewn carelessly across the surface of the water. Framing the picture was a stone wall jutting out from the shoreline. *Thank You, Lord, for the privilege of standing here where our forefathers landed,* she prayed, her prayer pouring out of a grateful heart. *Thank You for the gulf they spanned to bring us our freedom.*

She closed her eyes, inhaling the sea breeze and allowing the healing beauty of the moment to wash over her. Suddenly, without explanation, she sensed the tangible Presence of the Lord. Afraid to open her eyes, she felt Him approaching and began to tremble. Then, peeking from beneath her sunglasses, she "saw" inexpressible light—the glory of God—descending around her, enveloping her like a cocoon! She began to cry.

Don't be afraid. You are Mine...you are Mine, she heard the Lord say gently and with great compassion.

"I love You, Lord, but I don't understand." Still shaken, she couldn't help but be concerned for her unsaved husband and children. "Lord, what about Stephen? What about the children?"

This is not about them, Audra. This is about you.

"Then I heard Him speak again: *Job 23.* Immediately, gushing from my own spirit came the words, *Many waters cannot quench love, nor can the floods drown it.* I had not memorized that verse from Scripture (Song 8:7)," she insists. "It just popped into my mind, verbatim." But in that setting, seeing the vast expanse of ocean waters before her, those words were a healing balm.

"Then just as quickly as the Presence came, He left. I couldn't wait to get back to the van and look up the passage in Job. It read in part: 'He knows the way that I take; when He has tested me, I shall come forth as gold' (v. 10). There was much, much more, and I found out that I would need every bit of it in the next few months as I attempted to break free of that apostate church's satanic domination and control. But it took a visitation on the beach, the Shekinah glory of God, to bring me through, healed and whole.

"My husband is now saved. Our family is intact, no longer oppressed or cowering in fear. We are worshiping in a church in another state, and there is no power left in the witchcraft prayers prayed against us. Nine years after we moved from that church and state, we learned of the death of one of the pastors who had attacked us so viciously. My daughter, who, at age eleven, had suffered such horrible treatment from this pastor, said, 'Mom, I hope she repented before she died.' There was no trace of hatred, not even a hint of the desire for vengeance in my daughter. Only God could accomplish such complete healing in my child's soul!"

Praise God! He restores our souls.

He Restores Your Dwelling Place (Isaiah 58:12)

I have just had a long, lazy conversation with my friend Lizanne. She has a way, even on the telephone, of welcoming you into her heart—as if you were sitting on the plump cushions of one of the rocking chairs on her front porch, sipping a frosty glass of peach tea!

When we started talking about reclaiming the dream, she reminded me that God is the original Recycler and that she can look back from the vantage point of her years—six decades—and see the threads that have been woven together to produce the tapestry of her life. "And we know that all things work together for good to those who love God, to those who are the called according to His purpose" (Rom. 8:28). She can now see God's purpose more clearly. Even in the pit and the prison times, she could take hope because

"Through the Lord's mercies we are not consumed, because his compassions fail not. They are new every morning..." (Lam. 3:22,23). These verses, filtered through the lens of Lizanne's seasoned perspective, have taken on new meaning.

"I see three parts to my life," she says in that soft, Southern, ladylike voice. "There were the early days when my dad was in the Navy, and we moved every two years. There was midlife, with marriage and children and the need to pursue a career. And there are these golden years, when God has redeemed and restored the whole thing.

"Among my earliest memories was the time spent in my mother's home-town where things remained constant and secure. A dear couple, friends of hers, always made me feel so at home. I can see them now sitting in their rocking chairs on the front porch. Ever since, I've had a special place in my heart for rockers and porches. Maybe it was also because this couple always seemed to have all the time in the world for me—as if I were the most impor-tant person around.

"Later in life, after I received my education and married, whenever I thought of a job, social work topped the list. And so, while my children were young and my physician husband was busy with his practice, I volunteered in areas I enjoyed, including work with the elderly, children with mental retardation, and vocational guidance and foster care.

"A third interest was mountains. They held a special appeal for their beauty and their spiritual connection—one feels closer to God in the moun-tains, I think. And then there were all those Christian conferences I attended in the heart of the Smokies. My dream was to live there one day, preferably in a cabin tucked among the hills.

"But with all my dreaming, like Joseph, I encountered my share of pits and prison time. There was my daughter's hit-and-run accident in which she was seriously injured, but recovered. And then my husband Denny's heart attack at forty-seven. He was on disability for a time and was rarely without pain for the next seventeen years. These were times when God taught me lessons I might never have learned otherwise.

"For one thing, I learned about His provision. At forty, when I had to go to work after my husband's insurance plan dropped him, I found that every bit of the volunteer hours I had put in translated into college credit that would qualify me as a social worker! After securing my credentials, the job offered was locating and approving families for the adoption of children with mental retardation—only God!

"After Denny's death, I was sure I would move to the mountains—probably around Montreat where I had attended all those Christian conferences—but nothing seemed to work out. Then I met and married Bill. Bill lived in a neighboring county, and there were so many similarities in our backgrounds that I knew we were meant for each other. Guess what God provided this time? A 189-year-old log cabin, complete with a huge front porch, overlooking a lovely vista of forests and peaceful pasturelands!

"When we find ourselves in the pit, we can look up and see that God is at work, restoring and repairing. On second thought, He does much more than simply patch up our dream. He gives us a brand-new one. He gives us "...a future and a hope" (Jer. 29:11). He creates, then He re-creates.

"I have an Oriental lamp that needs some work, but when I took it to the shop recently to get an estimate on the cost, it was way too high. What I need requires restoring from the inside out. God takes our dream far beyond anything we could ask or think! I believe He works in mysterious and 'mischievous' ways, continuing to weave the intricate pattern of our lives, delighting in surprising us along the way. Someday we'll see the whole thing—the colors, the design, the dark moments, and the light. What a creative God!"

Lizanne has her dream home—the dream that dates back to her childhood—one that represents security, stability, and peace. There she communes with the Father from whom she draws her strength, and sits with friends on her porch, listening to their burdens and laughing in moments of delight.

That is your inheritance as well—to reclaim all that the Lord has planned for you. You, too, can be in the restoration business, proclaiming the goodness of God to your children and grandchildren, reminding them that He is working even when it appears everything has ground to a halt. He has promised to "...raise up the foundations of many generations; and you shall be called the Repairer of the Breach, the Restorer of Streets to Dwell In" (Isa. 58:12).

He Restores Your Joy
(Psalm 51:12)

I'm absolutely positive that God has a sense of humor! I can see it in so many situations and personalities and creatures. Just look at a mother opossum hanging upside down from a tree limb, her babies lined up all in a row beside her, or the giraffe with its too-long neck and its big brown eyes with those lush, sweeping lashes. I believe God also loves a good joke and even sometimes playfully tricks us with whimsical surprises. What about the fish with a coin in its mouth—just enough to pay one man's taxes? (Matt. 17:27.)

My darling friend Cathy has a story that runs the gamut from tragedy to comedy and back again. Unlike most young girls, she never wanted to be married. For one thing, as she describes it: "There was never enough love in our house to make it a home. There was no money, no parenting skills, no hope. Even though I loved life on the farm, my parents were always sick and, as the oldest child, I had to assume the parental role much too young. So the minute I could find a good excuse to escape, I did!

"I decided that since I wouldn't have a husband to support me, I'd better prepare to support myself. I went to school, worked hard for a master's degree in Christian education, then landed a wonderful job in a large church in Atlanta. Country girl in the big city! It was a great time. I thought I had it made."

Cathy paused. "Know how to make God laugh?" she asked. "Tell Him your plans."

By the time I had finished chuckling, she continued, "Remember what I said about marriage? Well, there was this minister on staff who was single at the time. We worked together and eventually we began seeing each other outside of office hours—just casually, at first. As our feelings grew stronger, I was ready to run in the opposite direction. Marriage was not in my plan. But apparently it was in God's.

"After we married in April of '86, we started our home—the home with all the love I had never known. Then on our fourth wedding anniversary, we found ourselves in the ICU of St. Joseph's Hospital, waiting for a new heart for my husband. Jerry had had a virus that attacked the heart muscle, and now he desperately needed a transplant. What was all this about? I was the one who hated pain and sickness and had never had a loving family. Now I had found the love of my life, and I might lose him to a baffling, freak illness! How could God do this to me?

"Jerry got his new heart, and several weeks later he was back in the pulpit. One day I even found him on the roof, cleaning out the leaves in our gutter! For 20 months we lived the good life. Then disaster struck again. His body violently rejected the heart. Now I had lost my husband, my best friend, and the only family I had ever known. I was a widow at 35, and I curled up in a fetal position and wanted to die myself.

"On one of those days when I was inconsolable, God reminded me of a rather unusual situation back on the farm. We had raised animals in those days—pigs, chickens, anything we could feed until they could feed us. Since we got our slop for the pigs from a restaurant in town, we usually found pieces of silver—knives, forks, spoons—in the bottom of the waste container, where the busboys had carelessly swept the utensils in with the crumbs. By the end of one summer, we had collected a place setting for eight, complete with serving pieces! Mother boiled them on the stove in bleach, and we used them on our table—much finer silver than we could ever have afforded. Silver in the slop!

"It suddenly occurred to me that I might never be able to answer the 'Why' questions: *Why did I have to grow up in a home without love? Why did Jerry have to die so young?* But I could answer the 'How' questions: *How am I going to get through this? How will I grow and learn? How can I help others out of their pits?* Everyone can find silver in the slop!"

Cathy never dreamed of a speaking and writing career. But her first book, *Silver in the Slop,* touched a nerve with thousands of readers, and she was soon in demand as a speaker. She is now writing her third book. Out of the depths of her own pit of despair and her prison of loneliness has come a ministry far greater than anything she could have imagined. God has brought her to a "wealthy place" of "rich fulfillment."

"I can't change the facts," Cathy says. "I can't bring Jerry back, but he didn't ask me to go with him, and I have things to do here. I have territory to reclaim. As Jesus said, '...In the world you will have tribulation; but be of good cheer, I have overcome the world' (John 16:33). I'm going to stick with His idea, His dream for my life. 'Silver in the slop can always be found if we have the patience to wait, to watch, and to recognize God at work in each moment of our lives. Remembering this, I rest in the assurance that God's blessings, sparkling and eternal, dwell in the loneliest night, the coldest winter, and the deepest distress.'"[6]

He Restores the Years the Locust Has Eaten (Joel 2:25)

Cathy is not the only one who grew up on a farm—so did I. I know what happens when the boll weevils get into the cotton or worms infest the corn. These garden pests devastate the crops. They devour them right down to the ground. They destroy them. Replanting those crops—restoring them—can take many seasons. But how beautiful when the cotton bolls are snowy white and full again, and the ears of corn are plump and ripe, promising a plentiful harvest.

Those years of famine in Egypt would have been disastrous had Joseph not been enabled by God to interpret Pharaoh's dream correctly. And now the prophesied seven years of plenty have come and gone, and the grain reservoirs are well stocked to provide for all who have need in Egypt or anywhere else in the then-known world. That's why we see Joseph's family from Canaan settling in Goshen, a fertile area in the northeastern Nile Delta of Egypt, approximately 900 square miles in size, truly the best acreage in the land of Egypt.[7] There they will be "near to me.... There I will provide for you," Joseph assured them.

Don't you know they must have been relieved? They would not die in the famine, but would live and prosper! In fact, later they would become so strong and numerous that the "children of Jacob—Israel" would pose a serious political threat to Egypt. But for now all is well, and everyone is happy.

That is exactly how I felt when God began to restore me from the pits and prisons of my life. I felt free, alive, able to breathe again, to live again. Even the air smelled different. God promises that in those areas that are most devastated you will be most healed—and most greatly used. In fact, note where the enemy strikes you hardest—and that will be your area of ministry.

My younger daughter, Margo, discovered that truth for herself during a divorce when she felt stripped of self-worth and grabbed for the last shred of hope. But I'll let her tell her story in her own words.

Margo's Story

"Okay, I'll admit it. I was always a shy person—so shy that when I was little, my sister would order my hamburgers at the fast-food restaurants. In fact, in the earlier years, she practically made all my decisions for me. She was the leader and I let her lead. She'd jump right in and fix things—big sister to the rescue. That is, until my divorce. I know she wanted to fix that, too, but it was one thing she couldn't fix.

"After struggling to pick up the pieces, I literally shut down. Every ounce of me was stripped down to the lowest form. I had always been artistically talented, but during this time I lost all creativity, all motivation to succeed. It was hard for me to see that God could, in any way, shape, or form, have any purpose for me. I was blinded and paralyzed with fear, gasping for air from reoccurring anxiety attacks. I felt so alone in this fight for my life.

"It wasn't that I didn't know the Lord. I come from a very loving Christian family, of course. But at this point I was running from Him and trying to take control of my own life—the control others had always had over me. That's when I started going to counseling and found a place where I could freely speak my mind. The world began to open up for me.

"After a few visits to the counselor, he looked at me and asked if he could be real honest with me. Of course, I said yes. He then looked me straight in the eye and said, 'Your problem, Margo, is that until you change you, it will be the same situation, just a different guy—the old revolving door.' I knew he was right, and I knew I had to do something about it. I had kept searching for some man who could make me happy, but no one measured up to the 'white knight' I was looking for.

"Another issue was my gifting in design. As the daughter of Ann Platz, one of the foremost interior designers in the Southeast, I was always terrified that people would expect me to be like my mother, and I knew I could never live up to her reputation.

"Actually, I loved going with her to book signings and speeches, where I saw the way her books and messages changed lives. I'd sit at the table with her and look into the faces of real people and know that what they were saying was straight from their hearts, terrible experiences, things you would never have expected just from looking at the outside. They probably thought that I didn't have a care in the world. If they'd only known.

"But in the last three years, I've sold out to the Lord. I prayed, 'Lord, take me, all of me, and use me for whatever You have for me.' And He has moved with favor right and left in my life and shown me His dream.

"The first real sign I was on His track and not mine was when I was asked to do a television special for HGTV (Home & Garden Television) that didn't involve Mom! It was my first time on TV, a huge project to undertake for a person who, in my own eyes, had no credibility and no self-confidence. When the producer called to tell me she wanted me to fly down to Jacksonville, Florida, to be on the show, unlike the old Margo, I didn't give her fifty reasons why I couldn't do it. I just jumped in. Here I was, actually tackling a TV special entitled 'Living With Color,' without riding on my mother's coattails! I could hardly believe everything that was happening!

"I knew that God had provided this opportunity for me. It was a dream job. I was to take a porch area and decorate it two different ways, using color. I was given three sources—Stein Mart, Pier I, and Pottery Barn—and allowed to borrow any accessory I needed. People just came out of the wood-work to help and encourage me. I learned that God can move in ways we cannot even imagine. His signature was all over that project. When you come out of your comfort zone into His plan, you go beyond your wildest dreams—from black and white to living color!"

As Margo's mother, recalling this triumph brings tears to my eyes. I can remember the time I got on my face before the Lord, wailing and pleading with Him to bring my daughter back to Atlanta, where we had an apartment in our new home, complete with kitchen and separate entrance. Don't tell me this was a coincidence!

I reminded the Lord that I had laid down my life for Him years before and promised to go wherever He sent me—into the inner city, to the prostitutes and drug addicts, anywhere—and that I hadn't asked Him for a favor before. But this was my Margo—she needed to be "near," where we could encourage and support her during this awful time, where she could be healed. Three days later, she picked up the phone in South Carolina, called me, and asked, "Mom, can I come home?" Praise the Lord! What a mighty God we serve!

Margo has since remarried. Nelson, whom you met earlier in this book, is the answer to all our prayers—a wonderful, godly young man who loves Margo for who she is. He affirms and encourages her and is the partner of her heart. They are on the brink of so much that is straight from the heart of God that it will make every girlhood dream Margo ever had pale into insignificance! As her mother, I can only thank God for being such a good Father and for sending John Platz to be her earthly dad.

Wherever you are in your life, whatever pit or prison you find yourself in, God is saying, "Come near to Me...I will provide for you."

He Restores a Hundredfold (Mark 10:29,30)

I have always been fascinated by the numbers recorded in the Bible and the fact that some are of greater significance than others—one, three, seven, twelve, one hundred. Just a quick search through Strong's concordance and a Bible dictionary yields some valuable insights. For example, the number seven—"a sacred number to the ancient Hebrew people...is often used in the Bible to symbolize perfection, fullness, abundance, rest, and completion...."[8]

It was also interesting to me to be reminded that God created all things in six days and rested on the seventh (Gen. 2:2,3); that this number held ritual importance in early Hebrew feasts and observances; that it plays a prominent part in many visions and dreams—Pharaoh's dreams of the seven fat cows and the seven lean ones, symbolizing the seven years of plenty and the seven years of famine, as well as the seven sheaves of grain. (Gen. 41:1-36.) And then there are the seven loaves and a few fish that Jesus multiplied to feed the multitude in Matthew 15, and the "seven last words of Christ" on the cross (found in each of the four gospels). You get the idea.

Apparently, this word *seven,* found in hundreds of passages in the Bible, most often has to do with what is expected *of* us—to restore abundantly when we wrong someone (Prov. 6:31), to forgive "seventy times seven" (Matt.

18:22), to show great honor for others, such as the seven days of mourning for Joseph's father when he died. (Gen. 50:10.)

We are limited in what we can do, but God is unlimited. The greater number, one hundred or hundredfold, seems to refer to what *He* is going to do for us. "Isaac [Joseph's great-grandfather] sowed in that land, and reaped in the same year *a hundredfold;* and the Lord blessed him" (Gen. 26:12). Isaac reaped a hundred times more than he had planted—but not because he was such a great farmer. It was the blessing of God. The favor of God was with Isaac as it was later with his grandson Joseph.

Now skip over to the New Testament: "Jesus answered and said, 'Assuredly, I say to you, there is no one who has left houses or brothers or sisters or father or mother or wife or children or lands, for My sake and the gospel's, who shall not receive a hundredfold now in this time—houses and brothers and sisters and mothers and children and lands, with persecutions—and in the age to come, eternal life'" (Mark 10:29,30). Our reward will be a hundred times more than anything we invest in the kingdom of God!

Take my new friend Jodi, for example, who has tested this truth and found it more precious than gold. Jodi and her husband both aspired to be astronauts before they married. Dave graduated from the Naval Academy and served in the Pentagon, and Jodi did research in the field of muscle physiology and the effects of weightlessness. But God had a different dream—a greater one, which He is still unfolding.

After marriage, the babies began to come quickly—one, two, three, four, five, six, *seven* blessings—and Jodi found herself consumed with organizing her inner space, caring for the precious little lives in her home. She home schools, devours the Word of God daily, and runs marathons. But there is still an active interest in space exploration. So much so that her husband gave her tickets to a shuttle launch for their eleventh wedding anniversary.

"Giving up my dreams to pursue a career in space exploration has been agonizingly difficult," she confesses. "There have been times I couldn't even watch a launch on TV or hear about various NASA projects because of the ache in my heart. So I wasn't too thrilled about the idea of seeing this launch in person. Still, when it worked out for the entire family to fly down in March of 2002, I decided it might be bearable. Especially when we were given access to the location usually reserved only for the families of participating astronauts.

"I wasn't expecting to feel or experience all that I did that day. And I had no idea how that experience would reach out and touch the entire NASA family at a later date. You see, that launch would be the last time anyone would ever see Columbia lift off, because in February of 2003, the shuttle broke apart upon re-entry. I used what the Lord showed me in March the year before to comfort the grieving families."

The following is a portion of a letter Jodi and Dave wrote expressing their sympathy and sharing their own personal faith:

February, 2003

Attending that launch was a dream come true for both of us, and its effect left us speechless and emotionally shaken for several hours afterward. ...We had wondered if it would be painful to watch when we so wanted to be a part of that moment. What we share now is an entry Jodi made in her journal.

"What I saw was something I never anticipated seeing—the glory of God in the most meager form of man's creativity. At liftoff, as the darkness turned to day in a brilliant glow more radiant than the most spectacular sunrise, and as Columbia was momentarily hidden in the clouds, the bright rays of fire and gas emanating from behind the cloud cover almost sent me to my knees. A thunderous roar shook the earth on which we were standing. What I was privileged to see was not just man's greatest technology, but rather a small taste of what it will one day be to stand in the Presence of our risen Lord. For one brief moment we saw His glory in tangible form."

May God be with you in these difficult days, and may your children take comfort in knowing how truly grateful a nation is for their precious sacrifice.

—Dave and Jodi Quint

This letter was sent to the flight director and the flight manager for the Columbia launch, as well as families of the fallen astronauts. Both NASA officials responded with personal notes. Jodi was awestruck! She has shared with us not for personal glory, but in amazement at how God has used her in ways far different—and greater—than she could have imagined. "How I longed to be part of the NASA family," she told me, "but it was not to be done my way. How faithful still is the God I serve that He would allow me to 'give life' to this organization in their time of need and crisis. How amazing the power and provision of a God who cares for His people."

I see Jodi being launched into the spiritual stratosphere as she "gives life" to her children, their children, and all the spiritual daughters who will come under her care. The story has not been fully told. There is more, much more for this woman of God with "stars" in her eyes. Her reach for the kingdom will be magnified a hundredfold!

Prayer for Restoration: Father of love and grace and beauty, Restorer of my dreams, thank You for loving me, taking me back, and restoring the years the locust has eaten. The pathway to You is timeless and proven. Thank You for the dream that originated in Your heart for me. Thank You for the resurrection power and the restoration power that renew my mind and rebuild my character. Continue to guide me, lead me, and steer me by Your Star directly to the door of Your home. In the priceless name of Jesus, amen.

"...Do not be afraid, for am I in the place of God?

"As for you, you meant evil against me; but God

meant it for good, in order to bring it about as

it is this day, to save many people alive."

GENESIS 50:19,20

CHAPTER 15

God Meant It for Good

"We know that all things work together for good to those who love God, to those who are the called according to His purpose."

ROMANS 8:28

Now we're getting to the good part—the part of Joseph's story where he takes off his mask, reveals himself to his absolutely horrible brothers, and they will finally "get what's coming to them." Isn't that what we've been waiting for? Justification at last! The payoff, the time when Joseph will at last be vindicated for all the years of false imprisonment, rejection, and abandonment.

But we have a plot twist. Joseph doesn't follow our script. He steps out of "character" and acts in just the opposite manner of what might be expected in this scenario. Now that their father Jacob (Israel) has died, the brothers are terrified that Joseph will wreak vengeance on them, after all, and they fall face down before him and beg forgiveness once again. Strangely enough, he doesn't retaliate. "...He comforted them and spoke kindly to them," offering his protection (Gen. 50:21). "...you meant evil against me; but God meant it for good..." (v. 20). Joseph got the big picture. He could see with eternal eyes.

Where are you in your journey, dear one? Have you come far enough to be able to look back and view your life from a different perspective than when you began? Have you observed God's hand in both poverty and plenty, whether physically, emotionally, or spiritually? Can you begin to detect a pattern emerging from the dark stains of your deepest sorrows, the muted tones of hope deferred, and the joyful splashes of faith, love, and anticipation? Will you now believe that God has meant all things for your good all along?

I have pondered and prayed over the New Testament Scripture for this chapter. The Romans 8:28 verse—words that are almost too familiar to be fresh and new—"...all things work together for *good....*" Just what is *good?* Does *good* mean happiness, satisfaction, winning the lottery, having all of your dreams come true? Or is there much, much more?

A precious friend sent me a quote from a devotional reading for the day that so captures my heart and brings life to this verse that I simply must share it with you:

Remember and be thankful.... Good does not mean pleasure.... Bright-being may not always be well-being, and the highest good has a very much nobler meaning than comfort and satisfaction. And so, realizing the fact that the best of things is that they shall make us like God, then we can turn to the past and judge it wisely, because then we shall see that all the diversity, and even the opposition, of circumstances and events, may cooperate towards the same end.... So the moments in my life which I call blessings and gladness, and the moments in my life which I call sorrows and tortures, may work into each other, and they will do so if I take hold of them rightly, and use them as they ought to be used....

In our lives it is good for us, sometimes, that we be brought into dark places; it is good for us sometimes that the leaves be stripped from the trees, and the ground be bound with frost.... It is good for us to be drawn, or to be driven, to Him; it is good for us to have to tread even a lonely path if it makes us lean more on the arm of our Beloved.... And for the present let us try to remember that He dwelleth in the darkness as in the light, and that we are to be thankful for the things that help us to be near Him, and not for the things that make us outwardly glad.[1]

Joseph knew all about being "stripped" and "bound" and "lonely." He knew about the darkness and the silences of God, when it didn't appear that anything "good" was happening. Most of us would have been thinking, *Where is the payday? When are things going to "turn out right"? Where is God?*

Sometimes we can't judge something until it is behind us. We can't know the joy that comes in the morning until we have passed through the dark night. Only in retrospect can we look in the rear view mirror and see the amazing hand of God in it all. That's when we cry, "Holy, holy, holy! He was with me all the time!"

Eternity Thinking

Good is a powerful word, a life-changing concept if we can just wrap our finite little minds around it. In fact, I believe we have to put on the mind of Christ and use eternity thinking. One Hebrew word for good, *towb,* is translated "beautiful, best, better, bountiful, cheerful, at ease...fair...joyful... pleasant...precious, prosperity...sweet, wealth."[2] *Good* is all the things we ever dreamed of—and more. Incorporated into that one word is the best of the best!

In our culture we strive for success. In the striving there is often anxiety, workaholism, stress, unhealthy competition, and ulcers! We have distorted the work ethic to become a "works" ethic in order to achieve the good life. We do "our best," seemingly unaware that God is sufficient. *Our* effort, *our* strength, *our* sweat, *our* achievement—with all that focus on self, we fall into the pit of idolatry! If we have God, we already have good. God is the essence of good. He doesn't do anything but good. God *is* good. And it doesn't get any "gooder" than that!

On the other hand, this society has dumbed down the word. We have so corrupted the meaning that we no longer know what is good. Some people even use the word *bad* to mean *good.* Look at Michael Jackson's best-selling pop album entitled "Bad." It is cool to be "bad." What confusion! Well, "God is not the author of confusion..." (1 Cor. 14:33). The Bible clearly warns, "Do not be overcome by evil (bad), but overcome evil with good" (Rom. 12:21). It is time we took back the territory of language, say what we mean, and mean what we say!

My sweet friend Rachel is just coming into a more complete understanding of how God has brought good from the bad circumstances of her life. She was born into a prominent Louisiana family, who successfully farmed the land for generations and were good stewards of God's blessings. Theirs was the portrait of Old South gentility—the matriarch and patriarch, a beautiful couple, reserved and aristocratic; the children, taught to keep their business to themselves, never to air their dirty laundry, and to smile...no matter what.

Gradually, the portrait of the "perfect" family began to crumble and crack. Rachel and her older sister did their best to smile when their wonderful, loving father began to change. She says that as a child, "My life was upside down at the age of six." Rachel smiled through his alcoholic rages. She smiled through the adjustments that had to be made when her mother was paralyzed after spinal surgery. She smiled when there was absolutely nothing to smile about. She smiled—until she could no longer fake it.

At eighteen, Rachel was a nervous wreck. Tranquilizers only made her feel disoriented. Counseling offered little more than a Band-Aid. She had attended church as a child, but while in college, she did what many college students do—she dropped out and slept late. Besides, she had followed instructions in the Bible and "knocked" (Matt. 7:7), but she felt that nobody had answered. She hadn't a clue where God was. As far as she could tell, He had a big flyswatter and was out to get her. It was all she could do to survive.

By this time her father was seeing someone else and eventually divorced her mother to marry the other woman. Right after her college graduation, with Rachel's little Toyota loaded to the hilt with everything she would need to start a new life in South Carolina, the last thing she told her sister through her tears was, "If Daddy kills himself, don't call me." Ten days later, after she had made the move, he did exactly that.

After his death, there were good days and bad for Rachel. When she found that she was having trouble in the grief process over losing her father, the minister of the church she was attending in South Carolina introduced her to another Anne (with an "e"!), a Christian education staff member. "She was the cutest redhead you'd ever want to see—and the first mature Christian I had ever met who wasn't a 'nerd'," in Rachel's words.

Her faith grew in quantum leaps as Anne discipled Rachel every Wednesday morning for weeks. It was during the morning Bible study sessions that Rachel was introduced to a life-changing verse: "Trust in the Lord with all your heart and lean not on your own understanding; in all your ways acknowledge Him, and He will make your paths straight" (Prov. 3:5 NIV). Rachel promised the Lord that she would trust Him and "if You will straighten my path and fix my crazy, chaotic life, I'll praise You for the rest of my life...but make it snappy!"

But it didn't happen overnight. There was one setback after another, the next being a diagnosis of bipolar disorder, with its wild mood swings, the same illness my daughter Courtney had. No longer able to function on her own, Rachel moved back to Louisiana to live with her mother. Two nervous breakdowns and a suicide attempt later, she came to the end of herself.

Along with the Good News of Jesus Christ that Rachel had learned from Anne was some good seed, hidden down deep in her spirit and just waiting to spring forth. Her godly grandmother, who had often kept Rachel and her sister during those early volatile years, had planted the Word of God in her heart. She clung to one verse, repeating it over and over: "I can do all things through Christ who strengthens me" (Phil. 4:13).

And there was her mother's example, her strong, longsuffering mother. A woman who, though abandoned by her husband and ill, woke up singing every morning.

"How do you do it, Mamma?" Rachel asked one day after moving back home to live with her mother in Louisiana. "How do you keep going? How can you stand it after all Daddy and I put you through?"

"You just do, Rachel. You have faith in the Lord, you forgive, and you go on, knowing it's going to be all right."

And it has been "all right." God led Rachel to a "cut-to-the-chase, no psychobabble kind of counselor," who proceeded to help Rachel understand why she had been terrified to trust God, fearing that, like her earthly father, He would disappoint her or "swat" her! Without this groundwork, Anne's rock-solid Christian guidance earlier, and the lifeline of God's living Word, Rachel would not have been prepared to handle her mother's unexpected death a few months later, after the "loveliest Thanksgiving we had experienced together in years."

Oh, there is more. "That verse I've always clung to? The Lord has truly strengthened me, and I'm growing stronger every day in Him. I can look back and see that everything that has ever happened to me is being used for good. My wonderful husband loves me like I've never been loved before. Our town has opened a domestic abuse shelter, named in memory of my mother, and last but not least—my secret ambition to write a book is being realized. I am co-writing a book on Southern customs with Ann Platz! My name will be on the cover along with hers. Now that is truly *good*—and another answer to years of prayer!"

Rachel has learned that all the *bad* things she experienced in those early days have been transformed to *good* by the power of the Lord who lives in her. Let me offer Rachel another verse to tuck away for a rainy day: "He has shown you, O man [you insert your name here], what is good; and what does the Lord require of you but to do justly, to love mercy, and to walk humbly with your God?" (Mic. 6:8). A perfect definition of good—justice, mercy, and humility.

When Your Name Is Cleared

Joseph was never memorialized with a building named for him. Nor did he write a book. Yet his sterling character stands as an example of all that is just, merciful, and humble. He was a good man.

But he was a man with a criminal record. He served several years in Pharaoh's prison. For that reason, his name had to be cleared before he could proceed with the calling of God on his life, before he could move into his ultimate destiny as the "savior" of a nation—a forerunner of Jesus Christ.

Earlier, when Joseph interpreted Pharaoh's dreams, Pharaoh himself cleared Joseph's name by placing the royal robe on him, giving him the official signet ring, and hanging the gold pendant around his neck. At that time Joseph also received a new name—Zaphnath-Paaneah—which, as we have seen, means "God Speaks and He Lives." But here is an interesting twist—an Egyptian name with an acknowledgment of the Hebrew God. Every time Pharaoh summoned Joseph, he was "bowing" to Joseph's God. Every time he used Joseph's Egyptian name in the presence of his advisors, his family, his servants, his officers, and any visitors to the court, Pharaoh was acknowledging that Joseph's God speaks and He lives. None of Egypt's pagan deities could speak. None of them were alive, only Joseph's God, the only true and living God. Hallelujah!

No matter where you have been or what you have done or failed to do, there is grace for you, too. If you know the Lord, your slate is clean, and you stand before Him, pardoned, forgiven, cleared of all charges, and given a new name.

He knows your name. Your name is significant to God. Being omniscient, "all-knowing," He knows you. He knows your past, present, and future. He knew about you from the foundations of the world. He knew when you would be born, your family pedigree, your hopes and dreams, your failures and flaws, and how you would walk into your destiny. He knows what you are doing and what you are thinking right this very minute. He also knows how your story will end. He is pulling for you to do *good*. No, that is not a grammatical error. He created you for good works that by them, you may glorify God. (1 Pet. 2:12; Titus 3:8.) This is part of the dream He has dreamed for you, and this is where I hope you are headed.

He has written your name in the Book of Life. As a believer, your name is written in the Lamb's Book of Life—God's eternal record of the redeemed. (Rev. 13:8; 17:8; 20:12,15; Ex. 32:32; Ps. 69:28; Mal. 3:16.) Not only that, but you are inscribed on the palms of God's hands! (Isa. 49:16.) This is your assurance that He will never forget you. Have you ever scribbled a telephone number on your hand when you didn't have a piece of paper handy or a note to remind you of an important point in a speech? I even recall a young lady who wrote down the directions to someone's house on the back of her hand, and another who used her palm as a calendar to record the date of an appointment! We've all done things like that.

But when I think of Jesus' nail-scarred hands and all our names recorded there, I could cry. This reminder of what He has done for us is sufficient evidence of His unconditional love and willing sacrifice. He has promised never to leave us and never to forget us.

He changes your name. With the clearing of all charges comes a new name. We have already seen how names in the Bible were used to signify some significant character trait. For example, Joseph's father, Jacob's, name meant "supplanter"[3] or deceiver. Jacob was true to his name and spent a good portion of his life deceiving people. But when he encountered God "face to face" in that famous wrestling match (Gen. 32:22-32), his name was changed to Israel, meaning "Prince with God."[4]

When your record is cleansed, you receive a new name that reflects your relationship with God. From that moment on, you are called by His name[5]— the name that is above all names. There is incredible power in the name of the Lord. Just a quick scan of the concordance in the back of your Bible, under "name," will yield rich insights:

"Our help is in the name of the Lord…" (Ps. 124:8).

"Your name, O Lord, endures forever…" (Ps. 135:13).

"The name of the Lord is a strong tower..." (Prov. 18:10).

"...I am called by Your name, O Lord..." (Jer. 15:16).

"That at the name of Jesus every knee should [shall] bow..." (Phil. 2:10).

My friend Floressa is a daughter of Zion who made a trip to the cross and changed her name and her destination forever.

The Unseen Hand of God

Floressa is a precious "completed Jew," meaning she was born Jewish, was brought up Jewish, and is saved by the blood of Yeshua, HaMashiyach—Jesus, the Messiah. We are sisters, daughters of the same Father and co-heirs of the inheritance of His Son. Her story reads like a Russian novel, with a cast of thousands, and as many plot twists as a Grisham page-turner!

Floressa's father was a Russian immigrant who brought his wife and six children to America by way of England. After a divorce, her father migrated south to Georgia, where he met the woman who would become Floressa's mother, a Christian, who was 23 years his junior. She quickly converted to Judaism, but sometimes took her two children to all-night gospel singings. At age eight, Floressa walked down the aisle in a South Georgia tent meeting, gave her heart to Jesus, then came home, forgot about it, and went on with her Jewish life. But God didn't forget.

Floressa shares, "There is no other explanation as to why my six older sisters and brothers—all of whom are about my mother's age and fully Jewish—accepted and embraced us so readily or why I survived a bad bout of TB when I was younger or how I made it through all the other stumbling blocks and challenges in my life. For example, over a period of nine years, my mother took in 67 foster children through the Jewish Children's Service. My brother and I spent our youth helping to raise these children. Since we were little more than children ourselves, this created many more challenges. I made it because God is good. He gave me the answers and picked me up and carried me over the rough spots.

"One of the roughest was when my husband's sister was abducted and killed. She was stuffed in the trunk of her car, and the car then was pushed over a cliff and set on fire. It was such a tragedy! Yet looking back, I can see God's 'good' that came out of this horrible tragedy. For example, we know several people who accepted Christ after Emelie's funeral. We also know of others who had gotten away from the church and began attending again. In our storm, God sent a rainbow.

Two precious friends, knowing my love for the garden outside my kitchen window, brought a beautiful bench in honor of Emelie and set it up outside the day before the funeral. The whole family went out and took lots of pictures around Emelie's bench.

"Later that night, my nephew, who had one of those new digital cameras, took one more picture of the bench alone. He was showing it to me when he noticed a spot above the bench. 'Don't worry about that,' he told me. 'We can airbrush that little flaw out.'

"I took a closer look and saw what appeared to be a perfect angel! To us God was saying that my sister-in-law was okay. It was as if she were saying, 'I love my bench! I'm God's newest angel.' He truly is watching over us. I can see His hand all through my life—in the good times and the bad."

While Floressa and I were talking by cell phone—compliments of the age of technology—she was driving to another city to celebrate her sister's ninety-third birthday! This Jewish sister, now on the threshold of heaven, married a believer and has become one too. But Floressa wants to reconfirm that this woman really does know the Lord and that they will be reunited, after death, for the rest of eternity. She is on assignment, carrying the Good News of a Jewish carpenter who died on a cruel cross for our sins, rose from the dead, and is now seated at the right hand of the Father.

The unseen hand of God is still at work in Floressa's life, weaving together the intricate threads of this family tapestry. When it is all done, it will be rich with Russian reds, highlighted with the white cliffs of Dover, and tinted with Georgia peaches. There will be a variety of textures in the hundreds of personalities in this extended family with their differing back-grounds and beliefs. But God meant it for good…and He is still at the loom, finishing off the magnificent piece with the scarlet thread of Jesus' blood.

Adversity in Reverse

She's a dynamo from Dallas—one of the most adorable women I know! She reminds me of a parfait—all the fruit of the Spirit topped with whipped cream; she can whip any adversity with a blink of her blue eyes and with all the patience and comeback-ability of Job! She's the one who wisely observes, "You can't be an overcomer unless you have something to over-come." And Kay has had plenty of experience in the overcoming department. Much of it has had to do with her profession.

As a single woman in sales, with great creativity and drive, she has always landed on her feet, even with the economy on a roller-coaster ride. For several years she worked in Dallas for one of the most popular Christian radio stations in the nation. She felt God's anointing on her job and things were going well. Then the downturn began, and the job dried up. With every door closed in the Dallas job market, and with her dad lobbying for her to make a move back home to Atlanta, she agreed—but only after putting out a "fleece."

"God," she prayed, "I don't want to move back, but if I get a job offer, then I'll know that's where You want me." Three interviews later, Kay had three job offers! She took one with another Christian radio station, and in six weeks, she had been promoted to sales manager. About this time her father was diagnosed with congestive heart failure. Since the two had some unre-solved issues, Kay knew that the Lord was providing time to reconcile, and their relationship was rebirthed. The day her dad died, Kay was there. He roused from his coma long enough to greet her and also kiss his bride of fifty years. Then he closed his eyes and went home to be with the Lord. (She tells her parents' beautiful love story in my book *A Match Made in Heaven*.) If Kay hadn't been in Atlanta those four years, she might have missed the bless-ing of that reconciliation.

Another time, when Kay was unemployed, she had wrecked her car, the bills were piling up, and she had no money. She fell on her face before the Lord on her bedroom floor. "You promised that You would supply all my needs according to Your riches in glory," she wailed. "You promised to be my Father, my Husband, my Provider. Lord, do something!" When she went to the mailbox, expecting to find more bills, she found a Christmas check for $500 from her brother. This was in July.

God was building a track record in Kay's life, and her faith grew stronger. At one point, she had just picked up a new company car from the dealer and was on her way to a friend's house when she hit a huge pothole in the road. She could feel the car scraping bottom. As she drove on, the car made an incredible noise, but she and her friend went on to a play they had been wanting to see.

The next morning, Sunday, Kay had a strong sense that she needed to be in church, but the church she attended was fifty miles away, and the new car was "broken." She dressed, then decided it might be a good idea to have the car checked at a service station before making the trip. She pulled in and explained her predicament. "I ran into a big hole last night with my car, and I wonder if you can tell me what's wrong. It's making a really weird sound."

The mechanic took a look and diagnosed the problem right away. "Yes, ma'am, I can tell you what's wrong. You've cracked the block."

I love the way Kay tells this story.

"Being blonde, I asked, 'How serious is that?'

"The mechanic looked at me as if he couldn't believe I could be *that* dumb! 'Really serious,' he said, still scratching his head. 'I'd say it means you need a new engine.'

"'Oh, well, thanks,' I said. 'I believe I'll get another opinion.' And off I drove, the car rattling louder than ever.

"At the second service station, the mechanic confirmed the verdict. 'You've cracked your engine block. You might make it three hundred miles, or you might only get to the end of the block. But you're eventually going to have to put in a new engine.'

"I couldn't waste any more time. 'Well, thanks a lot. I'm going to be late to church, so I'd better get going.'

"When I pulled into the church parking lot, the car was making such a racket that I'm sure I interrupted the praise and worship service. I walked into the back of the large, 5,000-member church just in time to hear the pastor say, 'I feel there are people here this morning who need prayer.'

"*Well, that definitely includes me,* I thought. I didn't even stop to find a seat, but proceeded down to the front. *I've wrecked the brand-new company car, and I'm going to lose my job if I don't get a miracle.* I had barely formed the thought before I was surrounded by praying people, pressing in for the miracle I needed. 'I feel God is going to use this car,' someone said. 'After the service, let's lay hands on your car and commission it into the ministry.'

"I was all over that idea. Afterward, I met the prayer warriors in the parking lot. They circled the car, laid hands on my car—the *company* car— and prayed. When I turned the ignition key, the engine purred like a kitten!

"On my way out of the lot, shouting, 'Hallelujah,' I heard that unmistakable still, small Voice. *Remember the story about the lepers? Only one returned to thank Me for healing him.* It took me a minute, but I got it. 'Okay, Lord, You're telling me You want me to go back to those service stations? I'll do it.'

"When I drove in three hours later, the car now behaving nicely, all the mechanics gathered around, their eyes as big as saucers, 'What happened to this car?' they asked.

"I went to church, and God healed it!"

"Why do you think He did that?"

"This was my chance. 'Well,' I began, 'for one thing, He saved my job. But there's something else. If I were God and I wanted to convince a few mechanics that I really do exist and that I am working in the lives of people today, I'd send a woman with a cracked engine block in to their service station, and then I'd make that engine as good as new. By the way, what's your relationship with the Lord?'

"I wish I could tell you that they all fell down on their faces and were gloriously saved on the spot. But I do still drive by those stations on Sundays, and I always stop in to fill my tank with gas before going to church—just so those mechanics can see for themselves that the car is still 'healed' and that God can do the same for them. What the enemy intended for evil, God meant for good!"

The Best Years of Your Life

Well, dear one, we have traveled together through the pages of this book, with many a look in the rear view mirror. We have relived moments of anguish and angst, pain and passion, death and devastation. We have caught glimpses of God's glory. We have seen His unseen hand at work, reconfiguring the jagged shards of our lives. We have reviewed years the locusts have eaten and time wasted with bad choices. We have identified the dream-stealers and considered how to reclaim the dream.

A verse in the Psalms, written by David, another dreamer and musician, is often quoted as a promise of God's provision. We love those words because they seem to guarantee that we will have everything we ever wished for. "Delight yourself also in the Lord, and He shall give you the desires of your heart" (Ps. 37:4). The little word *also* is an important clue that there is more here than meets the eye. For one thing, the Hebrew word for delight, which is *anag,* means "to be soft or pliable...."[6] Would this imply being receptive, moldable in the Potter's hands? And look at the verse just preceding this one: "Trust in the Lord, and do good; dwell in the land, and feed on His faithfulness" (v. 3).

If we "trust in the Lord...and feed on His faithfulness"...if we "delight" in Him (remember, that means to be pliable, receptive, moldable), then He shall surely give us the *desires* of our heart. The word for *desires* here is *mish'alah,* meaning "a request...petition."[7] Is it *whatever* request or petition—or dream—we desire, or is it what we desire *after* having been "softened," molded to conform to *the Lord's dream for us?* Isn't He really the only One who knows what we should be dreaming anyway, the only One who can grant the correct answer to our petition?

Oh, I wish you could meet my friend Fran. She is another who was born in Pharaoh's palace. Educated in the South in private schools, it appeared for a time that she was handed her dream on a silver platter. She married right out of college, and the beautiful couple seemed to have it all. What potential! What promise! Off to London with all the promise of success!

If you knew Fran, you would love her. She is absolutely angelic—the type of woman you want to protect, to shield from any pain or trauma. She should be sitting on a fine cushion, eating strawberries and cream. You would want to surround her with beauty and tranquility. She is too fine and lovely to taste of life's difficulties.

Because Fran was from a sheltered background, she was not prepared for disappointment when it came. After four children, her husband's emotional health deteriorated rapidly, and she was forced to bring up her family virtually alone.

For ten long years as a single mother, Fran was in the pit. But she was not sitting idly by or complaining about her lot or attempting to escape her pain through drugs or some form of fantasy. She was going to every Bible study in town, actively seeking a deeper walk with the Lord. Within her heart was the desire to be a whole family again someday, but she knew that wholeness needed to start with her.

One day, after a Bible study, she left only to find another car blocking hers. The owner was a handsome gentleman who had done a 360-degree turn to ask her out for dinner. She agreed, and the rest is history. A "whole" family again. A heart's desire realized. A dream come true.

Now Fran can look back on the strange pattern of her life and find the purpose. If she had not been deserted, if everything had gone smoothly, if she had not been forced to fend for herself, if her problems had not been bigger than she, if she had not spent what some would call the best years of her life alone, she might have missed the greater blessing. She might not know God as she knows Him today—as her Protector, her Defender, her Faithful Friend, her Comforter, her Husband, her Everything! In fact, looking back now, Fran can truthfully say that those "lost years," those lonely years, those years in the pit were "the best years of her life"!

How about you—can you begin to see that the patterns and pathways of your life were leading you straight to the royal house of the King, back to the original dream and the Dream-maker?

Prayer for Heavenly Thinking: Father God, we glorify You and thank You that You're the Lord of the journey. You never leave us. You never let go of our hands, You are always with us, even in the darkest night, when the fragile thread connecting us has worn thin. You do not allow the enemy to engulf us. You teach us heavenly thinking, with eternity's values in view, reminding us that You are strongest when we are weakest and that when the time comes for You to reveal what You meant for good, it will all make sense. Thank You for expanding our faith and showing us Your secrets. Move us into position to be launched into our destiny—for such a time as this. Prayerfully, in the powerful name of Your Son, Jesus Christ, amen.

"Joseph is a fruitful bough....

The archers have bitterly grieved him,

Shot at him and hated him,

But his bow remained in strength, and the

arms of his hands were made strong by

the hands of the Mighty God of Jacob...

By the God of your father who will help you,

and by the Almighty who will bless you

with blessings of heaven above...."

GENESIS 49:22-25

CHAPTER 16

The Joseph Anointing

*And God is able to make all grace abound toward you,
that you, always having all sufficiency in all things,
may have an abundance for every good work.
As it is written: "He has dispersed abroad, he has given
to the poor; his righteousness endures forever."
Now may He who supplies seed to the sower, and bread
for food, supply and multiply the seed you have sown
and increase the fruits of your righteousness,
while you are enriched in everything for all liberality....*

2 CORINTHIANS 9:8-11

I am a wealthy woman—rich in friends, beloved of my daughters, spiritual daughters, grandchildren, and John Platz, and redeemed by the blood of the Lamb. I have always felt the grace of God in my life, and on birthdays I adore looking back to count, not the years, but the blessings; to celebrate the knowledge that I, like Joseph, am a favored child of my Father; to delight in the riches that He has brought to my hands, into my arms, and before my eyes—the redemption of my soul, the restoration of my dream, the inheritance of a Father who owns the cattle on a thousand hills and has "...a future and a hope" for me (Jer. 29:11).

It is not confidence in myself I feel, but in the Lord who designed the dream. I marvel at how small my original plans were, how selfish and

narrowly defined, and how grand and great His are—how He multiplies a life
to touch the multitudes! My old plan was ineffective, so I allowed God to buy
it back—to redeem it—and to give me a new one, stamped with His seal and
signed in red, the blood of His Son, Jesus.

God is all about redemption. He takes useless, old dreams and makes
them new. He reclaims and renews those that have been lost or stolen by the
dream-stealers. In fact, the areas of your life that have been targeted by the
enemy are the very places where your ministry will be most effective. It is
here that you will have experienced the most healing and the greatest
bonding with God's heart. Through divine chemistry, your weakest places are
now your strongest.

But there is more. Once your feet have found firm ground again, once
you have entered into the fullness of your destiny as designed by the Dream-
Maker, once you have received all that God intended for you, you are ready
to be used as you have never been used before. You cannot give what you
have not received. Now you have a wealth of wisdom and knowledge and
revelation to share. The sky is the limit!

After the Famine

When the drought ends and the famine is over—when the new job is
landed, when the mortgage is paid, when the illness is healed, when there is
now life instead of death—there is always the temptation to use one's
resources selfishly and to take the credit for making it through the storm. Not
Joseph. From his youth, he has been a man of honor, integrity, diligence, and
wisdom. And with God's help, he devises a plan that will ensure ongoing
provision for the land of Egypt as well as his own family and the future fledg-
ling nation of Israel.

All is well for seventeen years. Under the wise leadership of Joseph, and
with the blessing of Pharaoh, the family "...dwelt in the land of Egypt, in the
country of Goshen; and they had possessions there and grew and multiplied
exceedingly" (Gen. 47:27). Just consider all that those words imply: prosperity, favor, marriage and procreation, increase, enjoying "the fat of the
land." Because of one man—Joseph—and his faithfulness, an entire nation
prospers and grows strong.

Sometimes the dream comes down to one man or one woman. Noah, who heard the voice of God, built the ark, and preached repentance to his neighbors for 120 years[1] without a single convert! Only he and his immediate family, along with two of every animal and bird as instructed by God, were saved on the face of the earth. Esther, the Hebrew beauty contest winner, pled with her husband, a pagan king, to spare her people. The fate of an entire nation rested on her slim shoulders, and she was willing to risk her own life to save them.[2] Jesus, the Son of God, bore the sins of all mankind—past, present, and future—on the cross. Even when He agonized in prayer in the Garden of Gethsemane as He faced the crucifixion, He was faithful to the dream. "Father, if it is Your will [desire, purpose, *dream*], take this cup away from Me; nevertheless not My will [desire, purpose, *dream*], but Yours, be done" (Luke 22:42).

Just as Jesus pressed on through the pain and agony of the cross for the "joy that was set before Him,"[3] Joseph endured the pit and the prison, fueled by his boyhood dream—the purpose and plan of God for a life that would impact every other life on the planet. He was truly raised up with an anointing for blessing. And it was a double anointing. Joseph was both a prophet—he could see God's vision, although he could not make out the details in the beginning—and he had an anointing very much like a modern-day apostle. He had the authority of God and the favor of Pharaoh to implement what God had given him.

After the famine, he used his natural gifts of administration and leadership to create provision for all the people. But he also used his spiritual gifts—discernment, interpretation of dreams, and godly wisdom—to follow God's commandments. He respected the authority of the land and was in submission to it, but he did not compromise his prior commitment to God. He stayed on purpose the entire time—from the pit to the prison to the palace.

Joseph's journey took him into dangerous territory—attempted murder, kidnapping, slavery, temptation by Potiphar's wife—through "wasted" years of waiting with no end in sight, and now into a place of supreme favor. Some people would have taken the money and run! But Joseph held fast the original dream and walked it out with integrity. He was not greedy. He did not spend these resources selfishly nor did he waste anything that came into his hands. He instructed his people to move into cities where they could be fed, then instructed them to sow seed for the years to come. Because all the land belonged to Pharaoh, they were to give him one-fifth of the crop yield, keeping four-fifths for their own use—both for provision and for replanting.

Joseph got the big picture. Looking back, he could see that the time of famine was a time of blessing; it caused him to lean on Jehovah-Jireh, the Provider. As my precious friend and mentor Prophet Mary Crum says, "Hardship can be learning ground, but Joseph learned his lessons so well, and the timing was perfect." Looking to the future, he helped his people use their resources wisely so that they would not be caught short in the next emergency. Joseph did not speak out of a spirit of scarcity, but saw God's sufficiency, His absolute abundance. He knew that the covenant God had made with his father, Jacob, beginning with his great-grandfather Abraham, was still in effect. Because of the promise, there was no panic in the hard times.

The Father's Blessing

A father's last words to his children are usually words to be cherished and remembered. I have already shared with you how my father blessed me on his deathbed and how I received the mantle of his authority. It was a precious moment, and I left that scene empowered to move into my dream and into my destiny.

Joseph, too, was empowered by his father's last words. When it came time for Jacob to die, he called in all of his sons. Joseph brought with him his two boys, Ephraim and Manasseh. To Joseph he said, "Behold, I am dying, but God will be with you and bring you back to the land of your fathers. Moreover I have given to you one portion above your brothers..." (Gen. 48:21,22). Along with the double blessing went an amazing declaration! Jacob repeated the one thing that had been constant throughout Joseph's life. In all his ups and downs, Joseph had known *Emmanuel*—"God is with us."[4] In plenty and in poverty, He proved to be more than enough.

Then Jacob/Israel, with his dying breath, spoke the words that would call into being prophetically the destiny of his twelve sons as patriarchs of their clans. They would forever after be known as the "twelve tribes of Israel." Sometimes with gentle scolding and at other times with tender blessing, the father spoke words of life to them. His particular blessing to his son Joseph chronicled the lean and hungry years as well as the years of abundance. "Joseph is a fruitful bough...the archers have...Shot at him and hated him.... But his bow remained in strength...made strong by the hands of the Mighty God of Jacob...By the God of your father who will help you, and by the Almighty who will bless you with blessings of heaven above...up to the utmost bound of the everlasting hills..." (Gen. 49:22-26). It was a special blessing, a comprehensive blessing that would sustain Joseph through the next sixty years of his life.

After Israel's (Jacob's) death, he was embalmed in the Egyptian tradition, which required 40 days, followed by a mourning period of 70 days, usually reserved for heads of state or people of great stature. At his earlier request, Israel's embalmed body was carried 300 miles back to Canaan to be buried with his people in the Cave of Machpelah.[5]

Author, Bible teacher, and evangelist F. B. Meyer wrote of this in his book *The Life of Joseph:* "And, indeed, that funeral procession must have been of a sort not often seen. There was not only the family of Israel but the officers of the court, and all the elders of the land of Egypt. In other words, the proud and titled magnates of Egypt, the most exclusive aristocracy in the world, were willing to follow the remains of a shepherd and a Jew to their last resting-place, out of honor for his son. 'There also went up chariots and horsemen, so that it was a very great company' [Gen. 50:9, author paraphrase]....a splendid funeral, because he had given to the land of Egypt so great a benefactor and savior in the person of his son...."[6]

The Father's blessing rested on the Son when Jesus died, too, but there was no great funeral procession for the King of kings. Only a handful of women and a few frightened men to take His broken body off the cross and prepare it for burial in a borrowed tomb. The rest had scattered to do their mourning privately and to wait for a knock at the door that would signal arrest, or worse.

No, there was no pomp and circumstance on earth when Jesus was buried. But in heaven, the Father was preparing a place of honor at His right hand to receive the Son. And the angels' voices were hushed for a time, as they held their breath in anticipation of the joyous reunion when He returned, having paid the price for all the sins of creation for all time!

Meanwhile between the cross and the crown, between the pit and the palace, there is kingdom work to be done.

The Joseph Anointing—Lead and Feed

With improved communications and technology, the world is growing smaller every day. Through e-mail alone, we are in instant touch with people in virtually every country. Missionaries, ministering in once remote areas, are now able to contact home base for needed supplies or reinforcements. People in war-torn nations or under threat of epidemic or natural disaster are able to broadcast their plight. We are no longer in doubt about the needs of the multitudes. We can hear their cries of pain and see the image of starvation—both physically and spiritually. There is no excuse if we fail to respond, no excuse at all.

God is raising up "Josephs" who will be able to lead and feed the peoples of the world. In defining the Joseph anointing, Prophet Mary Crum has some wise words: "This person has a Spirit-breathed knowledge of how to generate resources, accumulate them, increase them, and distribute them to further the kingdom purposes of God, which included, but is not limited to, feeding the hungry."

Generate—As with Joseph, who rose in the ranks to become second in command of all Egypt, the person with a Joseph anointing will know how to tap into the source of supply for the sake of others. He or she will be able to use personal funds or will be led to invest for maximum return. Whatever the area of influence and livelihood, God can use it to bless others. But *others* is the operative word. All of the wealth generated will not be used for personal consumption. Some of whom it may be said, "Everything he/she touches turns to gold," may actually have a Joseph anointing—one way in which God provides resources for building the kingdom.

Accumulate—Joseph was a dreamer and an interpreter of dreams, but he was never so heavenly minded that he was no earthly good. He was a man of purpose, a practical man. His interpretation of Pharaoh's disturbing dreams led to a very sensible plan for storing grain during the plentiful years so that there would be ample resources for distribution during the years of famine.

Dave Ramsay and Larry Burkett, Christian businessmen and authors, have written and lectured on the topic of using funds wisely, keeping a reserve fund for emergencies, saving for the "lean years," and giving liberally. What they are proposing is not necessarily a Joseph anointing, but simply good stewardship based on biblical principles. I highly recommend their books and seminar materials.[7] As we move into uncharted territory in the future, we will need to be equipped to take care of ourselves, our families, and members of the extended family of God.

Increase—Resident in the Joseph anointing is increase. God always expands and enlarges. He multiplies. It is important—as funds are accumulated and we begin to see the increase—to acknowledge His hand. We are warned in the Word not to say, "...My power and the might of my hand have gained me this wealth," but "You shall remember the Lord your God, for it is He who gives you power [means, endurance, capacity] to get wealth, that He may establish His covenant which he swore to your fathers..." (Deut. 8:17,18). Material blessings are included in the promises to the patriarchs and their descendants, but wisdom accompanies those blessings. As one well-known pastor says, "...God desires that we use our abundance to bless others.... Wealth is more than money and possessions. We need the wisdom both 1) to receive God's covenant of prosperity—to receive wealth without its controlling us; and 2) to see its breadth and intent for our whole being—that with wealth and health, peace and friends—we serve others. God's covenanted prosperity is always a means to an end and never an end in itself."[8]

Joseph, as he operated in the purposes and principles of God, received favor in spite of his circumstances. This may be true of the anointed believer, too. The stock market may rise or fall. You may be in prison or in Potiphar's house. But God can prosper you in the midst of it when your motive is to promote His kingdom.

Distribute—The "Josephs" are not greedy. They are not playboy-type spenders. They don't throw money away. They keep an accounting of expenditures and know where their resources are going. They are on track with God. Therefore, they know when He is moving on their hearts to make provision for someone or some people group.

"The poor you have with you always..." Jesus says in John 12:8, and then leaves it in the hands of His disciples to minister to them. Therefore, the

Josephs will always have some involvement with a larger cause in answer to God's call to supply the needs of the multitudes. I believe that the Josephs will be able to break a loaf of bread, and twelve basketsful will be left over![9]

God sometimes places people with a Joseph anointing, those who have a heart for a certain ministry, in the body of Christ to help fund someone else's dream. These "Josephs" are in covenant with the ministries and use their resources to support and encourage them—both in times of blessing and in times of famine.

Transfer of Wealth From the Wicked

The wealth of the world has been in the wrong hands for a long time. And it is obvious by now that the world does not have the solution to the problems of mankind. Only through discerning God's dream is a people or a nation able to provide wise leadership.

There is supernatural guidance and direction for those who seek the Lord—and a promised transfer of wealth from the wicked to the righteous. "…in my favor I have had mercy on you. Therefore your gates shall be open continually; they shall not be shut day or night, that men may bring to you the wealth of the Gentiles…[heathen, wicked]…" (Isa. 60:10,11).

Because of graft and greed, some so-called benevolent organizations have not funneled their funds properly, and many have continued to suffer while the rich get richer. When the money changes hands, it will come into the treasuries of the Josephs—and the "Josephines." They will be willing to carry out the orders of the Lord as His emissaries and distribute the wealth where it needs to go. Or, it may even be possible—as it was in Joseph's story—that some unbelieving "Pharaoh" will be moved to fund a believer's dream!

God's Networking

"I'm so glad to be here with you today! God sent me as a gift to you!" I began with enthusiasm as I greeted a group of nine teenaged girls, aged twelve to eighteen, who were incarcerated for various criminal charges in an Atlanta correctional institution. "What is one and one?"

"Uh…two." They regarded me with skepticism. What kind of trick question was this? Didn't everybody know the answer to that one?

"Wrong. It's ten thousand or maybe a million!"

"What?"

I smiled at their looks of consternation. "In God's hands, one and one can equal so much more than we could ever imagine! Just think what He can do with your lives and your dreams. It goes back to the story of Joseph, who started out as a shepherd boy with a dream of greatness. He was sold into slavery by his jealous brothers, was arrested and put in prison—just like you were, except that Joseph was falsely accused—then through God's favor, he was promoted to prime minister of Egypt!"

Their eyes lit up and they "got" it! I went on to share with them how special they are to their Daddy God—no matter what they have done or where they have found themselves—and before I left that prison, I led every one of those precious girls to freedom in Jesus as they opened their hearts and allowed Him to become their Savior. I told them that they cannot begin to fathom all that He has in store for them. I intend to stay in touch, because I know He has a future and a plan for each one of them and that He will multiply their dreams far beyond anything they could conceive on their own.

When I started out as a little girl, playing with color and decorating dollhouses, I had no idea that I would be here in this Atlanta prison fifty years later, helping the Great Designer in the transformation of nine troubled souls. I hadn't a clue that I would be writing books on "interior" design that are distributed more widely than I could have ever dreamed possible or speaking to thousands at seminars and conferences all over the country. But that is how God networks. He uses my life to touch other lives who will, in turn, affect still other lives. The potential for a ripple effect that will reach out to touch the nations is astronomical! Once again, that is God's math.

God does not compute in the same way we do. Therefore, when He asks for our time or our talents or a minimum of a tenth of our increase (Mal. 3:8-10), that is precious little when compared to what He was willing to give for the guarantee of our eternal life. (John 3:16.) He multiplies everything He touches.

And it's all about timing. "In the fullness of time" God sent His only begotten Son (Gal. 4:4). When the time is right, God will fulfill the dream He has placed in your heart. Events will take place—right on time. People will connect with you—right on time. The prophecy will begin to unfold—right on time. That's what happened to Joseph throughout his life, but particularly during the "forgotten" years—those two extra years after the butler was released and the baker was hanged. Joseph had asked the butler to "remember" him when he received his walking papers, but he forgot. Or did he?

I believe that this story turned out exactly as God intended it. He acted at exactly the right time. He moved on Pharaoh through his dreams, and Joseph was summoned to the court to interpret the dreams. Perhaps those two long years were needed for Joseph to rid himself of the last vestige of pride left over from his boyhood because his first words to Pharaoh prove his humble state. Remember? When Pharaoh asked him what the dreams meant, Joseph made a telling statement, "...It is not in *me;* God will give Pharaoh an answer..." (Gen. 41:16). All glory would go to God, not to the butler who finally remembered his promise to Joseph and told Pharaoh about him; not to the prison warden who recognized Joseph's leadership ability and placed him over the other prisoners; not even to the highest official in the land, with the power to pardon Joseph or to execute him.

Even from the beginning, God's network was in place, positioning the people who would lead Joseph into the fulfillment of his destiny. In each case, Joseph was faithful. He did his job well. Not knowing the outcome, but holding on to the dream, he performed every task with integrity and excellence. But this Jewish ex-convict could not have done a thing without the favor of God on his life.

Just consider all the times he could have been killed—in the pit, on the way to Egypt by the traders, in Potiphar's house by an angry husband who believed his wife's lies, in prison, or by Pharaoh himself. Even after his promotion to prime minister, Joseph could have been assassinated by someone who loathed the thought of a Jew rising to such power. Yet God's hand was on him all the way.

Joseph never became king of the country. He never became warden of the prison. He was simply faithful to his own calling and did his best where he was. He was a servant-leader. Remember that his most important "connections" were made while he was still in prison. Promotion comes from God. If we are faithful to the call, He will be faithful to promote us when the time is right.

Marketplace Mentoring

I believe that mentoring in the marketplace, which is any place outside the walls of the church, is the next big wave of the Spirit. I have seen glimpses of this as I travel and speak throughout the country. I hear from those who are eager to minister and feed others spiritually. I also hear the cry of the mature woman who knows that she is to lead while nurturing the younger women who look to her as teacher, friend, and mentor.

Marketplace mentoring is simply giving and serving right where you are, using your specific gifts to empower and encourage others toward spiritual maturity. Ministry has too long been associated with formal church roles and programs only. Ministry can take place anywhere you happen to be—in the home, in the schoolroom, in the workplace, at the corner market, on the golf course, "on the way."

"Jesus modeled ministry as He went about doing good," says Prophet Mary Crum. "Most of His ministry was not in the synagogues, but in the marketplace, the homes, and the highways and byways."

God is calling women today just as He has always called women. It was a woman who mothered the race and decorated the first garden apartment. It was a woman who cooperated with God, conceived by the Holy Spirit, and brought forth His Son. It was a woman who was the first evangelist. She witnessed the empty tomb and ran to tell the others that Jesus was risen from the dead. God loves women, and He trusts us with His very best ideas!

Now He is calling us—homemakers, businesswomen, mothers, teachers—whoever we are and wherever we are serving, to consider a "marketplace" ministry. Part of the marketplace He is referring to is the home. I believe that in these last days the home will be used in the same way that the New Testament homes were used—to house a portion of the church. Not to displace or replace the church, but as an auxiliary agent in supporting the church and reaching the unreached that only a feminine touch can provide.

Women have a wide sphere of influence, and we should be encouraged to step forward and receive our commission. There is a Joseph anointing for women to feed and nurture, a gathering anointing for pulling together diverse groups of people. Like the church, the home can be a hospital for hurting hearts, a refuge for weary souls, a way station for the wounded, a place of renewal and refreshing. I believe that it is time to bring our skills and talents back into the home and learn to use it for creative ministry.

There are some things women excel in, some touches that only women can give to bless a heart or a home. We can provide a resting place or a launching pad. We can encourage the defeated and applaud the achiever. We can try to out-serve one another, not caring who gets the credit. We can see the big picture that breaks down denominational walls and spans countries and continents.

Every woman is a unique piece of the quilt, crafted to God's specifications. She has been endowed with her own talents, her own gifts, her own personality, her own temperament, her one-of-a-kind style, and her own china patterns. You have been created for this hour, for this moment. No one else can accomplish exactly what God has called *you* to do.

Four super-spirits come to mind as women whose reclaimed dreams include a definite Joseph anointing—Ruth Ann, Stacy, Muriel, and Susan. The Lord has lifted them from the pit, custom-designed for each one by the enemy, guided them in the process of taking back territory, and anointed them for specific kingdom work.

Ruth Ann, once shy and retiring, is feeding the multitudes, literally and spiritually. Her passion, "The Great Banquet," is a wonderful plan in her denomination for strengthening and renewing the faith of believers through weekend retreats. The concept, taken from Luke 14:15-24, is a story Jesus tells of a man who prepared a great banquet and sent out an invitation, saying, "...'Come, for everything is now ready...'" (NIV). The idea is for people to come together to feast and fellowship at the banquet table of God. All are invited. Many will send their regrets. Ruth Ann is now a buoyant, joyful woman who hosts and helps in this outstanding ministry.

Stacy, a mover and shaker in the business world, is an eagle among eagles. Mentored by such outstanding leaders as Dr. Charles Stanley and John Maxwell, she is now strategically positioned by God to oversee 26 ministries with over 600 volunteers. When asked about her five-year plan (every company has one), she replies with typical humility, "I don't follow a plan; I follow a Person. And He says, 'This is the plan I have for you. It may be painful and it will not always be easy, but it is My plan. Walk in it." An anointed servant-leader, she is touching thousands for the Lord.

My books have garnered me many new friends from all over the world. One such friend is Muriel who lived in South Africa when we met a few years ago through e-mail. Upon reading my book *The Best Is Yet To Come,* Muriel e-mailed me to thank me for speaking straight to her heart throughout its pages. She told me of her search for her place of ministry at this time in her life. We are close in age and I could relate to her yearning to do something significant for the Lord. We began an e-mail friendship. Here is her story.

Muriel, born in Scotland and transported to South Africa with her husband and children where they lived through the dark days of Apartheid, was able to start her own business there, training uneducated African women from the rural areas to go back into their communities and start their own small businesses. "The joy of seeing the light go on in the eyes of those who were realizing for the first time that they had value and could make a contribution was so rewarding." With her children grown and her husband away on building projects in the Arab countries, Muriel is now back home, on a little island off the west coast of Scotland. There she is using her skills in training to fulfill another strong calling—a Joseph anointing—to lead and feed many more. "My journey is ongoing," she wrote recently, "so many hills still to climb."

Susan, whose life dream has always been to write and who was my writing partner on six books, was strongly influenced by the late Catherine Marshall, beloved Christian speaker and author. At her death, Susan wept and prayed, "Lord, I never thanked her for changing my life. If there is anything I can ever do for her, please let me know!" After that unusual prayer, she later met and married the well-known film producer, Ken Wales, who held the film rights to Catherine Marshall's book *Christy.* God's divine connections! Together, they brought that movie to the screen, and it has since been distributed worldwide, feeding countless precious souls around the globe with the life-giving story of salvation. Susan's dream to write was realized, as well as her desire to "repay" Catherine Marshall for the wisdom she had received through her writings.

From the Pit...to the Palace

As we come to the end of our journey with Joseph, I could not fail to include another dear friend with a huge Joseph anointing. Rhonda has known her share of deep pits and prison time. For example, she accepted Christ when she was in the pit of an adulterous relationship turned marriage. She could not have survived the next few years without God's hand on her life, carrying her through her husband's drug addiction, the loss of his son by another marriage, and the loss of both his parents within eight months. One nightmare after another, and then abandonment. Things could not have gotten any worse.

"Ten years ago, I was bankrupt, destitute, owed $60,000 to the IRS, with no source of income, no home, no car, no credit," Rhonda says. "I was at the mercy of the world. Yet I'm amazed at how the Holy Spirit spoke to me in those early years even when I didn't know Him very well. In my first Bible study, I was instructed by the Spirit to learn the names of God. In this exercise, I found out who God is and what we can count on Him for. He was preparing me even then for greater things. I had never been discipled, but when I was finally exposed to God's Word, I couldn't get enough of it!

"Six months later, I received an emergency call from my brother. He's pretty special; we share a kindred spirit. So I was devastated to hear that his wife, Kim, who was expecting their second child, was threatening to deliver prematurely. She was only 26 weeks pregnant.

"I rushed to the hospital and asked if I could go in and pray over her. I prayed in the name of Jehovah-Rapha, the Healer, and felt the Holy Spirit come over me in such a rush it took my breath! In my spirit I heard God's voice saying, *This baby is as strong as she is.* The baby, who was in the process of being born, was not supposed to live. He weighed only one pound, ten ounces. So tiny!

"I left the hospital and went to a church where I fell on my knees at the altar, 'Lord, here I am. I'll go wherever You want me to go if You will allow my brother to know his son for one day or even one hour.' Instantly I heard in my spirit, *Name the baby.'* The Lord was very specific. The name should be Ryan Christian, 'little king,' 'Christ-anointed,' and two years later, he's doing well. What a miracle! The Lord used my brother to draw me, irresistibly, to Himself. Now I thirst for even more—wherever He leads."

There is another piece of Rhonda's story you need to know. When she accepted Christ, she was involved in the dental industry, specifically in practice management. Seven years later, she was asked to come into a company, now as an independent contractor, and create their management consulting division. Within eight months, she had added over a million dollars of revenue to the company. God was beginning His sovereign work in her for His own purposes.

When she was at the end of herself ten years ago, Rhonda went into business, developing tools and training materials for relationship management for dentists and other small business owners. Within nine months she had retired her personal debt and doors began opening

"Two years ago, after being strongly influenced by Bruce Wilkinson's little book *The Prayer of Jabez,*"[10] Rhonda says, "God asked me to do more for Him and 'expanded my territory.' I let go of my secular business and went to Armenia to minister to women whose husbands had either left them or had been killed in war. I met with the woman in charge of a group called 'The Roman Virgins' and learned their history. She told me that in 300 A.D., the Roman Empire occupied a massive land area. Seven women, who were facing persecution in their own country for their faith in Jesus Christ, migrated to Armenia. On the way they knitted for a living and planted churches everywhere they stopped. In Armenia, the king was so taken with one of them that he wanted to marry her. When she rejected him because of her faith, the king was enraged and killed all seven. Two years later, realizing he had made a grave mistake, the king accepted Christ, and Armenia became a Christian nation.

"With my business background," Rhonda goes on, "I was intrigued with the idea of helping these abandoned women, widows, and children to support themselves through their knitting. The sweaters they create are carried by the most prominent ski resorts in the United States and around the world. Things began to click in. Maybe I could help. Maybe for the first time, I began to realize that my business savvy was instilled for the purpose of glorifying God. Then came the huge vision for completing a pastor's retreat facility that could be used as a knitting center until funding for a factory could be established. In this factory, the women would be able to mass-produce their sweaters. We are negotiating the property right now! But we will not stop with Armenia. God is now opening doors in Russia, India, East Africa, and Thailand as well."

God sends the manna, God sends the raven, and God sometimes sends women to feed His hungry people! Can you see His hand in Rhonda's life, dear one? All the jagged pieces of her broken dreams are coming together to create another beautiful mosaic that will bring Him glory and bless His people. And all of this has come out of a dream—a deep thirst for more of God. So much so that her ministry is called "I Thirst." Therein lies another story.

"After I gave myself to God at the altar that day, I didn't know the first thing about what I had promised to do for Him," Rhonda admits. "Through a divine connection with a national ministry, I began to thirst for more of the Lord. I asked my friend to pray about a name for an organization the Lord was laying on my heart, called 'I Thirst.' She responded, 'Rhonda, do you know who was all about I thirst? Mother Teresa. On a train one day, she saw a poor man in great despair, his hand stretched out to her, saying, "I thirst." In that man's face she saw Christ and how He thirsts for us. If He thirsts for us, how much more should we thirst for Him?'

"In the past few months, there has been more and more confirmation. Walking through a bookstore one day, I was drawn to a single book on a shelf. It was Max Lucado's *No Wonder They Call Him the Savior.* Chapter 7, 'I Thirst,' brought me to tears:

> I thirst.... That's not THE CHRIST that's thirsty. That's the carpenter. And those are words of humanity in the midst of divinity. This phrase messes up our sermon outline. The other six statements are more 'in character.' They are cries we would expect.... But 'I thirst'?
>
> Just when we had it all figured out. Just when the cross was all packaged and defined. Just when the manuscript was finished.... Just when we put our big golden cross on our big golden steeple, He reminds us that 'the Word became flesh.'
>
> He wants us to remember that He, too, was human. He wants us to know that He, too, knew the drone of the humdrum and the weariness that comes with long days. He wants us to remember that our trailblazer didn't wear bulletproof vests or rubber gloves or an impenetrable suit of armor. No, He pioneered our salvation through the world that you and I face daily.

He is the King of kings, the Lord of lords, and the Word of Life. More than ever He is the Morning Star, the Horn of Salvation, and the Prince of Peace.

But there are some hours when we are restored by remembering that God became flesh and dwelt among us. Our Master knew what it meant to be a crucified carpenter who got thirsty.[11]

And with those words, the dream is reclaimed. Jesus...the answer to our hearts' desire. Jesus...the hope of every childhood dream. Jesus...the expectation of restoration. Jesus...Rhonda's CEO and Business Partner, Margo's Knight in Shining Armor, Victoria's Deliverer, Cathy's Joy, Courtney's Conqueror, Mary's Vision, Martha's Comforter, Karen's Delight, Eliza's Word of Life, Charlotte's Wordsmith, Tracy's Wonderful Counselor, Betty's Creative Creator, Kay's Husband, Floressa's Messiah, Jackie's Healer, Muriel's Messenger, Lizanne's Love, Chandra's Provider, Barbie's Breath, Patricia's Teacher, Jan's Dream-Maker, Audra's Glory, Rachel's Abba Father, Stacy's Servant Leader, Jean's and Sandra's Redeemer, Jodi's Bright and Morning Star, Karen's Kinsman-Redeemer, Carol's Rock, Ruth Ann's First Fruits.

Jesus...the One who, having everything heaven had to offer, emptied Himself and gave everything for you and now abides at the right hand of the Father to watch over the dream He planted in your heart.

*L*ast *W*ords

It's time to go, but I leave you with a part of my heart. As I have written, I have envisioned your face as you read. I have prayed for you and asked the Lord to touch you where you hurt. I have asked Him to sink His truth deeply into your spirit where it may catch fire and blaze with new life. I have prayed for fresh revelation for you that will take these words far beyond my original vision. That's what God does with our dreams.

When Joseph was ready to die and it was time for his last words, he "...was now an old man. One hundred and ten years had stolen away his strength, and left deep marks upon his form....three and ninety years since he had been lifted from the pit to become a slave. Eighty years had passed since he had first stood before Pharaoh in all the beauty and wisdom of his young manhood.... With long life and many days God had blessed His faithful servant. And now, stooping beneath their weight, he was fast descending to the break-up [end] of natural life."[12]

One of Joseph's last acts had been the forgiveness—again—of his brothers, who were still carrying the unnecessary burden of their sin against him. He had already forgiven them once. And Joseph's behavior was a fore-shadowing of God's love through Jesus. As in the case of our relationship with Him, it is distrustful to bring up the same old sin over and over. It shows a lack of faith in His ability to forgive. "...having loved His own who were in the world, He loved them to the end" (John 13:1). Joseph also loved to the end.

As your dream comes into fulfillment, as you walk out your destiny, keep loving and forgiving. Let the beauty of Jesus spill out of all your broken places like the perfume in the alabaster box that Mary broke at His feet. Let the sweet aroma of your sacrifice bless all those you meet and mentor. Let your dream carry you to the end with honor and integrity.

As Joseph is dying, his children and grandchildren gather around him to catch his final words to them. He speaks of a time in the future when they will no longer enjoy the favor of Pharaoh, but will come out of the land "...to the land of which He [God] swore to Abraham, to Isaac, and to Jacob" (Gen. 50:24). It is the promise of home. They will be going home to the land of their forefathers.

Then he prophesies again—a promise that Joseph can declare with the authority of experience: "...God will surely visit you..." (v. 25). Just as God had been with Joseph throughout his journey, all the way to the end of his life, so He would be with Joseph's descendants—from Egypt to the Promised Land.

When our flesh and blood "are most impaired," how wonderful that our spirit "is most bright and most alive to the realities of the eternal world."[13] With Joseph's dim vision, he can see the hope of Israel—Jesus, the Messiah—in the shadow of his own life. It is a vision more bright and beau-tiful than anyone could dare to dream—the hope of heaven! And so may it be with you, dear friend.

Commissioning Prayer: Father God, Lord of the journey, Maker of the way, and Keeper of the dream, we come before You to bless Your holy name. You number the hairs on our heads. You ordain the length of our days. You have positioned us to touch the lives of others and make them whole. Thank You for the example of Joseph—the favor, the obedience, the integrity of his life— so beautifully displayed against the backdrop of a pagan culture. Father, direct us to the place where we, Your children, are to lead and feed the multitudes. The fields are white; the harvest is ripe. Thank You for every gift, every talent, every piece of the quilt that heals our hurts and restores our faith. Father, we thank You for Your faithfulness, Your mercy, and Your grace that accompany us on our life passage and will one day lead us straight to Your House where we will finally be at home with You for all eternity. In the name of Jesus, Hope of heaven, we pray, amen.

Questionnaire for Reclaiming Your Dream

by Ann Platz

I so want you to discover and reclaim your dream! I have designed a questionnaire for you to fill out in order to go back to your childhood and remember the essence of who you are. Please take your time answering these simple questions. You will find that this is fun and that you will be able to remember a lot, and amazingly, you will see many clues to reclaiming your dream. Enjoy this journey!

Name:_____

Describe your dream as a child of five years of age.

_____

_____

_____

1. In describing your dream, what did you want to be when you grew up? Your profession?

_____

_____

_____

2. Who were you playing when you played "dress up"? Who were your role models? Paint a picture with words of what you looked like and what your "dress up" clothes looked like.

_____

_____

_____

3. What were your playtime toys? Describe them.

_____

_____

_____

4. What were you creatively doing? Describe your crafts or what you were doing with your hands. How old were you when the dream started to leave...what age?

_____

_____

_____

5. Who were the dream-stealers, the people who "put out the fire" of your dreams and hopes?

_____

_____

_____

6. What did they say to you? Do you remember any words that were spoken to you to cause you to let go of the dream?

_____

_____

_____

7. How did you feel?

_____

_____

_____

8. When were you at the bottom like Joseph was in prison?

_____

_____

_____

9. Who was there with you? Who were your encouragers?

_____

_____

_____

10. How did you come back? What steps did you take? How would you compare your life with that of Joseph and his dream in the book of Genesis?

_____
_____
_____

11. Give me a little feedback on Joseph and his life. Do you relate to him?

_____
_____
_____

12. What was your hardest thing to do to reclaim your dream?

_____
_____
_____

What advice would you give a friend to reclaim their dream?

_____
_____
_____

13. What are some things that you would recommend to other women that they could do to restore their dream and then to help others restore theirs?

_____
_____
_____

Joseph and his coat of many colors

1. What is the greatest lesson you have learned from this story?

_____
_____
_____

2. Describe how you feel about his brother's actions towards Joseph?

_____

_____

_____

3. What did Joseph learn in prison?

_____

_____

_____

4. Does your life parallel with Joseph's? In what way?

_____

_____

_____

5. What are some other lessons you learned from this story?

_____

_____

_____

Endnotes

Chapter 1

1. Isaiah 46:9,10.
2. Jeremiah 1:5.
3. Hebrews 13:5.
4. Job 1:8.
5. Arthur T. Pierson, *George Müller of Bristol,* (Grand Rapids: Zondervan Publishing Company, 1984), p. 362.
6. Hebrews 11:25 KJV.
7. Joshua 14:10.
8. Genesis 37:3-10.
9. Genesis 37:18-28.
10. Genesis 39.
11. Genesis 41:39-44.

Chapter 2

1. Genesis 1:26.
2. Isaiah 9:6; John 16:7,13.
3. *Webster's Collegiate Dictionary,* Tenth ed., (Springfield, Massachusetts, 1993), s.v. "gift."
4. Ibid., s.v. "talent."
5. Ibid., s.v. "gift."
6. 2 Timothy 1:6.
7. Tim LaHaye, *Spirit-Controlled Temperament* (LaMesa, CA: Post, Inc., 1966). Much of the material in this chapter is based on Dr. LaHaye's book, filtered through the lens of my observations and experience, both professional and spiritual.
8. LaHaye, *Your Temperament: Discover Its Potential,* (Wheaton, Illinois: Tyndale House Publishers, Inc., 1984) p. 24.
9. For the complete story, see Judges 4 and 5.
10. John 19:26,27.
11. Psalm 84:11.

Chapter 3

1. Jim Monsor, *Spiritual Mountaineering,* N.p., n.d.
2. Genesis 37:7,9.
3. James Ryle, *A Dream Come True: A Biblical Look at How God Speaks Through Dreams and Visions,* (Orlando, FL: Creation House, 1995). A must-read for those interested in exploring this controversial topic.
4. Ibid.
5. Ibid., p. 39.
6. Ibid., p.43.
7. Ibid., p. 51.

Chapter 4

1. 2 Corinthians 10:4; Ephesians 6:10-18.
2. Revelation 3:12; 21:2.
3. Beth Moore, *Praying God's Word,* (Nashville, TN: Broadman & Holman Publishers, 2000), p. 290.

[4] Genesis 39:9.

[5] *Merriam Webster OnLine Dictionary,* copyright © 2002, available from <http://www.m-w.com>, s.v. "yield."

[6] Esther 2:12.

[7] James 1:2.

[8] Elisabeth Elliot, *Discipline: The Glad Surrender,* (Grand Rapids: Fleming H. Revell, 1982), pp. 154,155.

Chapter 5

[1] This paragraph contains the author's paraphrased narrative of the early life of Jesus and is based on Matthew 1:18-25, Mark 6:3, and Luke 1:26-38.

[2] Oswald Chambers, "Reading 85—The Submission of Life," in *My Utmost Devotional Bible,* (Nashville, TN: Thomas Nelson Publishers, 1992), p. 283. Used by permission of Discovery House Publishers, Box 3566, Grand Rapids, MI 49501. All rights reserved.

[3] Genesis 12:14-20.

[4] Genesis 26:7-11.

[5] Genesis 25:25,26.

[6] *Jamieson, Fausset, and Brown Commentary,* (Electronic Database: Biblesoft, 1997), s.v. "Genesis 25:26." All rights reserved.

[7] Genesis 29:20-30.

[8] Genesis 27:1-37.

[9] *New Unger's Bible Dictionary,* originally published by Moody Press of Chicago, Illinois. Copyright © 1988; s.v. "BETHEL." Used by permission.

[10] Genesis 32:24-28.

[11] John 6:35.

[12] Pat Robertson is a well-known religious leader, author, and religious broadcaster who is founder and chairman of the Christian Broadcasting Network, and founder and host of The 700 Club Christian television program.

[13] Based on excerpts from the book by Frances J. Roberts, *Come Away My Beloved,* (Uhrichsville, Ohio: Promise Press, 2002), pp. 170,171.

[14] Ibid., pp. 120,121.

[15] The material on Joseph's brothers is based on information from Trent Butler, Ph.D., gen. ed., *Holman's Bible Dictionary,* (Nashville, TN: Holman Bible Publishers, 1991), various pages by name in alphabetical order. Used by permission.

[16] Roberts, p. 25.

Chapter 6

[1] The statistics and quote appearing here were taken from the National Center for Children in Poverty (NCCP) Web site of Columbia University, available from <http://www.nccp.org/pub-cpf03.html>.

[2] Not her real name.

[3] Psalm 37:23.

[4] Isaiah 54:5.

[5] Frances J. Roberts, p. 8.

[6] Rex Reed, M.D., *What the Bible Says About Healthy Living* (Ventura, CA 93003: Gospel Light/Regal Books, 1996), used by permission.

[7] Ibid., pp. 11,12.

[8] Ibid., p. 13.

9   Much of the material in this section is taken from "Understanding Depression—Yours and Theirs," offered by Clemson Extension and revised by Brenda J. Thames, EdD, Program Development Specialist, and Deborah J. Thomason, EdD, Family and Youth Development Specialist, Department of Family and Youth Development, available from <http://www.cdc.gov/nasb>, S.V. "depression."

10 Ibid., p. 2.

11 From a fact sheet published by the National Institute of mental health (NIMH), Publication No. 01-459, available from <http://www.toddlertime.com/bipolar/what-is-bipolar.html>.

12 2 Chronicles 20:17.

13 Courtney is aware that the doctors' report is not the final word; God's Word is. Nothing is impossible with Him, and there are testimonies of total healing from bipolar disorder. In the meantime, however, she is adjusting to living *with* the disease while praying for the completion of God's healing work in her life.

14 Sometimes divine healing happens instantly, where the symptoms disappear immediately, but often supernatural healing takes place gradually, over a period of time. Supervised prescription medication may be an important first step in God's individualized plan for divine healing.

15 While Courtney did not choose to kill herself, fearing God's displeasure, she was too ill at the time to realize that unsupervised use of drugs and alcohol would add a dangerous dimension to her problem. Thankfully, God extends His grace and mercy!

16 Joel 2:25.

17 From a paper submitted to the Office of Disease Prevention and Health Promotion (1993), available from <http://www.tobaccodocuments.org/lor/87679958.html>.

18 Luke 12:7.

Chapter 7

1   Revelation 12:11 tells what Jesus' blood can do for us: "And they overcame him [Satan] by the blood of the Lamb...."

2   Ephesians 6:11,13,17.

3   Satan is referred to as the Beast, one of his end-time evil henchman, many times in the book of Revelation, including Revelation 11:7, 13:2-4, and 17:7,8.

4   Ezekiel 28:12,13.

5   Based on information from Herbert Lockyer Sr., gen. ed., *Nelson's Illustrated Bible Dictionary,* (Nashville, TN: Thomas Nelson Publishers, 1986), p. 952, S.V. "Satan." Used by permission of Thomas Nelson, Inc.

6   Webster's, Tenth ed., S.V. "pride."

7   Nelson's, pp. 657, S.V. "Lucifer."

8   Ibid., p. 434, S.V. "Beelzebub."

9   Ibid., p. 299. S.V. "devil."

10 Revelation 12:3.

11 Unger's, S.V. "DEVIL."

12 Brown, Driver, Briggs and Gesenius, *The KJV Old Testament Hebrew Lexicon,* "Hebrew Lexicon entry for Heylel," entry #1966, S.V. "Lucifer," available from <http://www.biblestudytools.net/Lexicons/Hebrew/heb.cgi?number=1966&version=kjv>.

13 I believe that you will be greatly encouraged about the potential for reclaiming the media for kingdom purposes by reading the Bob Briner book *Roaring Lambs: A Gentle Plan To Radically Change Your World* (Grand Rapids, MI: Zondervan, 2000).

14 Ten Bible references on hell are: Matthew 5:22,29,30; 10:28; 23:15,33; Mark 9:43,45,47; Luke 12:5.

15 Thayer and Smith, *The KJV New Testament Greek Lexicon,* "Greek Lexicon entry for Geenna," entry #1067, s.v. "hell," available from <http://www.biblestudytools.net/Lexicons/Greek/grk.cgi?number=1067&version=kjv>.

16 Matthew 8:12; 13:42,50; 22:13; 24:51; 25:30; Luke 13:28.

17 Nelson's, p. 473.

18 "Sometimes Satan is represented as transforming himself into an angel of light...and sometimes...as a roaring lion: denoting the efforts which he makes to alarm and over-power us. The lion here is not the crouching lion—the lion stealthfully creeping toward his foe—but it is the raging monarch of the woods, who by his terrible roar would intimidate all so that they might become an easy prey." *Barnes'Notes,* by Albert Barnes, D.D. (Electronic Database: Biblesoft, 1997), s.v. "1 Peter 5:8." All rights reserved.

Chapter 8

1 A hard tough chalcedony (or translucent quartz commonly pale blue or gray with a wax-like luster). It has a reddish color and is generally used in jewelry. Merriam-Webster, s.v. "carnelian."

2 "A semiprecious stone that is usually rich azure blue...." Ibid., s.v. "lapis lazuli."

3 Based on information from Lionel Casson, *The Pharaohs,* (Chicago: Stonehenge Press, Inc., 1981), p. 23.

4 James E. Strong, "Hebrew and Chaldee Dictionary" in *Strong's Exhaustive Concordance of the Bible,* (Nashville: Abingdon, 1890), p. 19, entry #899, s.v. "garment," Genesis 39:13.

5 Kay Arthur, *Sex...According to God,* (Colorado Springs: Waterbrook Press, 2002), pp. 6,7.

6 Jack W. Hayford, Litt.D., gen. ed., *Spirit-Filled Life Bible,* (Nashville, TN: Thomas Nelson Publishers, 1991), p. 1797.

7 Arthur, pp. 212,213.

8 Based on a definition from Nelson's, p. 100, s.v. "Body Armor."

9 Webster's Tenth ed., s.v. "righteousness."

10 From the hymn "My Hope Is Built (The Solid Rock)," words by Edward Mote (1834), music by William B. Bradbury (1836); available from <http://www.cyberhymnal.org/htm/m/y/myhopeis.htm>.

11 Shirley Arnold, from a letter to women as quoted in Jack W. Hayford, Litt.D., ex. ed, *Women of Destiny Bible* (Nashville, TN: Thomas Nelson Publishers, 2000), p. 1451.

12 Based on a definition from Nelson's, s.v. "ARMS, ARMOR OF THE BIBLE."

13 Based on a definition from Strong's, "Greek Dictionary of the New Testament," p. 47, entry #3185, s.v. "greater," John 5:20.

14 Based on a definition from Nelson's, p. 556, s.v. "JESUS."

Chapter 9

1 Charlton Laird, *Laird's Promptory,* (New York: Henry Holt & Company, 1948), p. 211, s.v. "deferred."

2 Acts 2:30-36.

3 Nelson's, p. 773, s.v. "cupbearer."

4 This excerpt by Chuck Colson was taken from "True Power and Security," *The Transparent Leader* by Dwight L. Johnson (Eugene, Oregon: Harvest House Publishers, 2001), p. 23.

[5] Genesis 39:22.

[6] 1 Corinthians 13:2.

[7] John Maxwell, *The Maxwell Leadership Bible,* (Nashville, TN: Thomas Nelson Bibles, a Division of Thomas Nelson, Inc., 2002), p. 49.

Chapter 10

[1] John 20:24-29.

Chapter 11

[1] Sherrill Whiton, *Elements of Interior Decoration,* (Chicago: J.B. Lippincott Company, 1944).

[2] Holman's, p. 1103, s.v. "PHARAOH."

[3] Ibid.

[4] John Maxwell, "Profiles in Leadership: Pharaoh," from *The Maxwell Leadership Bible,* p. 50.

[5] Genesis 41:8.

[6] Based on information from *Spirit-Filled Life Bible,* p. 65, s.v. "41:16, An answer of peace" (marginal note at the bottom of the page).

[7] Based on definitions from Strong's, "Hebrew and Chaldee Dictionary," p. 54, entry #3559, s.v. "establish," Genesis 41:32.

[8] Ibid., entry #4116, p. 62, s.v. "shortly," Genesis 41:32.

[9] Based on information in Nelson's, p. 991, s.v. "SIGNET."

[10] Holman's, p. 885, s.v. "LINEN."

[11] Ibid., p. 1433, s.v. "ZAPH(E)NATH-P(A)ANEAH."

Chapter 12

[1] *Merriam-Webster OnLine Dictionary,* copyright © 2002, s.v. "pro," available from <http://www.m-w.com>.

[2] Charles Swindoll, *Joseph: A Man of Integrity and Forgiveness,* (Nashville, TN: W Publishing Group, a Division of Thomas Nelson, Inc., 1998), p. 99. Used by permission of Thomas Nelson, Inc.

[3] This information is based on material from Trudy Weathersby, "Kübler-Ross Revisited," "5 Stages of Grief," and "Coping With the Five Stages of Grief and Bereavement," available from <http://www.dying.about.com/cs/stagesofgrief/>.

Chapter 13

[1] Beth Moore, *Living Beyond Yourself: Exploring the Fruit of the Spirit,* (Nashville, TN: LifeWay Press, 1998), pp. 112.

[2] "Come Home," words and music by Will L. Thompson, in *Sparkling Gems, Nos. 1 and 2,* by J. Calvin Bushey (Chicago, Illinois: Will L. Thompson & Company, 1880), available from <http://www.cyberhymnal.org/htm/s/o/softlyat.htm>.

[3] "Roe v. Wade, court case of 1973 in which the Supreme Court of the United States ruled that a woman has a constitutional right to an abortion during the first six months of pregnancy." Taken from the encyclopedia article, *"Roe v. Wade," Microsoft® Encarta® Online Encyclopedia 2003,* (Microsoft Corporation: 1997-2003) available from <http://encarta.msn.com/encnet/refpages/RefArticle.aspx?refid=761595572>. All Rights Reserved.

Chapter 14

[1] Genesis 47:11.

[2] Webster's Tenth ed., S.V. "restore."

[3] Strong's, "Hebrew and Chaldee Dictionary," p. 107, entry #7310, S.V. "wealthy," Psalm 66:12.

[4] James Robison, *Spirit-Filled Life Bible,* p. 2012, S.V. "The Biblical Definition of Restoration (Job 42:10-12)."

[5] Strong's, "Hebrew and Chaldee Dictionary," p. 107, entry #7307, S.V. "breath of God," Genesis 7:22.

[6] Cathy Lee Phillips, *Silver in the Slop,* (Canton, GA: Patchwork Press, Ltd., 1999), p. 4.

[7] Based on information from Nelson's, p. 438, S.V. "GOSHEN."

[8] Ibid., p. 968, S.V. "SEVEN, SEVENTH."

Chapter 15

[1] Alexander MacLaren, *Expositions of Holy Scripture,* (Grand Rapids: Wm. B. Eerdmans Publishing Co., 1938), selections from pp. 4-15.

[2] Strong's, "Hebrew and Chaldee Dictionary," p. 45, entry #2896, S.V. "good."

[3] Ibid., p. 51, entry #3290, S.V. "Jacob."

[4] Based on a definition from Nelson's, p. 531, S.V. "JACOB," when his name was changed to Israel.

[5] 2 Chronicles 7:14.

[6] Strong's, "Hebrew and Chaldee Dictionary," p. 89, entry #6026, S.V. "delight," Psalm 37:4.

[7] Ibid., p. 73, entry #4862, S.V. "desires," Psalm 37:4.

Chapter 16

[1] *Adam Clarke's Commentary* (Electronic Database: Biblesoft, 1996), "Genesis 6:22." All rights reserved.

[2] Esther 7:3,4.

[3] Hebrews 12:2.

[4] *International Standard Bible Encyclopedia,* S.V. "Immanuel."

[5] Genesis 50:25,26.

[6] Adapted from *The Life of Joseph* by F. B. Meyer, (published by Emerald Books, P.O. Box 635, Lynnwood, WA 98046, 1995), p. 142. Used with permission.

[7] See your local bookstore for materials by Larry Burkett and Dave Ramsay.

[8] Frederick K. Price, "Prospered to Bless," *Spirit-Filled Life Bible,* (Nashville, TN: Thomas Nelson Publishers, 1991), p. 267, S.V. "KINGDOM DYNAMICS," Deuteronomy 8:18.

[9] John 6:11-13.

[10] Bruce Wilkinson, *The Prayer of Jabez: Breaking Through to the Blessed Life* (Sisters, Oregon: Multnomah Publishers Inc., 2000).

[11] Max Lucado, *No Wonder They Call Him the Savior* (Sisters, Oregon: Multnomah Publishers, Inc., 1986), pp. 60,61.

[12] F. B. Meyer, p. 142.

[13] Ibid., p. 145.

Prayer of Salvation

God loves you—no matter who you are, no matter what your past. God loves you so much that He gave His one and only begotten Son for you. The Bible tells us that "...whoever believes in him shall not perish but have eternal life" (John 3:16 NIV). Jesus laid down His life and rose again so that we could spend eternity with Him in heaven and experience His absolute best on earth. If you would like to receive Jesus into your life, say the following prayer out loud and mean it from your heart.

Heavenly Father, I come to You admitting that I am a sinner. Right now, I choose to turn away from sin, and I ask You to cleanse me of all unrighteousness. I believe that Your Son, Jesus, died on the cross to take away my sins. I also believe that He rose again from the dead so that I might be forgiven of my sins and made righteous through faith in Him. I call upon the name of Jesus Christ to be the Savior and Lord of my life. Jesus, I choose to follow You and ask that You fill me with the power of the Holy Spirit. I declare that right now I am a child of God. I am free from sin and full of the righteousness of God. I am saved in Jesus' name. Amen.

If you prayed this prayer to receive Jesus Christ as your Savior for the first time, please contact us on the web at **www.harrisonhouse.com** to receive a free book.

Or you may write to us at

Harrison House
P.O. Box 35035
Tulsa, Oklahoma 74153

About the Author

Warm, hospitable, and gracious, Ann Platz epitomizes the qualities that people admire most about the South. Raised with a deep appreciation for the art of beautiful living, she grew up in an ancestral plantation home in Orangeburg, South Carolina. In the mid-'70s Ann moved to Atlanta, Georgia, where she resides with her husband, John. She is the mother of two daughters, Courtney Jones and Margo McDonald. Together, she and John have six grandchildren.

Ann has been well-known in the South as an interior designer for over 25 years and is a popular and delightful lecturer. Speaking on topics from design and etiquette to the deeper things of the Spirit, Ann warms the heart with her effortless southern elegance and storytelling wit.

She is the author of six other books, including *Social Graces* and *The Pleasure of Your Company.* Her design credentials include a governor's mansion, country clubs, and historic houses, as well as two *Southern Living* idea houses. She and John are members of Mount Paran Church of God. They are active in the Christian community of greater Atlanta.

To contact Ann Platz
please write:

Ann Platz
1266 West Paces Ferry Road, #521
Atlanta, Georgia 30327-2306
(Fax) 404-237-3810

or visit her on the Web at:
www.annplatz.com

*Please include your prayer requests
and comments when you write.*

Also From Harrison House
by Ann Platz

Guardians of the Gate

Additional copies of this book
are available from your local bookstore.

www.harrisonhouse.com

Fast. Easy. Convenient!

- ◆ New Book Information
- ◆ Look Inside the Book
- ◆ Press Releases
- ◆ Bestsellers

- ◆ Free E-News
- ◆ Author Biographies
- ◆ Upcoming Books
- ◆ Share Your Testimony

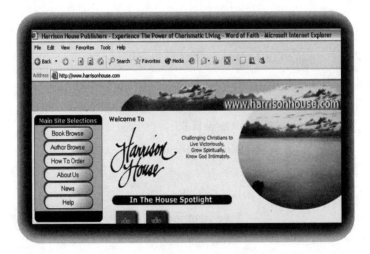

For the latest in book news and author information, please visit us on the Web at www.harrisonhouse.com. Get up-to-date pictures and details on all our powerful and life-changing products. Sign up for our e-mail newsletter, *Friends of the House,* and receive free monthly information on our authors and products including testimonials, author announcements, and more!

Harrison House—
Books That Bring Hope, Books That Bring Change

The Harrison House Vision

Proclaiming the truth and the power
Of the Gospel of Jesus Christ
With excellence;

Challenging Christians to
Live victoriously,
Grow spiritually,
Know God intimately.